BASKETBALL
for Women

Becoming a Complete Player

Nancy Lieberman-Cline
ESPN and Prime Sports Network

Robin Roberts
ABC and ESPN

with
Kevin Warneke

Human Kinetics

Library of Congress Cataloging-in-Publication Data

Lieberman-Cline, Nancy, 1958–
    Basketball for women : becoming a complete player / Nancy
Lieberman-Cline [and] Robin Roberts with Kevin Warneke.
        p.   cm.
    Includes index.
    ISBN: 0-87322-610-0 (paper)
    1. Basketball for women.   I. Roberts, Robin, 1960-   .
II. Warneke, Kevin.   III. Title.
GV886.L44   1996
796.323'8--dc20   95-17945
                                                                 CIP

ISBN: 0-87322-610-0

Developmental Editors: Mary E. Fowler, Julia Anderson; **Assistant Editors:** Henry
Woolsey, Ed Giles; **Copyeditor:** Bob Replinger; **Proofreader:** Jim Burns; **Indexer:**
Joan Griffitts; **Typesetting and Layout:** Ruby Zimmerman; **Text Designer:** Stuart
Cartwright; **Cover Designer:** Keith Blomberg; **Photographer (cover):** Patrick
Murphy-Racey; **Illustrator:** Paul To; **Printer:** United Graphics

Human Kinetics books are available at special discounts for bulk purchase. Special
editions or book excerpts can also be created to specification. For details, contact
the Special Sales Manager at Human Kinetics.

Printed in the United States of America   10 9 8 7 6 5 4 3 2

Human Kinetics
Web site: http://www.humankinetics.com

United States: Human Kinetics, P.O. Box 5076, Champaign, IL 61825-5076
1-800-747-4457

Canada: Human Kinetics, Box 24040, Windsor, ON N8Y 4Y9
1-800-465-7301 (in Canada only)

Europe: Human Kinetics, P.O. Box IW14, Leeds LS16 6TR, United Kingdom
(44) 1132 781708

Australia: Human Kinetics, 57A Price Avenue, Lower Mitcham,
South Australia 5062
(08) 277 1555

New Zealand: Human Kinetics, P.O. Box 105-231, Auckland 1
(09) 523 3462

CONTENTS

FOREWORD

Women's basketball has made great strides in the last quarter century. More women and girls participate in the sport than ever before. Games are shown on national television. Top 25 polls for colleges and high schools are published regularly in most newspapers. And the old six-player game—played until 1994 in Oklahoma—has given way to a more competitive, up-tempo, full-court brand of ball.

Despite these advances, we've only scratched the surface. Players like Nancy Lieberman-Cline, Cheryl Miller, Lynette Woodard, and Sheryl Swoopes have given us a glimpse of what's possible. Their brilliance was reflected in their total game, not just one facet. They could shoot, pass, handle, and defend. Plus they played smart and were team leaders. The total package.

What we need to elevate our game to new heights is to develop multiple skills in players. This will take an even greater commitment by women and girls who coach and play basketball; more time on the court; better instruction, better practices, better conditioning; a tough mental approach that distinguishes the serious, competitive athlete from the recreational player.

Women's Basketball: Becoming a Complete Player is for players to ex-pand and improve their individual and team performance. The book motivates the serious player to work on all areas of her game, and not to be satisfied with her current level of skill, conditioning, or knowledge.

Coaches will want every player on their team to have a copy. A roster full of complete players would make our job much easier, right coaches? When I recruit players to the University of Tennessee or am involved in selecting players to participate on all-star teams, I look for more than just physical talent. I look for players with multidimensional games; players who can turn to option B when option A isn't working; players who push themselves to be the best they can be.

Nancy Lieberman-Cline and Robin Roberts are a perfect pair of authors for this book. Both have excelled in their basketball and professional careers. And their book will help you excel, too.

Pat Summitt

PREFACE

Basketball for Women: Becoming a Complete Player is a testimony to how far women's basketball has come during my 25 years in the game as a player, instructor, and broadcaster.

The purpose of this book is to help you take your game to the next level. It's a practical but challenging guide. How much it helps you will depend on how committed you are to the game. Maybe you are a high school freshman or sophomore fighting for playing time on your team. Maybe you're already a starter on your team looking to sharpen your skills. Regardless, this book can help you get the most out of your talent and skill. It can help you reach your potential.

Many female basketball players have had the proper mental attitude and physical ability to compete at the highest level of the game. However, they haven't always had the opportunity, instruction, or training. The good news is times are changing. And as times change, those players with the proper mental attitude and physical ability are finding more and more opportunities to excel.

If you have questions about playing the game—Where can I play? How can I get into pickup games? How do I play against guys? Should I play against them at all? How can I be more coachable? How do I accept a role on my team? How do I prepare to compete?—this book will help you find the answers.

Specifically, in chapter 1 you'll learn about the great pioneers of our sport and discover the keys to your own success. In chapter 2 you'll learn the importance of being mentally ready to play. Methods and programs for physical preparation—flexibility, strength training, and endurance—are presented in chapter 3.

In chapters 4 through 8 you'll learn how to become an offensive threat. You'll find instruction and drills for gaining the best position, footwork, dribbling, passing, shooting, and setting screens.

And don't forget about defense! Chapters 9 and 10 will teach you effective positioning, footwork, and rebounding—the dirty work. If you have a solid work ethic and a willingness to accept the challenge of becoming a defensive stopper, you'll love this part.

In chapter 11 all of the techniques and tactics taught in the first 10 chapters are put into perspective—the bigger picture. No matter how good you are individually, basketball is a team sport. You must use your talent to benefit your team. You'll learn the keys to being a true team player. You'll also get some advice about such things as being a positive role model, how to get along with your teammates, and what it's like to be recruited to play at the next level.

Basketball is a great sport for many reasons. It's one of the few sports that allows girls and women to compete side-by-side, face-to-face with their opponents. It gives players the opportunity to contribute to their team's success through individual achievement and performance. Cornette Irby, one of my former Foot Locker Scholarship athletes, knows this. She wrote to tell me about her improved ballhandling skills as her team's point guard and her progress as a student—three As and three Bs for the first 6 weeks of the semester. She attached her honor-roll ribbon to the letter. Cornette's going to be successful someday—possibly on the basketball court, but definitely in life.

Basketball's multifaceted dimensions provide thrills and excitement that can last a lifetime. Above all, basketball gives you a chance to dream. Go ahead. Dream high.

Nancy Lieberman-Cline

Since basketball has truly been a major part of my life, it only seems natural to put all I've learned in a book for others to use and share. My hope is that my son T.J. will pick up this book often enough to work on his skills and have fun with the game that has brought me so much joy.

God Bless,
Nancy

INTRODUCTION

I remember that day in 1974 when Mildred Asheper, the athletic director at Far Rockaway High School, called the U.S. Olympic Committee. She talked with Bob Paul. He had received calls like this before: a coach or athletic director telling him that she had an athlete—a high school athlete—who she thought could make the Olympic women's basketball team. I was that athlete, and this time Bob's caller was right. I came home from Montreal in 1976 with a silver medal. Afterward, Bob told me that I was a success story. I was the first high school athlete to make a women's Olympic basketball team.

Basketball has truly been a blessing for me. During my career I've realized many dreams and learned many lessons. My coaches and teammates were my teachers and role models. They inspired me and guided me when I was developing as a player. This book is my way of motivating and instructing the next generation of women basketball players. It is my contribution to the game that gave me so much.

Basketball and competition build confidence, self-esteem, and trust in yourself and your coaches. It also provides opportunities to learn immediately from your experiences—win or lose. Basketball can teach you the best lessons of all—not just how to be a better player, but how to be a better person.

Think about your basketball skills. Are you a solid performer? Do you want to achieve greatness? Are you doing what it takes to excel? Hard work, discipline, and training can be fun and rewarding. Basketball is a game that constantly challenges you. Be ready. Tell yourself: "I'm a winner. I'm willing to give it my all." Then, do it.

That's the attitude it takes for you to get to the next level. It's the whole package—attitude, ability, desire, and effort. All the great women basketball players have shared the goal to be the best. Lucy Harris, a former Olympic star and three-time collegiate national champ, had challenges and took them all on. Her work ethic, discipline, and mental attitude always took her to the top. The same is true for Cheryl Miller, Lynette Woodard, Ann Meyers, Dawn Staley, Sheryl Swoopes, and the rest. Some were great scorers, some were unbeatable rebounders, and others were great ball handlers. Some had the total package. I know the next group of women's basketball stars will be even better.

You can be in that group, but it will take hard work and a love for the game. Give yourself every opportunity to find out just how good you can be. Put yourself in a position for good things to happen. That's what ESPN's Robin

Roberts did. Robin helped write this book and has applied her intellect and athletic ability to achieve tremendous success. While on a tennis scholarship at Southeastern Louisiana University, she earned a spot on the women's basketball team. And she excelled, even though at 5 feet 10 inches she had to play the post against much taller opponents. She's a wonderful example of someone who seized an opportunity, not only on the court, but also in the classroom. She graduated cum laude. Today, she's seizing another opportunity as one of the country's best sports broadcasters.

You are the only one who knows how hard you're willing to work and how far you want to go. Be efficient and gamelike in your approach to practice. Approach your development systematically. Great players never become great in one season. It takes years of effort, determination, and practice. Work on your weaknesses as well as your strengths. Overcoming your weaknesses might be what it takes to make you the best player on your team, or even all-state.

Watch players you like and admire. Imitate their moves and techniques. If you have cable television, watch as many women's games as you can. Go to women's college and high school games with your parents, coach, or friends. Other women are out on the floor—faking, shaking, talking, driving, stopping, and popping—someday that can be you! Treat your development seriously.

Once you have made a commitment to your game by practicing, training, sacrificing, and being a student of the game, you will find that you have improved yourself as a person because of your dedication and commitment. You've heard it said many times before: Sports build character and commitment. That means you have to sacrifice your time and give your effort to improve. When you apply dedication of these qualities, the benefits carry over into everyday life. Your discipline, responsibility, and ability to set realistic goals will be put to good use whether you're on or off the court. Before we start, here are some tidbits of information to think about. Statistics compiled by the Women's Sports Foundation show that girls who participate in high school sports are three times more likely to graduate, 80 percent less likely to have an unwanted pregnancy, and 92 percent less likely to get involved with drugs.

These statistics don't lie. As much as I hope this book helps you become a better basketball player, I hope it helps you become an even better, more confident person. There's nothing you can't accomplish if you only believe in yourself.

When you are playing, focus on doing whatever it takes to get the task done. Remember, when you look out on the floor you don't see players of different religions, races, or with higher or lower grade-point averages. You see other athletes. They're your classmates and friends pursuing the same goals and dreams as you. That's winning.

Nancy Lieberman-Cline

CHAPTER 1

Taking Your Game
to the Next Level

Taking your game to the next level of performance takes patience and focus. You should feel comfortable with yourself and your choices. It's OK to be feminine. You don't have to give up your femininity or try to hide it to succeed on the basketball court. Some women believe that in order to be taken seriously on the court, they can't be attractive. That's not true. We have to be proud of who and what we are.

At the same time, we need to be aggressive, physical, and not afraid to mix it up on the court. Sound confusing? It's all part of the identity crisis women have had to face since they began playing basketball some 100 years ago. We've been told to be dainty and docile, not aggressive and athletic. Senda Berenson, the daughter of a Russian peddler who prized education, faced this dilemma when she first took a liking to a new indoor game that inventor James Naismith called basketball. Berenson, frail as a child, enrolled at the Boston Normal School of Gymnastics to improve her strength. She thrived, and later was selected to fill a vacancy at Smith College as its gymnastics teacher. At Smith, Berenson experimented with the curriculum and ended up changing the course of women's athletics. Naismith's basketball intrigued her, but she did not want to be accused of promoting exercise that could be considered unfeminine. Berenson resolved the problem of society's stereotypes about women through compromise. She divided the basketball court into three sections and modified the rules. That way, physical contact between players was minimized.

A ROLE IN HISTORY

Women's basketball today is more uptempo than it once was. We push the ball up and down the court, and use our speed, quickness, the transition game, trapping defenses, and the three-point shot. It wasn't always that way. Basketball competition at first was played on the intramural level (on the three-section court and by the rules Berenson developed). Within several years, the first game between two colleges was held. The three-section court later was replaced by one divided into halves, with players specializing either on offense or defense on their side of the court.

By the early 1900s, women's basketball had reached every continent. Soon, the Amateur Athletic Union (AAU) formed and began organizing national championship contests. By the 1950s, Wayland Baptist College in Texas and Nashville Business College in Tennessee emerged as the dominating schools in women's collegiate basketball.

A basketball Hall of Famer, Nashville's Nera White may have been the game's first women's superstar—although she received little recognition because of a lack of media exposure in the '50s and '60s. She could easily hit from half court. Her speed and strength were amazing. She was a 15-time all-American selection and was most valuable player of the AAU tournament 10 times. In 1957, she was a member of the USA team that participated in the world championships. Not surprisingly, she was the best player.

The modern era of women's basketball began in 1969 with the first National Intercollegiate Women's Basketball Tournament. Carol Eckman organized the tournament and her school, West Chester State College, hosted the event. Thanks to Eckman's effort, women's basketball no longer had to rely solely on the AAU for tournament competition. Eckman's influence on the game extends even further than the tourney, as several of her former players are now National Collegiate Athletic Association (NCAA) Division I coaches.

Another pioneer in women's basketball is Bob Spencer. When Spencer started a women's basketball program at Kennedy College, he had no idea he would someday be one of the winningest coaches in women's collegiate basketball. He later took over the women's basketball program at Fresno State University and was the first collegiate women's coach to win 500 games.

Title IX

Women's basketball received a boost in 1972 from Title IX, the gender equity law that prohibits discrimination based on gender in educational programs and activities at the collegiate level. With regard to athletic programs, Title IX addresses three basic equal opportunity program requirements: participation opportunities, scholarship dollars, and other athletic program benefits.

Schools are obligated to provide athletic opportunities for men and women in proportion to their enrollment in the general student body. If a college has 55 percent male undergraduates and 45 percent female undergraduates, athletic participation should reflect this mix. This does not mean that a school must provide an equal number of teams. Rather, the number of athletes should reflect this ratio.

In addition, scholarship dollars must be provided to male an female athletes proportional to their athletic participation. If a school is spending $400,000 per year for athletic scholarships and half of these athletes are women, then half the amount should be funding athletic scholarships for women. Equal opportunity also applies to program benefits—equipment, uniforms, and supplies. An institution must spend whatever is required to provide female basketball players with the same quality uniforms and equipment provided to male basketball players.

The game took another direction in 1982 when women's basketball became part of the NCAA. The women's game receives more exposure, funding, opportunities, and credibility as part of the NCAA. The game received still another boost through its partnership with CBS, which began airing regular-season games on television. In addition, more national awards are given to players who excel on the court and in the classroom. Finally, the NCAA established its women's basketball tournament, which began with 36 teams, later expanded to 48, and now invites 64 squads—the same as the men's tournament.

Some Comparisons

Women's basketball often must deal with fans who compare it to men's basketball. This is certainly not a negative, although women's basketball will continue to forge its own identity. Because of the physical differences between men and women (and the height of the rim), women have not mastered the dunk or the ability, as they say, to play above the rim. Men's basketball has taken years to achieve the status it now enjoys. As female basketball players become better athletes, our game will take on these and other new elements.

In order to improve, today's players face highly skilled competition and must possess solid fundamentals, good communication skills, mental preparedness, a solid work ethic, and physical ability. You must be eager to learn, listen, and apply new knowledge and skills to your game.

Women's basketball has been fortunate to have its superstars: Nera White, Dawn Staley, Anne Donovan, Katrina McClain, Sheryl Swoopes, and many others. As we get bigger, quicker, and are able to jump higher and shoot better, the beauty of it all will be the day when coaches and players reminisce about yesterday's stars: "Yeah, I remember Staley, Swoopes, McClain, and Donovan. They were good, but wait until you see the players I watched today. They're really going to be great."

Memorable Moments

Women's basketball has achieved many milestones in addition to Title IX:

- Senda Berenson introduces basketball to Smith College students in 1892, and the first official women's basketball game is played at Smith College in 1893.
- The first official publication, *Basket Ball for Women*, is published by the Spalding Athletic Library in 1901, with Senda Berenson as its editor.
- The first AAU National Women's Basketball Championship is played in 1926.
- Two-court, six-player basketball is introduced in 1938.
- The USA women's basketball team competes in the Pan-American Games in 1955.
- Two-court basketball with roving players and a three-bounce dribble is introduced in 1961.
- The first National Intercollegiate Women's Basketball Tournament is played in West Chester, Pennsylvania, in 1969.
- A five-player, full-court game is introduced using the 30-second clock in 1971.
- The first AIAW National Collegiate Championships are played in 1972.
- The first Kodak All-American Team is named in 1975.
- The first Olympic competition in women's basketball is held in 1976 in Montreal.
- The Women's Professional League opens in Milwaukee in 1978.
- UCLA's Ann Meyers is signed by the Indiana Pacers in 1979 to try out at a free-agent camp.
- The first nationally televised game is aired in 1979. Old Dominion defeats Louisiana Tech in the AIAW finals.
- In 1980, Cheryl Miller is the first woman to dunk in a high school game.
- The Women's Basketball Coaches Association is formed in 1982.
- The first NCAA National Championship for women is held in 1982.

- The United States wins its first olympic gold medal in women's international basketball in 1984. The U.S. squad defends its gold in 1988. The Soviet Union had dominated women's basketball since 1958.
- In 1985, Kansas' Lynette Woodard becomes the first woman to play with the Harlem Globetrotters.
- In 1986, Nancy Lieberman becomes the first woman to play in a men's professional league—the United States Basketball League (USBL). She plays for the Springfield Fame in 1986 and the Long Island Knights in 1987.
- At the 1990 NCAA tournament in Knoxville, Tennessee, 16,595 fans watch the championship game and 17,601 watch the semifinals. The most pleasing aspect is that Tennessee is not even in the tournament.
- In 1991, the NAIA Championships expands to 32 teams.
- Lisa Leslie sets a record by scoring 101 points in the first half of a high school game in 1991.
- In 1992, Kodak sponsors the first all-American game for girls' high school players. Katie Smith and Crystal Robinson are named MVPs.
- The Women's Basketball Hall of Fame is established in Jackson, Tennessee, in 1993. The Basketball Hall of Fame in Springfield, Massachusetts, has enshrined Nera White, Delta State Coach Margaret Wade, Ann Meyers, Carol Blazejowski, Lucy Harris-Stewart, Anne Donovan, and Cheryl Miller.
- The 1993 women's Final Four in Atlanta sells out, drawing more than 17,000 fans.
- Collegiate women's basketball has its own preseason classic in 1993—the State Farm Women's Basketball Hall of Fame Tip-off Classic. Inaugural participants are Texas Tech, Ohio State, Tennessee, and Vanderbilt.
- The 1994 NCAA women's Final Four in Richmond, Virginia, sells out a year prior to the tournament. More than 13,000 fans attend.
- In 1995, Liberty Sports purchases the Women's Basketball Association.
- The 1996 women's Final Four in Charlotte, North Carolina, sells out. More than 23,000 tickets are sold.

GETTING STARTED

We must have self-confidence, desire, and discipline to succeed. We must prove that we can play the game. Your first step is to get out on the court and compete. Get physical. Gain experience. Play hard and challenge one another. Be competitive. Zero in on weak parts of your game and have the discipline to work on them until you conquer them. Winning is important, but it's learning how to make positive gains through a loss that makes you a champion.

Learning how to be a solid one-on-one player who can take an opponent to the rim, shake the defense for a jumper, or penetrate, draw the defense, and dish off to a teammate means everything. How bad do you want it? We all have desire to be better and to win. That means playing in the heat, playing outdoors, playing with no air-conditioning, playing not only on wooden floors. Play two-on-two or three-on-three. Work on your movement, read situations, and take the rock one-on-one for the score. It's a great feeling.

Identify Your Goals

Learning how to set realistic goals and then achieve them is the most important thing you can do as a young player. How do you start? Let's say your goal is to make all-state. You need to honestly assess your level of ability. Think of it as a scouting report. What are your strengths? Weaknesses? Are they physical? Mental? Set up a plan and evaluate the following eight areas of your game:

- Shooting
- Passing
- Ballhandling
- Rebounding
- Defense
- Conditioning
- Mental approach
- Coachability

Now, on a scale of 1 to 5—with 5 being the highest—rate yourself. If you give yourself a 5, explain why you believe you are that good. If you give yourself a 3, in what areas are you strong and in what ways are you weak? If you give yourself a 1, evaluate your deficiencies. Now you have the proper information to create a plan to achieve your goals for making the all-state team. You can designate the areas for improvement and create a plan for action.

Let's say you realize you need to improve your ballhandling, improve your shooting going to the left, and improve your rebounding. List how you can improve each skill, as in the following example.

- Ballhandling—You dribble too high in traffic. You have a tendency to pick up your dribble when pressured, get trapped by the defense, and turn the ball over.

- Shooting—You need to square up your shoulders and stop fading away.

- Rebounding—You don't box out properly. You turn and go to the ball and don't always make contact with an opponent.

Now you are breaking down each skill and thinking the game through. Your scouting report will be your guide to your plan of attack.

Establishing personal goals and being a team player aren't contradictory. You should want to be a team player. It can be taught by your coaches, but it's much easier when it's something you want. Now, being a team player doesn't mean you shouldn't set goals for yourself; certainly you should, as long as they involve other players. Be sure to set goals in the right areas.

In addition, set minigoals for yourself during each practice. Are you having problems using your left hand? Are you not finishing easy shots? Do you get discouraged? Think about areas of weakness and make it a goal to improve with each practice or game. Mental challenges keep you focused. You won't have time for your mind to wander in games or during practice.

Establish Your Priorities

Once you are sure what you want as a basketball player, define the road to achieving your goals—for yourself, your team, your family, and your friends. Limit other activities, when possible, that might take time away from practice. Focus on your game and manage your time. We all wish we had more time. Give yourself adequate time to practice, to work on conditioning, to study, and to spend time with your family. Have a plan! Be organized. For me, the order is clear:

1. God
2. Family
3. Work/school
4. Basketball

If you can identify the important long-term objectives, the road will be much clearer. If you are organized and devoted in your approach to faith, family, and school—basketball will fall in place.

Spiritual commitment gives you a chance to focus on what is truly important. Athletics are important, but not more important than believing and learning more about your particular faith. Spirituality teaches you to realize how important family values are, as well as the importance of making proper choices with your time—mentally and physically. The gray areas are taken away.

Spiritual commitment allows you to understand your priorities: what you think is most important at the time and what is truly important. Spiritual commitment gives you respect, fear, discipline—everything you need to build a solid foundation for improvement.

School challenges you to think for yourself when you are faced with difficult problems. School is a wonderful source of information that allows you to test your mental approach to situations and come up with the correct decisions. School also makes you organized. You must learn time management because of all the demands on your time.

When you have gained the ability to learn and think out situations at home or in school, the final piece of the package becomes sports. Sports, more specifically basketball, teaches you responsibility, teamwork, trust, commitment, and a competitiveness that allows you to want to win at any level. When you can apply these ingredients, you have a solid foundation to go beyond the basics in everything you choose to take on.

Developing Your Plan

Now that you have identified what your goals are in terms of improvement and the order in which you will undertake them, let's develop your plan for overall improvement. Have your coach or mentor work with you as you share your evaluation of your strengths and weaknesses. Ask your coach to share some drills with you in each of the areas you have listed. Now, take a step back and review. First, you know your problem areas. Second, you are getting the proper information to establish a plan for improvement. Coaches are a great source of knowledge. They also are objective. You want to have three to five drills to work on in each skill area. This way, you won't be doing the same drill over and over. Diversity will keep challenging you and keep your interest level up. Different drills can achieve the same results. Determine how much time you can devote to your game each day. It may be 60 minutes or 2 hours. You decide. Remember, you have other commitments during your day to think about: school, family, practice, and others. Find a good time to fit basketball in. Make sure it is a time when you can concentrate totally on your game. One day, you might want to use your time to work on drills in four categories. The next day, the other four. Maybe you need work only on ballhandling and shooting. Now that you have developed your plan, let's put it into action.

Taking Action

Basically, taking action is practicing. And practicing might mean watching films or working on your conditioning. Taking action can make the difference in your basketball career. You're not just talking about improvement, you are actually working on your skills. It sounds easy. It can be. That's how the great players became great.

Start by getting to the gym or court early enough to stretch and loosen up. If you are with a partner, make sure she also has an organized plan for her areas of improvement. You want to push each other's intensity. Remember, you can push yourself when practicing on your own.

Be prepared. Have the correct number of balls you will need. Maybe it's just one. Get into the drill immediately. Remember, make it gamelike. Be quick. Explode. Be focused and concentrate on each skill and the drill you have chosen. Try not to cut corners. Don't make your goal just to get through a drill if it takes away from your form.

Practice on the not-so-glamorous part of the game. And remember repetition is key. Practicing your shooting is important, but you must practice dribbling—shaking someone one-on-one using great skills.

Or, you must practice being a great penetrator so teams will have to double-team you. Then, you can make a sweet pass to a teammate. Maybe the clock is winding down and you're behind by 1. You play great defense and pick up a charge. You put your team in a position to win. That's why you become fundamentally sound by practicing each of these different areas of the game. You have more advantages on the court. The more skills you have, the better position you are in to succeed and, ultimately, to win.

Players get named to all-state teams by doing the extra things: putting in hours of practice and repetition. Players earn college athletic scholarships by doing more than the average players. You must push yourself more than others. You reach another level of performance and you reach your goals by dedicating yourself to hard work and practice, by studying the game, and by having fun.

Sacrifice.   Taking action also means sacrifice, which means giving up personal glory. It means putting your team's success first. It also means organizing your time to make the most of your day. You can eliminate distractions from your hectic everyday schedule. Stay focused on a few areas: academics, practice, games, and family. Academics are extremely important. In order to be a good team player, you must be on the team. Stay eligible! Show your teammates that you have balance in life. It will reflect how your teammates look at you. Use your time wisely. There are only so many hours in the day. I'm not saying live your whole life around basketball. What I am saying is if you want to be good or great, you must determine what your priorities will be.

 Finding an Edge

When I was playing at Old Dominion University, I was always looking for an edge. I was never satisfied with my play. I always wanted more. In a sense, this may sound as if I were greedy. I was. Being the best was important to me. My teammates were good, very good. I wanted to be better than them and my opponents. If a teammate was a better outside shooter, my goal was to improve my shooting to match hers. If we had a drill, I wanted to be first in line. I wanted to win every wind sprint and suicide. Being number two for me was only acceptable after I gave my effort to be first.

Growing up in New York, I knew at age 10 that I wanted to be the best basketball player in the world. That was my goal. I made sacrifices to enhance that dream. I didn't go to parties or watch a lot of television or movies. I was always in the gym or schoolyard shooting, playing, practicing my ballhandling skills, and thinking the game. I loved it. And you know what, I never thought of playing basketball 5 or 6 hours a day as a sacrifice. It's what I wanted to do. It has helped me with the work ethic I have today in all areas of my life. My passion for basketball has given me an understanding of how I want to live my life.

Student of the Game.   You've probably heard the phrase "You've got to be a student of the game." When you are in the classroom, you're there to learn. The same is true when you're on the court. There is so much valuable information available. Watch college and high school games. Single out players and study their moves. Tape women's games on television and watch them again and again. Listen to what the commentators are saying about the players when they analyze the action. The commentators may be breaking down a defense or offense you haven't mastered. Read basketball magazines and watch instructional tapes. There's nothing better than participating in summer camps and clinics to improve and challenge yourself against other players. Do these things—they will help you improve. If you're willing to learn, you're going to get better.

To truly be a student of the game, you must have an overall approach to improvement. Of course, getting out and practicing the fundamentals is vital. But so is having knowledge and an understanding of the game.

The information you need is close by. Use your coaches as sources of information. Don't be shy about asking for their time. The game will be much simpler if you understand it. Coaches can objectively evaluate your skill level and your mental approach to games and practices. With the information they share, you can determine where your strength and weaknesses lie. Once you know these things, a plan for improvement can be put together. It's important to listen. That allows you to learn. View your coaches, or whoever your mentor is, as someone who can help you get better. Take their comments positively. Try not to take any criticism personally. Your coaches are just being truthful and helpful.

And coaches, your responsibility is to be there for your players. Teach them the skills necessary to improve, but also teach them about the mental aspect of the game. Be available to work with players who hunger for more time and improvement. Take pride in them as they reach another level of performance. As you know, being a coach is a demanding role. Players watch you and emulate your characteristics, mannerisms, and overall philosophy. They're around you a lot. Be solid role models for your kids. Go the extra step. Take them to clinics and encourage them to work hard but enjoy the game.

Make improvements in your game as well. Go to clinics, talk the game with other coaches. Watch high school and college games. Your overall improvement and learning will enhance your ability to teach and communicate to your team, no matter what level you are coaching.

The relationship between a coach and player is special. The time, respect, trust, and achievement the two share will last a lifetime. Coaches are changing the lives of their players. What could be a greater feeling than knowing you are helping mold a young lady's future?

 ## Listening and Learning

Can you imagine being just 17 years old and having already played for legendary coaches such as Cathy Rush, Billie Moore, and Sue Gunter, not to mention outstanding AAU and high school coaches? Each presented me with so much information. Sometimes it was confusing, but I didn't let their different styles frustrate me. I tried to be flexible, which was a key learning point. I couldn't be stubborn when it came to improving my skills. If a coach suggested I try a new technique, I needed to be open to the advice. Refusing to try would have been a major mistake.

Your Vision.   Have you ever been on the court by yourself shooting? In your mind the clock is counting down—5, 4, 3, 2, 1. You shoot and make the shot at the buzzer. You win the game. How many times have you missed that last shot? In your mind, not many. That's your vision. You are seeing yourself in a successful moment. Mentally, you've done it so many times that when you have to respond in a game situation, you've been there before. You can practice having vision. It's confidence—muscle memory of being successful in your own mind. It's a tremendous advantage to have. It can be developed. It only takes mental practice. Here are four steps you can use for success:

1. Think of game or practice situations on or off the court in which you want to be successful.

2. Create mental games with yourself on or off the court. For example, you're at the foul line with 1 second left and your team is down by 1 point. The fans are going nuts. You step to the line for two foul shots. You nail the first one and shoot the second one to win the championship for your team. You see it going through the net. You make the shot. It's a great feeling.

3. Use mirror vision. Stand in front of a mirror. Work on whatever skill needs improvement. Maybe it's your shooting form. Shoot a ball and check out your form. Is it what you thought it was? If your form is incorrect, you now can see it and make the correction. For example, is your elbow out, or in the correct L position? The mirror doesn't lie.

4. Dream on. Every night while lying in bed before you go to sleep, envision a part of your game. Maybe it's picking up a charge or grabbing a rebound. Maybe it's shooting. Make 100 shots to perfect your form and follow-through before you go to sleep. Always visualize success. It will help you when you get to the court. Your confidence will soar as you work your vision of what you can accomplish.

Today's young players have many great women to look up to for inspiration. The list is constantly growing. You have Sheryl Swoopes, Lisa Leslie, Natalie Williams, Teresa Edwards, Heather and Heidi Burge, Dawn Staley, Katie Smith, and Charlotte Smith. For me, it was Ann Meyers, Lucy Harris, Carolyn Bush-Roddy, Trish Roberts, Nancy Dunkle, and Julienne Simpson. For players before that, it was Brenda Moeller, Cherie Rapp, Dottie Macrae, Nera White, and Patsy Neal. We learn from generation to generation. That's the beauty of history and vision. If you see the standards set, you can aim higher and try to improve the game.

Practice, Practice, Practice.   Those are the words you most often will hear from coaches. Practice is the place you can be in control of your actions and your rate of improvement. Practice gives you a chance to work on individual and team skills. It teaches you chemistry and timing, which are so important when playing a team sport.

Politics and Vision

We get vision from the people who came before us. I would never have thought that one day a woman could be president of the United States had it not been for Geraldine Ferraro, who was the Democratic vice-presidential candidate in 1984. She opened the door for other women to succeed in politics and government. Thanks to Ferraro, women can aspire to lead our country and someday will. She didn't win the election, but she gave women vision.

You can take so much knowledge away from a practice session. You have answers to many questions: How did I match up against the other players? What were my strong points and weaknesses during practice? Was I competitive? Do I want to be the best? Was I coachable? Was I focused? Did I make myself and my teammates better? What was my level of intensity? These are all real questions you should think about when getting ready to practice. Your answers will reflect how you play in games. Do you want to rule? Here are some things that will help you dominate on the court:

- Think about practice before you get there. Be ready to compete!
- Arrive early enough to relax. Get warmed up properly and stretch so you are ready to start when practice begins, not 10 or 15 minutes later.
- Work on your weaknesses. Turn them into strengths.
- Be a positive person. Encourage others. Don't get down on your teammates or yourself after a mistake.
- Be a leader. Set an example of focus, enthusiasm, and intensity in all practices.
- Listen to the coach. Ask questions if you are not sure about a drill or situation.
- If you are practicing by yourself, have a plan of what areas you want to cover. Be efficient. Don't waste time.
- Most importantly, even in practice, play to win. It will raise the level of all your teammates.

Motivation

Motivation is the key to any challenge. If you are competitive enough to want to be better, maybe even the best, then you have the ability to be motivated. Motivation is the reason you put more time and effort into your individual game. Motivation is your desire to achieve personal and team success. Robin Roberts was motivated to be one of the best rebounders at Southeastern Louisiana University. Jody Conradt is motivated to be the all-time leading active women's coach with more than 650 career wins. Did you see Sheryl Swoopes dazzle the crowd at the 1993 NCAA Women's Final Four with 47 record-breaking points in the championship game? Someone, somewhere—it could be you—should be motivated to break her record one day.

Your motivation should be fueled by the goals you set. These are examples of goals you might set:

- Work on weaknesses.
- Make the all-state team.
- Win a championship.
- Receive a full scholarship to college.
- Play in the women's Final Four—and win it!

Be focused and motivated to practice, work hard, and achieve every goal you set. Motivation comes from seeing other athletes' success. Now, we have something to shoot for. Being motivated for success is a great feeling, even as you work toward your goals.

Positive Influences

As players, we spend most of our time with coaches. We watch how they talk, walk, and dress. We even pick up on their mannerisms without knowing it. Coaches are a great source of information. Many times you think you know what the coach wants, but maybe the timing or the options are hard to understand. Ask questions! It's much like being in the classroom. Listen, ask the teacher questions, get the explanation. Then, apply it.

We all have our own stories of who guided us at certain times in our careers. For me, I'm a lucky lady. My AAU coach growing up, La Vosier LaMar, taught me not to fear anyone and to respect everyone. So many others influenced me. Brian Sackrowitz and Larry Morse,

The Reports Didn't Lie

Scouting reports can be valuable tools for winning. Marianne Stanley, my coach at Old Dominion University, would order not only scouting reports about our opponents, but also reports about Old Dominion. This gave us a chance to see how other teams viewed our strengths and weaknesses. She allowed us to read our individual reports. Scouting reports listed my left hand as weak and that opponents should give me the outside shot. This was different from how I viewed my game. They became two areas I worked on consistently on my own during practice. By my senior year, my left hand and outside shooting were no longer listed as weaknesses. As a matter of fact, they became strengths. I had new options and was more unpredictable on the court. The more options you have, the more chances you have for success.

---

my high school coaches, taught the street player in me discipline, teamwork and, of course, the fundamentals.

At the 1976 Olympics, Billie Moore and Sue Gunter of Louisiana State University shared their wisdom and patience with me. University of Tennessee coach Pat Summitt, who was a teammate on the 1975 and 1976 USA teams, taught me toughness, how to be mentally and physically ready, and, more than anything else, pushed me to achieve. Marianne Stanley, my coach at Old Dominion, gave me the thinking part of the game. She also showed me how to make each of my teammates better. She taught me how to be a leader.

I will always have a soft spot in my basketball heart for University of Iowa coach Vivian Stringer. She gave me an honest chance to make the 1989 U.S. National team. The USA had just opened the Olympics to professional athletes. I hadn't played for my country since the 1980 Olympic Trials. At age 29, I made the team.

Greg Williams of Colorado State taught me to be a true professional when I was with the Dallas Diamonds in two women's pro leagues. I would be committing an injustice if I left out Henry Bibby and Dean "the Dream" Meminger, whom I played for in the United States Basketball League (USBL). They were in a difficult position, having a woman on their teams. They needed to win, play the best players, keep the media and fans happy, and find playing time for me. They accomplished all that, but it was a difficult task. During our time together, Bibby and Meminger learned to handle new situations. I learned to understand coaches better. More than anything, I learned to soak up as much knowledge and information as I can from each coach for whom I've had the pleasure of playing.

Soaking Up Knowledge

When I was at Old Dominion, I'm sure my coach thought I was a nuisance. I didn't care. I was there to learn, and she was one of the best. Look at Coach Stanley's credentials: a three-time all-American who at age 24 became head coach at one of the best women's basketball schools in the country. Coach Stanley had played basketball at Immaculata College in Pennsylvania for Cathy Rush, the John Wooden of women's basketball. I couldn't pass up the opportunity to learn from Coach Stanley. I figured I might not get another chance to learn from such a basketball expert, one who had learned from another legend. I wanted to be like a sponge and soak up all the information she had to share. I asked a lot of questions—probably to the point of being annoying. "What do you see?" "How do you do that?" She always answered and I always listened.

Summary

Taking your game to the next level means understanding who came before you and set the standards for you to surpass. Remember these points:

- Women's basketball has a rich history. You can learn from the persistence of these sports pioneers.
- The keys for success are self-confidence, desire, and discipline.
- Put your plan for success into action.
- You must be a student of the game to succeed. Identify the roles of players and coaches; everyone has an important role.
- Develop your vision for your game. See yourself succeeding.
- Practice, practice, practice.
- Your motivation will determine how far you will go.

CHAPTER 2

Developing a
Winning Attitude

The mentally strong succeed, and exceptional basketball players have outstanding mental strengths. Winning mentality is the ability to know you are going to win and succeed in what you are trying to accomplish because you have prepared yourself mentally.

Developing a winning mentality is a quality you can acquire—one that can separate exceptional athletes from average ones. You can build that mental attitude by working hard to improve your game. It is a mix of confidence, knowledge of skills and strategies, creativity, desire, discipline, persistence, being in top physical condition, and being a good communicator.

Winning starts in the mind. It's knowing you have prepared yourself thoroughly for the challenge ahead. It's the positive attitude you show the minute you hit the practice court or begin competition. You are ready to do battle against your teammates or with your opponents. You have worked on your skills. You are in excellent condition, which is part of your confidence. You are willing to be competitive in all aspects of basketball. Mental attitude makes you confident you can make your teammates better. You want to be the one who they can look to. You'll win it or lose it and handle the consequences. Your confidence also comes from knowing the offense and defense your coach has taught.

You can develop this attitude by experiencing success. If you continually are able to hit the winning shot in practice, pickup games, or competition, you will feel confident in your ability to do it again and again. Where does all this start? When you practice, are you mentally focused? Do you challenge yourself?

For me, it was my walk, my talk, and my ability to look players in the eye and communicate an air of confidence. My work habits were so demanding I always felt I was better prepared than my teammates or opponents. I developed my game while playing, thinking about my game, watching basketball on television, and listening to it on the radio. I emulated players and tried all their moves. I tried to incorporate different styles into my game. The more I practiced, the more successful and confident I became. This mental attitude kept me from putting limitations on myself. It didn't matter who I played against: younger, older, bigger, stronger, boys, girls. I was never intimidated. I was prepared to give my best effort and my confidence soared. I was always picked in street ball games to play with the guys. They wanted me because I could play and I had the right attitude to win. That made all my hard work in practice worth it.

So often it's your mental attitude that determines how hard you work at the game or in life. Exceptional players have certain strengths. The mix consists of desire, attitude, discipline, persistence, self-confidence, and being a good communicator with your teammates and coaches.

THE MENTAL GAME

This part of basketball can separate you from others. If you can see situations on and off the court, you will be able to make proper decisions based on what you think and actually do when you are playing. The mental aspect of the game allows you to be aware of what is happening. Knowing you can outsmart an opponent with strategy or deception is a great edge to have. There are four elements to the mental portion of your game:

- Thinking the game
- Confidence
- Knowing skills and strategies
- Creativity

Each component can be used to your advantage. All it takes is effort. Remember, the most talented athlete isn't always the best player or the winner. Sometimes, the basketball player who thinks a better game comes out on top.

Thinking the Game

Play games with yourself. Take a piece of paper and draw a miniature court. Run your offense or defense as you think it's meant to be run. When you put it on paper and you're drawing the screens, cuts, and dribbles, you start to look at timing and mentally go through your options. OK, we're stuck. Let's reverse the movement and check the weakside options. Let's say the defender overplayed the wing. I could fade to the corner for the shot. It might be open. This process also works with defenses. If I rotate up on the trap, what passing lanes are open? If it's in the corner, I'd better get off the ball and rotate to protect the basket.

Thinking basketball is the ability to react spontaneously on the court, better and more quickly than your opponents or teammates. You have studied the offenses and defenses and you can read situations as they develop.

You can think the game by knowing your options on the court, by having the ability to see where players are, and then by doing what you can to create situations within your team's game plan.

Thinking is knowing what's going on. Know how much time is on the clock—both the game clock and the shot clock. You may need to decide whether you should call a time-out. Was it a smart time-out to burn? Can you play with three fouls? It all comes down to what you do repeatedly. Are your choices sound?

You can learn the thinking part of the game. Usually, you learn this from your mistakes. That's how you find out if your choices on the court are correct. Thinking goes hand and hand with solid fundamentals. If you have both, you'll be able to think what you need to do and then execute. I often think back to the 1984 Olympics and about Teresa Edwards, the youngest player on the team. She was smart, fast, and a great defender. She always knew where to be on the floor. She had one weakness: When she was in position for a three-point shot, she couldn't knock them down. It was the part of her game that wasn't up to par with the rest. She made herself into a great player by knowing she had a weakness. She's now a three-time Olympian, and one of the best clutch three-point shooters in the world. She knew she had to work hard on her outside game to be the best.

Confidence

Confidence means knowing you will be successful. Success and hard work breed confidence. The more you experience being successful, the better you are going to feel about yourself and your skills. If you have made jumper after jumper from the corner in practice, you will remember that success when it's time to take that shot in a game.

A serious athlete must have confidence to know she can win. Martina Navratilova, by the early 1980s, already was one of the greatest tennis players in the history of the game. Yet, midway through her career she still didn't believe she was a winner. She didn't believe that she could win consistently. She didn't train for success. When she changed her training habits in 1981 and began believing she could win consistently, she went into every match believing she couldn't lose. That's the attitude you have to take with you on the basketball court. If you think you can defeat your opponent, you already have an edge.

Confidence allows you to control your success and setbacks. If you know what you're capable of accomplishing on the court, you're going to be self-assured when it's time to test your skills. Let's say you can bench press 135 pounds 10 times in a row. If you're asked to lift that 135 pounds—or even a little bit more—you're going to be confident that you can accomplish the task. It's the same on the basketball court. If you constantly hit your free throw shots in practice, you can be confident that you're going to hit them in a game.

Confidence allows you to walk on the court, size up your opponent, and say to yourself that there's no way you're going to lose to this person or team. You're going to play to the best of your ability, and it's going to be up to your opponent to outplay you to win. It's important to prepare properly and take care of all the elements you can control. The rest you can't worry about.

Building Confidence.   You began building your confidence the first time you picked up a basketball. It might have been with your parents or with some friends. You checked out the game. You may have thought: "I like this game. I think I'll give it a try."

As your basketball career progressed you began to get an idea of what you do well. At the same time, you probably discovered what areas needed some work. If you targeted those weaknesses and worked until they were eliminated, you accomplished two important things. First, you mastered your weaknesses and became a better all-around player. Second, you saw what you could accomplish with a little work and determination. That builds confidence.

Your progress will help your confidence soar. You will be a more well-rounded player. You will know it and so will your opponents. You will be much more difficult to guard. Take them inside, outside, shoot over people, or drive around them. If that doesn't get your confidence going, nothing will.

Another way to build your confidence is to find and develop your specialty. Everyone remembers Kareem Abdul-Jabbar's sky hook. Whenever the Los Angeles Lakers needed a basket, they turned to Jabbar and his sky hook. You need to determine what part of your game is strongest and then polish and accentuate that skill. That way, you always have an "ace" to turn to in a tight situation. This doesn't mean you can neglect the other parts of your game. Sheryl Swoopes

Working for a Shot

When my collegiate basketball career ended, despite what I had already accomplished, I was not a great outside shooter. Perimeter defenders backed off me a few steps, knowing that I was likely to pass or drive rather than shoot a jumper. I had succeeded as a penetrator and opportunity-type player. Many of my easy baskets were off steals and turnovers. Those days, I realized, were coming to an end.

In 1980, I signed a contract to play in the Women's Professional Basketball League. I knew my game might not be good enough to get me through. One of my coaches, Greg Williams of the Dallas Diamonds, told me quite bluntly: "Nancy, you need an outside game."

That summer was one of the most challenging, yet rewarding, periods of my life. My former college teammate Rhonda Rompola, who's now the coach at Southern Methodist University, and I played every day. Without exception, I took 400 to 500 shots a day. In college, we didn't yet have the three-point shot. Now, in the women's league, we would. I needed to be ready to add the three-point shot to my game. So every day, when I was practicing my shooting, I made sure that 150 of those shots were from three-point range.

That first year in the women's league was a good one for me. I averaged 30 points a game. I shot 56 percent from the floor and 40 percent from three-point range. I had the confidence to pull up and shoot from the outside. I had another weapon.

---

from 1993 NCAA champion Texas Tech is not a one-dimensional player. She has many talents. But with a game on the line, Swoopes and the Lady Raiders knew they could rely on her outside shot.

Confidence comes from winning. First, you have to know how to win. We're not talking strictly in terms of points on the scoreboard and who finishes ahead. If you have a bad attitude but you control it during a game, then you're a winner. If you often disagree with the referees, but control your temper during a game, you're a winner. If you're constantly worrying about your statistics, but concentrate on working with your teammates so everyone plays better, then you're definitely a winner.

If you think of success and winning in terms of progress and achievement, you can be a winner every time you take the court. Just make sure that you don't waste your time and you'll always improve.

Finally, a confident basketball player is one who has done her homework. You should want to learn everything you can about the game. It is important to know your offensive and defensive strategies by heart. We'll talk more about how knowledge of skills and strategies sharpens your mental game. For now, remember that you can play your best if you are sure of yourself, are relaxed, and know what you should be doing. There's no excuse for the player who isn't prepared. Knowledge comes from practice. So pay attention. When your coach is talking, listen. Your coach may be sharing valuable information to help you understand a drill or strategy. Even if your coach is speaking to another player, it never hurts to listen.

Incorporating Confidence Into Your Game.   Turning yourself into a confident player isn't easy. It all begins with pride. You should be proud of your team and yourself. It has to come from within. Pride comes from constantly challenging yourself and your teammates to get better. That pride and hard work will turn into confidence, and

 ## His Airness Versus Lady Magic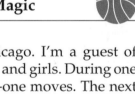

It's July 1993, at Elmhurst College near Chicago. I'm a guest of Michael Jordan at his basketball camp for boys and girls. During one of Michael's lectures, he talked about one-on-one moves. The next thing I know, it's me and Mike going one-on-one with 450 campers watching. My goal was not only to make Michael sweat, but also to make him work. He's a talker. He talks trash. And, he's full of confidence. He was trying to intimidate me, seeing if I would accept the challenge. I'm thinking no way am I going to roll over and let him have his way. I wasn't about to let his reputation and his confidence sway my confidence. Obviously, I'm overmatched. I did manage to make some moves and slide by for a lefty running shot off the glass. Not only did it put a smile on his face, but the shot drew a cheer from the kids. OK, I lost 10-2, but I was giving it my best—mentally and physically. I think my effort and confidence surprised everyone. It wasn't about the score and who won and who lost. It was about earning Michael's respect and keeping my own. I had the confidence from years of experience to play him to the best of my ability. I couldn't ask more of myself.

your opponents will sense that you are sure of yourself. It shows in the way you hustle on and off the court. It shows in the way you keep your cool when a referee's call goes the other way.

Confidence, however, doesn't mean cockiness. Some players cross the line and are no longer confident, just cocky. They showboat and they sacrifice the good of their team for their own glory. They seek attention first and worry about others second. It might be easy to show off your skills just for the sake of letting others see what you can do. But that doesn't make it right. Don't dribble behind your back just because you feel like doing it or you believe it might impress someone. Have a reason. You need a reason to pass behind your back or dribble between your legs. If it's the best option to gain an edge on your opponent, then go ahead. If you're doing these things just to show off, it will someday backfire on you—that's not being a good team player. Players who show off live for the moment—the spectacular. Strive for long-term consistency and quality. Now that is really spectacular.

A confident player is difficult to stop because she is feeling good about her game. Confident players carry their teams to victory. You're sure to build your confidence if you focus on improvement and progress. After each game, evaluate your performance. Watch the game film, if possible. Focus on what you did well and not so well. Remember those things and think about them before the next game. Learn from your mistakes. Watch what you did before you made a mistake and try to figure out what you can do to prevent yourself from making the same mistake again. If every time you missed a free throw, you noticed (on film) you were staring out into the crowd or looking around, you would know you have to work on your concentration. When you do things well, get a mental picture of exactly how you did it and how you felt. If you're a confident player, you'll be able to take a good, hard look at your performance and take steps to make it even better next time.

Knowing Skills and Strategies

When it comes to skills and strategy, basketball players don't have it easy. There's much more to the game than Xs and Os. You have to know when to press and when to trap. You have to know how to break a press and how to work that trap. Football players, in some ways, have it much easier. They specialize. They have to know offensive or defensive strategies and plays, but usually not both. In basketball, you must know both if you want to compete. In the early days of basketball, girls played offense or defense in six-on-six competition. They specialized in one portion of the game. With today's uptempo, transition-style of basketball, you need to be proficient at both or you'll be left behind.

When you're young, you are responsible for learning some of the basic skills you need to compete. High school and college coaches have less time to teach these days because of all the rules changes restricting practice time. These rules allow you more time to handle your academic requirements. If the next step for you is to play college basketball, get your fundamentals down and play the game as often as you can. College coaches don't have as much time these days for players who can't dribble the ball with both hands or who don't box out well. You don't have to be perfect, but you must have the skills that they believe they can work with. Years ago, a player who was extremely tall, but clumsy, was considered a project; coaches wouldn't expect this person to contribute to their programs right away. These days, with so many talented players in high school and junior high, there's not much time for projects. Scholarships are expensive and valuable for a player's education and development. The best advice I can give you is to learn these skills—the basics—early so you are ready for high school ball and you can spend time polishing your skills instead of learning them.

Building Knowledge of Skills.   Understanding basketball skills and strategies can occur in many ways. As you experience situations on the court or watch games, you see how other players react and what decisions they make. You will find out if you can achieve the same results once you get on the court. I'm a firm believer in watching the game and listening to coaches or successful players. Building knowledge is gathering information. If a play is stopped, consider your other options to keep the play successful. You should be able to read situations on the floor and make split-second adjustments. It could be on the offensive or defensive end. An important aspect of basketball is to avoid predetermining what you are going to do. You must have flexibility. Sure, you might know what offense you need to run against a 2-3 zone defense. But maybe the inside has been taken away and the outside shot on the weak side is available. Use it if it's there. Stick to your game plan if you see it can work. Your skills play a vital part in this combination. You may want to make a certain move or pass. Now you need to have the proper fundamental skills to make it work. The worst feeling is to see a potential situation and not be able to complete it because of a weakness in your game.

There are many skills you need to learn to become proficient at basketball: footwork, jump stops, defensive stance. The list goes on. This may sound a little tedious, but there's no getting around learning these skills. This also may sound like learning skills takes the fun out of the game. That may be somewhat true, but before you can scrimmage, and definitely before you're ready for a game, you have to know these skills.

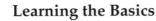

Learning the Basics

Since 1979, Louisiana Tech has had one of the most consistent women's basketball programs in the country. Tech has won three national championships and would have had a fourth had North Carolina's Charlotte Smith not hit a three-pointer at the buzzer to win the 1994 NCAA title.

Why has Coach Leon Barmore's team been so good? The basics. He has been a believer in the inside game for years, featuring high-percentage basketball. Tech's guards know that a simple entry pass into the post area can lead to victory. They work at it. They practice the ball fake and the bounce pass over and over. Simplicity and repetition have been the keys to successful team play, no matter who's on the court for Louisiana Tech.

When you are working out by yourself or with a friend, you can continue to make workouts fun and competitive while still using the skill correctly. As your skills improve, you will begin to see how these skills combine as major aspects of the game. For example, you may be a great shooter. But if you have problems shaking the defense or have poor footwork, you may never get a chance to perform the skill in which you excel.

You can learn the skills and their uses. I may be getting a little bit philosophical, but it's important that you know the "why" behind basketball skills and strategies. You need to know the philosophy, or purpose, behind using a bounce pass in a certain situation or the purpose of boxing out rather than crashing the boards for a rebound.

Communication between players and a coach is key. If you completely understand how to do something, you will be able to do it. If you're not sure, that's where guessing starts. Guessing does not contribute to your game.

With so much information available, you can gain insight about basketball skills and strategies. You can attend clinics, read books, call coaches, network with other players and experts, watch high school, college, and professional basketball on television, and watch videos. The resources are unlimited. How does a player get better? Get some references. Look to the experts. Find the people who know. When I wanted to learn more about shooting, I watched my former teammate and current SMU head coach Rhonda Rompola. She had perfect form, follow-through, and results. I also read the "Shot Doctor," Ace Hoffstein, who wrote the book *(Hoops) I Missed!* Ace is one of the best at teaching shooting and I respect his advice.

I probably own every book and video on the market. I began building my basketball library long ago and am always adding something to it. I want to keep up with the latest changes. Young players may need to rely on their parents and coaches to help them find the latest information on basketball. A good place to start is your local library. I'm sure your coaches subscribe to coaching magazines. Ask them to let you read their copies.

Here's some advice:

• **Watch the Game**—Watch it in person or on television. Watch good high school or college teams play. Mental imagery is important. You can see others who mentally play the game. They won't be hard to spot. They will be the players who make good decisions on the floor and have low turnover ratios.

• **Tape the Game**—Have your own library of tapes to watch. There happens to be a tremendous amount of women's college games on cable and more recently on network television. At your leisure, you can watch a particular game or player. You can use slow motion—if your VCR has it—to watch specific moves or plays.

• **Read About the Game**—Read any basketball material you can find. These could be instructional books or magazines, or even autobiographies. You'll get a sense of how others coach the game, and situations and games others have been in.

• **Talk the Game**—Find teammates or other basketball players who want to talk the game. This is very informational. The more you talk, the more your focus is mental. I love to find basketball junkies. It's the purest form of staying in tune to the game. It's fun to hash out the game you're going to play or an opponent you will be guarding.

• **Read Scouting Reports**—Read not only about your opponent's tendencies, but see what others think about your game or your team.

Never Stop Learning

Because I've played through the '70s, '80s and '90s—whew, that's a long time—I've seen drills, skills, and strategies change. Women's basketball is a more athletic, uptempo game today than it was 20 years ago. It certainly is crowd pleasing. I have found a way to stay current with all the new offenses and defenses by interviewing coaches and players. While this is part of my job as a television and radio commentator, I'm always learning. Auburn's Joe Ciampi runs his 2-3 zone differently than Texas Tech's Marsha Sharp. Each is quite successful and each has a different philosophy and scheme. One style might be to force you to shoot more from the outside with a player running out on you. The other style might be to invite double-teaming once the ball gets to the inside post. The thinking might be slightly different, but both are effective strategies for each team. Watch for subtle differences when you are viewing a game.

Incorporating Knowledge and Skills Into Your Game.   There are different ways of incorporating knowledge of the game and what skill to use and when to use it. See what works for you. There are basic decisions to make on offense and defense. Depending on your coach's style, you should have options to utilize. It always helps to find out what works or doesn't work in practice. Some of the drills your coach might put you through can be competitive-type drills that highlight a combination of thinking or reacting, then using the proper skill to complete the drill. Remember to keep your mind sharp so you don't get sloppy on the court. Also be competitive in all drills, but have fun doing them.

Start the process by evaluating what kind of player you are. Start with the basics. Are you a post player or a guard? Are you an inside or outside player? Are you a scorer or a rebounder? Are you a team leader or a role player? Now, define your strengths and weaknesses. Through this process, you'll begin to understand the skills you need to accentuate your strengths and correct your weaknesses. You can target these skills and work on them in practice.

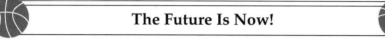

The Future Is Now!

In 1974, a friend read in the *Long Island Press* newspaper that tryouts were being held for a USA team that was playing exhibition games against a Russian team. We went to Queens College on a Saturday morning. I couldn't believe it—250 girls were there. Tryouts lasted all day. Finally, after many cuts, my number was still around. The committee selected 10 players out of 250. I, as a 16-year-old high school sophomore, was 1 of the 10. We went to a 3-day precamp tryout in New Mexico. There had been three other tryouts like ours. Forty women went at it for 3 days. Ten were selected to move on to the tryout camp with all the veteran players. I was one of those 10. After 3 days, I injured my ribs—the diagnosis was that they were broken. A member of the selection committee and the head coach drove me to the airport so I could go home. Alberta Cox, the coach, looked at me and said with a warm smile: "Nancy, you work hard so you can make the 1980 Olympic team." I was startled. I looked at her and said: "Coach, that's 6 years away. I'm going to make the 1976 team." She thought I had potential for the future. I wanted to reach that potential right away.

Want to be a better shooter? Incorporate all the necessary skills—concentration, coordination, rhythm, and many others—into improving your shooting. Even if you are not going to be a post or power forward, work on rebounding. Learn how to box out. My responsibilities as a point guard include shooting, bringing the ball downcourt, passing off to teammates, and directing the offense. With my experience, it's easy for me to define my style and evaluate my skills. As a teenager, it's not so easy. Good advice is to experiment. Find out where your strengths lie through the process of elimination and eventually you'll be able to define your game.

If your coach tells you that you have potential, ask him or her what you can do to realize that potential. Make your coach be specific. All potential means is that at some point—maybe next year, maybe in 20 years—you may excel at the game of basketball. Potential means you haven't yet lived up to others' expectations. All you need to do is worry about living up to your own expectations.

Try not to be stuck with the "potential" label. Keep working and don't be satisfied. Use potential as motivation. Enjoy the challenge of being better or working harder than your teammates and friends. Only you can make it happen. Set goals for yourself. Motivation and goals go hand in hand. When your skills and mental game come together, you will see tremendous improvement in your overall game.

Using the skills and strategies you've been taught means making the most of your time. Be positive. Always walk away with something positive. There are times when it's not easy. There are times when you get down and think it doesn't matter. It does! If you are getting to the next level, you're encountering better players. If you are a sub, push the starters to be better. It will help you and the team. Be competitive with them. Respect them, but don't back down. If your coach puts you in a game during garbage time, be the "garbage queen." Get the most you can from the time you get to play. Don't allow the situation to pull you down.

Playing My Best

In 1975, I played for the U.S. squad in the world championships in South America. I wasn't playing much, so I sat at the end of the bench and pouted. In international basketball, it's more difficult to substitute because there are fewer breaks in the action. But I didn't realize this; I only knew that the coach wasn't letting me play. I remember telling Pat Summitt, my teammate, who coaches at the University of Tennessee, that even if the coach put me in, I wouldn't go. Summitt set me straight. She told me that even if I only played 10 seconds, I was going to give it my best. She told me that I had to make the most of my playing time—long or short—because game experience is where you test all the skills and knowledge you've learned. That lesson still is with me.

Think of your basketball skills as the foundation of your game. Above all, you want to be solid in the fundamentals. Think of it this way. Before you can work calculus problems in school, you have to know algebra. And before you can handle algebra equations, you have to be able to add, subtract, multiply, and divide. Your basketball skills are the addition, subtraction, multiplication, and division. You put those skills together and you're ready to learn basketball strategies. Finally, you're ready for competition. Start early, so you won't have to play catch-up.

Creativity

Many women enjoy watching basketball. When they're not playing, they're watching—high school, collegiate, and professional basketball. One reason to watch is because you can learn something every time. Another reason is that you can enjoy watching. Basketball is entertaining, it's fun. It's also amazing what some players can do.

Basketball players are stronger and better athletes than their counterparts from decades past. That means there's much more they can do on the court. Basketball is in an era of marketability. Athletes must, in a sense, sell themselves on the court. They must promote their talents. If basketball isn't interesting, people won't come to watch. You always see a crowd whenever Tennessee plays Georgia, Stanford plays USC, Texas plays Texas Tech, or other top rivals meet in women's basketball. These teams are enjoyable because they play a fast-paced, uptempo brand of basketball. They also have players who know how to entertain crowds.

Being creative on the basketball court is an important part of your game—but remember it's only one part. Being creative in the right situations can make you a more valuable part of your team, make you a better player, and get your teammates and the crowd fired up.

Building Creativity.   Basketball is supposed to be fun. You often hear professional basketball players say they'll keep on competing as long as the game is fun. They've got the right attitude. Sure, it's a business for them. But basketball is a game too, and people who play it are supposed to enjoy themselves—even the professionals. Making basketball fun takes a little creativity on your part. Play mind games with yourself. You've seen the television commercial about the little boy who picks up a discarded basketball on the playground. He begins an imaginary countdown, dribbles, and shoots what he hopes will be the winning basket. We all smile after the boy misses but claims he was fouled. Even when the boy missed his shot, he found a way for his story to have a happy ending. That's what basketball is all about. I'm sure you have played those same games with yourself—shooting the game-winning basket just before the imaginary buzzer sounds. Funny thing, as you get better you expect to make more and more of those game-winning shots. Don't be surprised when you start making them in real games.

Creativity comes through practice. There's no other way. Creativity gives you options. You perfect those options in practice. You have the ball above the key. What are your options? You can go forward, double clutch, and try to draw your opponent into committing herself. You can go right, go left, or you can step back and pop a jumper. Doing those things doesn't just happen. They are acquired skills. And as you've heard several times already, you acquire those skills through practice.

The truly great women's basketball players come from different backgrounds and environments. But there's a common thread—the blacktop, school yards, and parks. Call them what you want. That's where freedom and creativity are nurtured—playing one-on-one, two-on-two or three-on-three. When you get it, you can't lose it. These are great places to learn the sights and sounds—learning basketball and the game's lingo. You develop shots and moves you never knew you had. Maybe it's a drive, a spin, and a finger roll to finish the play. It's all part of experiencing what your limits are and can be.

 Not a Surprise

At Old Dominion, my teammates and I would often practice taking half-court shots (after practice, of course). Many of us routinely knocked down a few. We were relaxed and confident.

During my senior year, I happened to make half-court shots in two straight games. Of course, I just looked at my teammates like "What did you expect?"

I remember asking Harlem Globetrotter legend Meadowlark Lemon how he made those incredible hook shots all the time. The crowds were always shocked when he did, but Meadowlark wasn't surprised when they went in. He said "Nancy, I've been practicing those shots for years. I expect to make them."

Get a VCR and tape some women's college games. Get your remote and slow down the action. Watch some of the sweet moves that are made and how they develop. In 1992, the University of Virginia had one of the best backcourts in the history of women's basketball. With three-time All-American and two-time Player of the Year Dawn Staley and her teammate Tammy Reiss, Virginia was exciting. The two were great for the game; they were well worth the price of admission. Not only did they have style, they were also true winners. Dawn could do it all—slice through the defense with incredible ballhandling skills or make a no-look pass to the Burge sisters on the inside. If the defense went with Dawn, there was Tammy Reiss to knock down the perimeter jumper. Inside or out, both had the ability to break down the defense and get the ball to an open teammate.

If you work at a skill or shot long enough, you'll be able to tell if you feel comfortable and if you're improving. The important thing is to use your creativity when practicing on your own. Use it in free time and in pickup games. Work it until you're ready to show it in team practice and competition.

Incorporating Creativity Into Your Game.   Adding creativity to your game is an extension of building your creative skills. It's developing your options. If you can pass with your left and right hands, shoot with your left and right hands, take the ball to the hoop, and hit from the outside, you're going to be difficult to guard. The more options you have, the more opportunities you have to be creative.

People think being creative is driving to the basket, spinning 360 degrees, and laying the ball in the basket. They're right. Being creative, however, is also reading defenses well. Stanford's Jennifer Azzi wasn't flashy. But she was the best at getting the Stanford offense in high gear. She could spot weaknesses in an opponent's defense and take advantage of those weaknesses. Sheryl Swoopes wasn't flashy—just amazing. She was one of the most difficult players to guard. She was dangerous in so many ways that opponents didn't know how to stop her. Whether it was handling the ball, moving without it, rebounding on the offensive end, she found ways to score and hurt Texas Tech's opponents.

I remember a play that Swoopes, Krista Kirkland, and their Texas Tech teammates worked to perfection. No matter how many times they ran it, their opponents couldn't counter the attack. Swoopes would post low on one side of the basket with another Tech teammate. Two teammates would post low on the other side and then clear out to the corner. Swoopes would cut hard to the high post, looking like she would receive a pass from Kirkland. Swoopes' defenders began to overplay her. They'd cheat to try to deny the pass. Then, Swoopes and Kirkland knew that if Swoopes faked high, she'd be all alone if she cut back toward the basket. The result was an easy backdoor layup.

Some people aren't going to be as creative as others. Don't force it. Stay with your strengths and do what you can to incorporate them into your game.

My former coach at Old Dominion, Marianne Stanley, saw that our team was talented and creative. She let us make our own decisions. She gave us parameters. She didn't force us to run a set offense with no variations. She gave me the green light to make decisions. Sure, we could beat our opponents playing a half-court game because we had outside shooters and we had strength inside. But we wanted to beat them down court. Coach Stanley let us improvise; she let us be stars. In many ways, her coaching style in the late 1970s was ahead of its time.

Coaches such as Rick Moody at Alabama, Jody Conradt of Texas, Joe Ciampi of Auburn, and Tara VanDerveer of Stanford are changing the game of basketball with the way they run their offenses. Their plan is to look for the three-pointer first. These coaches and many others begin by recruiting the top outside shooters in the country. Then, they encourage them to look for the three-point shot. If they don't beat their opponents down court for a layup, they look for an open three in transition. If it's not there, they run their half-court offense, still looking for an open three-point shot. Their players aren't afraid to shoot from the outside. They don't have to worry about being taken out of the game if they miss several shots early. They know that if they miss four times, they'll have a chance to make the next four. Remember that you can't do something if you don't try it. Many of these coaches have enough confidence in their players' outside shooting to let them try.

Remember, when it comes to creativity, don't get impatient. Just because you can't match your friend's moves doesn't mean it has to stay that way. You'll catch up if you practice. Another important thing to remember is that creativity doesn't always mean flashy passes and flashy moves. Some of the most creative players in the history of basketball weren't the ones who had 40-inch vertical jumps or could dunk in a dozen ways. Being creative on the ballcourt means using all your options and making the best decision for the moment.

KEYS TO SUCCESS

A winning attitude means better conditioning and better preparation. It means having the confidence to know that in easy or tough situations, you'll make the right decision for you and for your teammates. It's also that aura about you—no matter if you are outspoken or shy. It's your look, the way you walk, and how you perform. The mindset of a winner is a great asset to have working for you.

It's essential that you develop this part of your game and feel comfortable about your efforts. Many of the top players have an extraordinary mentality. Through hard work and extra effort they have become superstars.

Desire

Success on the basketball court begins with desire. No one said success was going to be easy. Hard work and discipline are the elements for success! There's no room for shortcuts, if you want to be great.

To want greatness means you have a desire to be better than the others around you. Having that desire enables you to work out longer, stay focused on your goals, and do the things that enhance your game. That could be wanting to find better players to practice and play with, or seeking out camps, summer leagues, or places to get extra court time.

Desire is hurdling obstacles to reach your goals. It doesn't matter if it's too hot, too cold, or too windy. Desire is eliminating excuses of why you can't practice. Desire is your effort to find opportunities to work your game. You can do it if you really want to.

Building Desire.   When you watch others achieve a high level of success on the court, it helps you build desire. See how they have achieved it and dedicate yourself mentally and physically to wanting to be that good. You build desire from the ground up. It's the little things you do that give you the love and dedication needed. Focus your time around the game; make sacrifices in your daily schedule so you have proper time to work on your game or watch others play. Desire means you must allow yourself to dream of greatness: to know and see that it can be done. Competitiveness will also fuel your desire for success; each level you get to in your game will make you want to reach the next. If you dream about making the all-star team, or the state finals, you should never expect anything less than what your goals are.

Incorporating Desire Into Your Game.   This means challenging yourself. Get out there and get better. Self-improvement is in your hands. Do the basic drills with intensity. I always recommend playing against players who are better than you. It makes you strive for another level. You have to be focused and concentrate harder. Desire to improve is your love for the game. That's right, the game. Go out and practice it, play it, compete. It could be at the school yard, the YMCA, the gym, or in tournaments such as Hoop It Up, the national three-on-three tournament. They're everywhere. Find one and challenge yourself to be better.

Discipline

Discipline and desire work together. It takes discipline to stay 15 minutes after practice and shoot another 40 or 50 free throws. It also takes a little desire to want to stay after practice when your teammates are on their way home.

Discipline doesn't just dictate when and how much you practice. It also dictates what you practice. We all have parts of our game that are better than other parts. Some people are better at being defensive stoppers, while others excel at perimeter shooting. So why not practice only those things that you do best? The biggest reason is that you won't be your best if you work only on your strengths. Instead, you have to focus your time and energy on your weaknesses. Pick the parts of your game that are the weakest and spend your time changing those weaknesses into strengths. Repetition is a key. If you have trouble going to your left, spend more time using your left hand. Use your imagination to create gamelike situations when you might need to rely on that particular skill and how you would respond.

Discipline also means putting your team first. The better you are individually, the more valuable you will be to your team. That means practice and sacrifice. It takes discipline and good decision-making skills to know when to pass up the 15-footer and find your open teammate for the layup. Your coaches can help you become a more disciplined player. There are many knowledgeable coaches that you come across. Soak up their wisdom, styles, and philosophies. Apply the ones you like and tuck the other information away for another time.

I Thought I Had to Score to Be Noticed

I started my freshman year at ODU in 1976 as a heralded Olympian with a silver medal. I thought I had to score 20 points or more a game to live up to what was expected of me. I also thought that's how I would get noticed for individual honors. Although ODU would be on its way to its best season, I become my own focus. It was me first, my teammates second. As my sophomore season approached, Coach Marianne Stanley asked me to pass more and make my teammates more valuable and better players. I couldn't understand at first what she was saying. What, me give up scoring? Coach was saying, "Nancy, we will be better as a team if you become more of a team player. Score less, we will win more often." She was right. In each of my next three seasons, my scoring average dipped sharply. But our winning increased greatly: 30-4, NWIT champions; 37-1, national champs; and 34-1, national champs. We won as a team and I still achieved my individual goals and so did many of my teammates.

Discipline means being an individual and it can certainly be applied to putting your team first. Yes, it's very important to want to be good, very good. But you can achieve that in many ways. Can you make your teammates better? Can your ability, attitude, and leadership help others on your team get better? Absolutely. In a team sport such as basketball, the more weapons you have on the court, the better chance you have to win. That's why team play usually wins out over individual success. Discipline also can mean sacrifice. You may want to take a certain shot, but maybe a teammate has the better percentage shot, underneath. Sure, you've hit that shot before with someone hanging on you, but now's the time to make the right decision. Give it up. You may score fewer points, but you may help your team more when you hit the open teammate instead of taking your shot. That type of play can go a long way toward winning. It shows your teammates that you trust and believe in them and that they can be counted on. It builds a solid respect and communication among the players. Believe me, when the game is on the line, you'll have your chance to win it or lose it. Coaches respect team players. It shows your willingness to do what's best for the team.

Building Discipline.   Repetition is the key to building discipline. Discipline is mental. Before you do something or say something, you think it. You must build discipline first. Now you can apply discipline in what you expect your work habits to be. How do you treat and talk to teammates and opponents? Do you apply discipline when listening to your coaches? You should. You build these traits by being focused, having a basic plan of attack, and carrying out that plan without deviation.

Incorporating Discipline Into Your Game.   This means control. Don't force a situation on the court if it's not there. If you are a great 15-foot jump shooter, don't allow the defense to push you out to 20 feet for your shot. Be disciplined enough to know you can work for the shot you want to take. Don't be satisfied. You can also incorporate discipline into your game by being on time to practices, games, and meetings. How do you handle yourself on the court with teammates, opponents, coaches, and officials? Are you courteous? Do you lose your cool? It's all part of discipline. You're in control of your actions.

Donovan and Nissen

Old Dominion University had a problem my senior year in 1979-80— a very good one. We were the defending national champs and coming to Old Dominion was the National High School Player of the Year, heavily recruited 6-foot-8 Anne Donovan. At any other school, starting would have been a lock. At Old Dominion, we had 6-foot-5 all-American senior Inge Nissen. I waited eagerly to see those giants battle for supremacy in the paint. It became quite clear that the vet wasn't giving her spot to the rookie and that the slender rookie wasn't afraid to go right at the veteran. Each worked diligently on favorite moves and tried to develop a new one to use against the other. Anne found the Jabbar hook shot and Inge worked on increased mobility and her outside shot. The time and discipline each "twin tower" used to expand her game and help the other improve were big reasons Old Dominion went on to win its second-straight national championship. It took a lot of discipline for Inge to realize Anne could and would block her shots underneath. It took discipline for Anne to realize she'd better play defense with her feet moving because Inge was so quick off the dribble from the high post.

You can put discipline into or out of your game. It's up to you. Are you in control on the court or out of control?

Persistence

Persistence is your attitude. It's your frame of mind. It's not being satisfied. If you are persistent in basketball or in life, you can be successful. That quality will help you with skills and strategies. Eventually, you will figure out why you are successful on the court. Desire and hard work are a function of persistence. It's the only way to achieve success. Persistence has a domino effect. Everyone benefits except maybe your opponents. You've got the desire to play your best and if your opponents can't match that desire, watch out.

Building Persistence.   You build persistence when you are willing to settle only for the best. There will be times in practice when hard work, repetition, and persistence pay off. Continue working when you think you can be better at a skill, drill, or learning the game. Don't be afraid to ask questions of coaches, mentors, and players. Get it right in your mind. That's how you can build persistence into your game. It's always doing, asking, and making sure it's correct. No matter how much or hard you work at something, apply those habits all the time. You'll be amazed at how being persistent can change a coach's or teammate's opinion of you. If you play hard for 2 hours in practice, your persistence should show your coaches you can give the same effort in a game. Take that focus and desire and use it every time you practice or play.

Incorporating Persistence in Your Game.   This means being repetitive in drills, games, watching tapes, and reading about whatever area you are trying to improve. Don't let anyone talk you out of wanting to do more. Your game, as we have talked about, has strengths and weaknesses. Everyone has some of both. When you are working to improve, don't get discouraged. Continue to be persistent with your goals and desire to improve. Look at the positive changes you are accomplishing. Persistence is as much mental as it is physical. It's a battle you must keep winning.

A Little Persistence Pays Off

I was playing in the USBL for the Long Island Knights in 1987. Our team was loaded with talent, including Michael Ray Richardson, a three-time NBA all-star, and Geoff Huston, a former NBA regular. Both had played with the New York Knicks. Remember, I was the only woman playing in this league.

We were playing the Rhode Island Gulls and talk in the locker room before the game turned to the Gulls' 5-foot-3 Tyrone "Muggsy" Bogues. Richardson, the former NBA all-star at 6-foot-3, was telling anyone who wanted to listen how he was going to post low against Bogues and knock him across the head with a forearm if Bogues got too close to him.

The first time Richardson had the ball, he obviously was thinking of how he was going to put his plan into action. Bogues, however, had other ideas. He stripped the ball from Michael Ray and raced down the court for an easy basket. The next time Michael Ray got the ball, it was the same story: a steal and two points. The third time, Richardson pump faked and Bogues stole the ball. Here's a player going against a three-time NBA all-star and getting the best of him. Three possessions, three steals. Richardson told our coach Dean Meminger that he wanted out of the game—right now. I had been on the bench telling Dean I could guard him. "I know I can, let me try," I told Coach. Dean kept saying no. I kept up my persistence. I wanted a chance.

After Richardson took himself out of the game, Coach looked down the bench and asked who wanted to guard Bogues. No one volunteered, so I did again. My persistence and desire to play paid off.

Shortly after I entered the game, Huston and I were working to trap Bogues as he worked his way down court. Bogues started to spin when he saw Huston close in. I took advantage of Bogues' momentary distraction and stole the ball. As I raced down court, I didn't forget that Muggsy was close behind. Although I am a half-foot taller than Bogues, I didn't forget that he has a 40-inch vertical jump. Instead of risking getting my shot blocked by my much-shorter opponent, I drove to the basket and passed off behind my back to Huston, who was trailing on the play. Two points.

I don't mean, by telling this story, to sound like I'm bragging. I merely want to show how players who may not be as tall or as strong as their opponents can compete as long as they have desire and are persistent. Bogues didn't let his size stop him and I didn't let being the only woman in a men's league slow me down.

COMMUNICATION

Communication is a major asset to winning. It's important to have an understanding of what your coaches and teammates think and feel. That eliminates the unknown. If you completely understand, it becomes easier for you to be properly prepared to play the game.

You can be a good leader through communication. It can be how you talk, a pat on the back, a wink or a smile. Some players don't have the same ability as you. You can bring their level up with how you communicate with them. A subtle word of encouragement or pointing out a better way of using her skill can help a teammate. How you say it can hurt or embarrass a teammate. Remember, once you say something to someone you can never take it back. Take time to understand how and what others are thinking and feeling. Spend time with each of your teammates. It could help you know how each will respond in different situations. Some are more tolerant or sensitive than others. You might not always hang out with all your teammates, but there's information you can get from spending some quality time with them. This information can help you and the team on the court. This type of time can let you know how teammates feel about winning and losing. Do they like the system? Are they confident? Do they like hard passes or bounce passes? Besides, communication skills will remain with you long after your playing days are over.

Teammate to Teammate: Can We Talk?

A positive compliment can go a long way. Criticizing a teammate should be the job of a coach. Suggesting to your teammate an option she didn't think of can be achieved in a positive manner. If it's done in a negative way, you run the risk of being tuned out. We all know when we make a mistake. Try not to compound it. There is definitely room on the floor to use communication for success. For example: "Jackie, great pass to Nikki in the corner. If the defense reads it next time, look under the bucket. Yolanda is wide open on the switch." Give your teammates positive options if you sense they're available. If you are not sure of a situation, don't give an answer. Go to your coach for help.

Keep it Positive

Communication was a problem for me during my freshman year at Old Dominion. My skill level was different than that of many of my teammates. Instead of being patient, I was critical. "Why can't you handle the pass, grab the rebound?" "Come on, you have to make the layup." I was extremely critical of their mistakes; this was poor leadership on my part. I was making the problem worse because I was hurting their confidence. Not only did they have to contend with their own performance, they also had to deal with me.

My coach during my sophomore year, Marianne Stanley, showed me that a positive approach would be better suited to the team's development. Instead of saying, "Sue, how could you miss that pass?" I complimented her for busting down the court and trying for it. "Hey, no problem. Sure, it was my fault. I'll get it to you next time!" That change worked wonders for my relationship with my teammates and their level of confidence.

Coaches Coach—Players Play

Your job as a good teammate is to try to raise not only your level of play, but also your teammates'. Be a positive force on the floor. It's the coach's job to teach and instruct. It's the players' responsibility to carry out the plan. Encourage your teammates to stick with what the coach is teaching. Be a supporter, not the teacher.

On the Court.   Sometimes, the court is the most difficult place to communicate with each other and your coach. The pace is frantic, emotions are high. Crowds can be loud at times. Many games have been won or lost with a team's momentum. Whether you are up or down, pull your teammates together in dead-ball situations—after a foul and definitely after a shooting foul. Get your strategy in order.

Be Yourself.   Being yourself sounds easy and it is. As you watch many of the great stars of collegiate or Olympic basketball, you may think: "I wish I was her." I hear that quite often—players want to be like Olympians Katrina McClain, Suzy McConnell, or Teresa Edwards. It's OK to want to be the best. But you need to be yourself. Develop your own style, moves, and on-court attitude. Take the good things about these players. But don't want to be them. Women's basketball needs lots of new stars. There will be plenty of time for you to figure out how big, how fast, and what position you will play. Continue to work at your overall game no matter what. Who knows how far you can go? Remember, you should always want to "Be your own hero!"

Officials—They've Got a Tough Job.   This is one tough area. No matter what you believe, the officials truly try their best. Yes, they will miss calls. In many cases, however, the calls will even out. Be respectful of the men and women with whistles and stripes. The worst thing you can do is get a bad rep as a complainer or whiner. It will only draw attention to you. Let the coach deal with the officials. Be a good sport when faced with calls you believe are incorrect. Remember, the officials are human and are using their best judgment. They will never please everyone.

BEING A TEAM PLAYER

If you are the star of your team, project leadership on and off the court. It's not a bad thought to take a teammate to the side and compliment her on a great effort, or even verbally praise her in front of the others. That can build an individual's and a team's confidence and pride. It can bond teammates.

If you're not sure of your coach's preferred system or play for you, go directly to your coach and ask. This way, you'll know exactly what is expected of you as a player.

Teamwork

If there is a word to describe winning, it's teamwork—everyone blending together, sacrificing areas of their game to make the coach's philosophy and system successful. That means believing in each other and not always being concerned with individual achievement. The greatest feeling in improving as a team is achieving it together. If you believe playing together is the most important aspect, your thinking is correct. You win as a team and lose as a team. That's where trust and relying on each other comes in.

Filling my Role

My first year in the women's professional league with the Dallas Diamonds, my coach Greg Williams came up to me after a game in New Orleans. I was down. We had lost. I played terribly that night and hadn't quite adjusted to what my place on the team was. I wanted to be a team player by passing, but I was forcing my passes too much. Coach Williams said: "Lady Magic, we know you want to make your teammates better, like you did in college. But this is the pros and we are paying you to score. I'm running plays for you and you keep passing up easy shots." It was at that moment I realized my value to the team was more scoring than passing. This defined my role and answered many of the uncertainties I was feeling. With that, the Diamonds went on to play in the championship series against the Nebraska Wranglers. I was scoring points because that was my contribution to the team's success.

The Team Is Always First.   It always amazes me how University of Tennessee Coach Pat Summitt's teams continue to be true champions. It's not only the three NCAA titles; it's the fact that very few players on her teams have extraordinary scoring averages. Yes, Tennessee has its all-Americans, but each of these outstanding players' objectives is to win the national championship. If they achieve individual success, it's a bonus.

In 1984, the United States Olympic team finally won its first gold medal in women's basketball. In 1988, the team went to Korea to defend that medal. It was one of the most talented USA teams ever: Teresa Edwards, Katrina McClain, Andrea Lloyd, Cynthia Cooper. I could go on and on. As a group, each respected her teammates' talents. Each player's goal was to work together—no matter who played the most minutes. It was gold medal first, individual recognition second. It worked and the USA team earned a second consecutive gold, which proved a team will, in most cases, beat an opponent featuring a great player. It was a beautiful sight to see the greatest women basketball players in the world team up for the overall success of their country.

Filling a Role.   Doing your part takes no ego and lots of confidence and pride. There's nothing better than for your coach to clearly explain what your role on the team is—what you can do to contribute to the overall success of the team. Look at this role definition in a positive way. Basketball is a team sport; each player is very important. You are simply a piece of the puzzle. And remember, role players are looked upon as elite figures on a team. So set that ego aside and do whatever is asked of you by your coach. You might be asked to score, set monster screens, play tough defense or, maybe, a combination of these areas. You are capable of giving your coach and team the

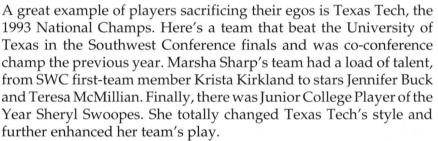

Just Plain Happy for Her

A great example of players sacrificing their egos is Texas Tech, the 1993 National Champs. Here's a team that beat the University of Texas in the Southwest Conference finals and was co-conference champ the previous year. Marsha Sharp's team had a load of talent, from SWC first-team member Krista Kirkland to stars Jennifer Buck and Teresa McMillian. Finally, there was Junior College Player of the Year Sheryl Swoopes. She totally changed Texas Tech's style and further enhanced her team's play.

Sheryl's game drew national attention as she broke virtually every scoring record at Tech and in the Southwest Conference. The final touches were added her senior year: National Player of the Year, Southwest Conference Player of the Year, and on and on. I couldn't believe how sincere and caring Sheryl's teammates were. They were all solid players in their own right. They cheered and cried for joy each time Sheryl broke a record. I never saw any jealousy—just plain happiness. This attitude must have had a lot to do with Marsha Sharp and her assistants' approach, and the players believing in her system. Sheryl's ability to share her honors and try to put the spotlight on her teammates must have been appreciated. Sheryl, no doubt, was the star—but the championship was truly a team effort.

advantage they need. You must be able to explain what your role will be to help your team win.

Sometimes, it's easier to be a role player or a substitute. Less can be better. Less responsibility can mean more results. If you come off the bench, it's not a negative. Watch the game. Read the tempo and flow. What does your team need? Is it rebounding? Are your teammates up or flat? Subs need to uplift a team. You're the spirit if the starters are tired or struggling. If the starters are hot, it's your job to keep the fire going. Give your best—for 1 minute or 30 minutes. It's effort that counts.

Enthusiasm for Your Teammates' Accomplishments.   There's no greater feeling than when you are sincerely excited about your teammates' achievements. Then, all the hard work and preparation has been worth it. It shows respect for their hard work and accomplishments. They appreciate your support and how you respond to them. I've seen players play well and their teammates fail to show support. It's selfish to not want a teammate to do well. Even if it's not you, it's for you. Keep the team goal in sight. There will be a point when you'll need and want your teammates' support, as you have given them.

Summary

Perhaps what you need is the mental edge. No matter what your level of talent, playing smart and staying focused can be exactly what you need to win. These are some things to remember:

- Develop a strong mental attitude.
- Hard work and repetition lead to developing desire, discipline, self-confidence, and persistence.
- Learn your basketball skills early. You can then incorporate strategies into your game.
- Team players have winning written all over them. It takes sacrifice, learning your role, communication, and teamwork.
- As a student of the game your focus doesn't waver.
- Motivation keeps you focused on continued achievement.

CHAPTER
3

Training for the Game

Nancy Lieberman–Cline and Martina Navratilova

As we've seen, attending to your mental game is a necessary step in making your basketball efforts pay off. Another important step involves improving your physical condition. Here are 10 points to think about as you begin your road to achieving top physical condition:

1. Accept every challenge.
2. Have a good mental and physical approach.
3. Set your goals high.
4. Don't be afraid to succeed.
5. Play to win.
6. Have heart and desire.
7. Help people get better.
8. Have a sense of humor.
9. Don't worry about things you can't control.
10. Accept the challenge to play against people who are better.

CONDITIONING FOR BASKETBALL

Proper conditioning should have an objective and purpose. Just think how you will feel to know your hard work and dedication have helped you improve your running, quickness, jumping power for rebounding, and overall flexibility to reduce injuries and recover quickly when injured.

Basketball is not the slow, deliberate game it was several decades ago. You have to be in top physical condition to excel at the fast pace of today's game. That takes dedication and hard work. Your conditioning can help you eliminate turnovers or sloppiness due to mental and muscle fatigue. You must be able to prepare your body to withstand the 32 or 40 minutes of a high school or college basketball game. We've all seen teams that can keep the score close in the first half but run out of gas toward the end of the game. Keeping fit for those final minutes—and beyond—is what this chapter is about.

We often see athletes make foolish training decisions. Young women work out 6 days a week to stay in shape and on the 7th day they eat and drink irresponsibly, don't get enough rest or sleep, and end up losing all of their training gains. If you are a serious athlete, you must be committed to your mind and body—full time. You have to want to get better. Remember that the harder you work off the court, the easier it will be on the court.

Wearing Them Down

Conditioning was one of the strengths of the 1978-79 Old Dominion women's basketball team that won its first AIAW national championship. We trailed Louisiana Tech by about a dozen points at halftime, but we weren't discouraged. We knew we could wear teams down with our size and conditioning. For us, the game turned into a mental and physical battle that we knew we could win. We did, by 10 points. I attribute the 20-point swing to conditioning, depth, and execution.

The four main aspects of physical training are enhancing your flexibility, building your strength, improving your endurance, and being aware of other training issues, including diet, that can make a difference in your athletic career. We'll talk briefly about each of these areas and point out some other important training considerations before looking at a training program and some conditioning exercises you can use to achieve a new level of physical conditioning.

Your conditioning program should concentrate on the following areas of fitness:

- Strength training
- Flexibility
- Cardiovascular fitness
- Nutrition
- Rest/recovery
- Speed and agility
- Plyometrics or jumping ability

Pre-Hab Conditioning

You've heard of rehabilitation and rehabilitative training. I'm a big supporter of "pre-hab" training. If you're a one-sport athlete, you might think that as soon as the season's over you don't have to worry about physical training until next season. In today's high level of competition, athletics are full time, even though you may take a break from your specific sport and focus on another. Cross training is the key. You'll reach your potential if you continue to train. The off-season is the time to hone in on your weaknesses and turn them into strengths. If you're a multisport athlete, you have an advantage. You have the luxury of keeping in shape while you play other sports. Your disadvantage is not being able to personalize your training to improve your basketball game. It's OK to use other sports to supplement training, but be sure to leave time to work on your main sport.

Pre-hab, simply put, is preventive steps to keep you as healthy as possible. Pre-hab training means that you never fall out of shape. You'll always have a foundation for your physical training and you're doing all you can to prevent injury. Too many great athletes have lost their jobs to someone else because of injury. Many athletes get hurt because their bodies are not ready to handle the strain of intense off-season or preseason conditioning. Your chances of injury will be reduced if you stay in pre-hab condition.

When you do get injured, the trainers and doctors take over. They will put you through many tests to make sure what the injury might be and how to best get you on the road to recovery. Trainers and doctors can be an injured player's best friends.

Staying in pre-hab condition means working out and training hard. An off-season spent on the couch watching television and eating junk food will erode your foundation of physical conditioning. When it's time to get ready for the coming basketball season, you don't want to have to start from scratch. You can increase your exercise program as the season draws near. When it's time to step on the court for the first day of practice, your teammates and coaches will notice.

Training Frequency

There are three main seasons to the basketball year: off-season, preseason, and in-season. The off-season lasts roughly from late spring to August. You should be training to train during the off-season. This means getting in shape and building your fitness foundation in preparation for the coming season. You should work to increase your flexibility, strength, and endurance while improving your basic basketball skills. You should also correct any poor nutrition habits you may have.

The preseason usually includes September and October, starting 6 to 8 weeks before your first official practice. Now you are strong mentally and physically. You are training to compete and raising your level of performance in all areas. You should maintain your flexibility and continue to increase your strength and endurance; at the same time you continue to refine your basketball skills.

In-season stretches from November to March, with April off. You are ready for competition. You've trained hard, worked on your skills, and now are ready to show your teammates, coaches, and competitors you have put in your time. You are ready for every challenge. Continue to maintain flexibility and strength, while increasing endurance. Your coach is responsible for training during this period.

ENHANCING YOUR FLEXIBILITY

The off-season is the time when most of your progress, strength, endurance, speed, and quickness will be achieved. You don't have to hold back on anything because you have time to work on your overall conditioning, flexibility, and basketball skills.

I suggest that when the season ends, you take 7 to 10 days to have fun and let your mind and body recover before you get back to work. As your training progresses, you will be making changes in your conditioning as you near the season.

This is a terrific time to work on flexibility, which will help you reduce the chance of injuries. Let's start by addressing prevention of those injuries. Flexibility is the ability of the joints to move through a full range of motion. Range of motion refers to the degree to which there is movement around a joint. Pain-free mobility of the muscles and bones requires that you maintain a full range of motion at all joints. Flexibility will give you an appearance of ease, smoothness of movement, graceful coordination, self-control, and total freedom. It will help you perform more skillful movements with greater self-assurance and amplitude. Flexibility can mean the difference between an average and an outstanding performance.

Flexibility is especially important in basketball because of all the movement you must make on the court: stopping, starting, leaping for a rebound, making a move to the basket, playing defense. The more flexible your body is, the quicker it can react to the move you are asking it to perform. If you are tight and stiff, your reaction time is greatly reduced. Think of your body as a rubber band. The more flexible it is, the more it can stretch and do whatever you need it to do. If it's tight, it will stretch only so far without breaking. Basically, without flexibility you have limited your physical ability to perform.

In 1990, while training for the Goodwill Games, I worked with Auburn University coach Joe Ciampi. I followed stretching routines provided by Auburn's strength and conditioning staff. The exercises made a difference in reducing my chances of injuries.

It is important that your muscles are warm before you start to stretch. Proper breathing while stretching can allow you to relax and stretch farther than you think you can. Stretching can be uncomfortable if you are tight. By taking deep breaths and blowing out while in the stretch position, you are relaxing your body. Remember to always breathe while stretching.

Improving and maintaining your flexibility can be accomplished through simple stretching and calisthenic exercises. These can be incorporated into your weight training regimen and endurance exercise workout—topics we'll address later in this chapter. It's absolutely mandatory that you spend time stretching before you begin any workout. One torn muscle can put you on the sidelines for months. Take a few minutes before each workout to make sure your muscles are loose and ready for work.

How to Stretch

As with most things, there is a right and wrong way to stretch. A relaxed, slow approach is what I have found most useful. Many times players will bounce while stretching, and that can cause injury. If you bounce throughout your stretch, your muscles will tighten, not relax. Remember, your body needs time to loosen up each of the muscle groups before it can perform to its maximum. The old adage "No pain, no gain" should not apply to stretching. The last thing you want to do is injure yourself while stretching.

Stretch lightly. Hold your stretch for approximately 10 to 20 seconds. Remember, no bouncing. Go easy and breathe out as you extend your stretch. As you start to feel tension, hold your position, and keep breathing. The muscle will continue to loosen as you hold the stretch. Then, relax after about 20 seconds.

Use repetition. Do each stretch two or three times. Each time you will try to extend the stretch farther. Again, hold it at the point of tension. Don't force your stretch. Ease back if you are uncomfortable. It could take time for you to recondition and loosen various muscle groups.

Breathe and count. This combination is so important. The breathing allows you to relax and exhale all the tension as you are stretching. When we feel pain or tension, we often hold our breath. That will only make you more tense. Breathe normally and count slowly. Don't rush through the 10 or 20 seconds of stretching time.

Warming Up and Cooling Down

The warm-up is essential in preparing muscles to work and stretch without being injured. Walking or jogging are good ways to warm up. The warm-up increases your heart rate, breathing, and blood flow and raises your body temperature. Warm up your body for about 5 minutes *before* beginning any stretches, to avoid damaging cold muscles. Cooling down after working out helps your breathing and heart rate return to normal and inhibits blood, which has been pumping to your working muscles, from pooling in your extremities. You should cool down for 5 minutes at the end of your workout by simply decreasing the intensity of your activity or by walking. Continue to cool down with stretching exercises.

To begin your warm-up, jog around the court three times to get your blood flowing. The blood flow will reduce stiffness and send oxygen to all areas of your body. Now your muscles are warm even before you stretch.

- Start at the top of your body. Move your neck from side to side and around front to back a few times. This is relaxing.

- With your arms out by your side, make small circles, five to the front. Now, reverse your motion and make five circles in the opposite direction.

- Now increase the circles: five large circular motions one way, then five in the opposite direction. This will loosen your arms and the shoulder areas.

- Put one arm out in front and pull it across your chest using your other arm. Keep stretching the arm straight across your chest. Then, change arms and repeat. This stretches the shoulder in another area. Repeat two or three times with each arm.

- Put one arm straight in the air, then place it behind your head.

Bend it at the elbow so your arm and hand is pointing down your back. Place your opposite hand on the elbow and push down slightly. You will feel a stretch in your triceps area (upper part of your arm), which is your follow-through when shooting.

- Reverse arms and repeat two or three times.
- Bend at your waist, keeping your legs together. Try to touch your toes. Do not lock your knees; keep them bent slightly—we don't want you to hyperextend your knees and cause injury. Try bending slightly in each direction: front, back, side to side. This will stretch your lower back and side muscles.
- Stand with your legs shoulder-width or slightly more apart. Turn your body to either side and you are stretching the inside of your legs.

For endurance training, the same warm-up can be used. This warm-up will prepare you to take the court, hit the weight room, or speed around the track. It may take time and concentration, but stretching will reduce injuries and give you a longer career. The more you play and train, the more essential it is to properly stretch.

After you have finished your workout and while you are still warm and stretched, it's time to jog a few laps to properly cool your body. Then, do some light stretching before you are finished.

It's important to know the correct techniques for stretching. Remember:

1. Stretching reduces muscle tension.
2. With proper breathing, you can learn how to relax while stretching.
3. If you stretch properly, your coordination will improve on the court. Your movements will be freer and easier.
4. Stretching also allows you to have a sense of awareness for your body—what hurts, where you are tight.
5. Pre-hab reduces the number of injuries you will have.

I've picked five simple stretches that you should incorporate into your stretching routine. They'll help you get loose and prevent nagging injuries.

ACHILLES TENDON STRETCH

Stand upright four or five feet from a wall. Bend one leg forward and keep your opposite leg straight. Lean against the wall while keeping your body in a straight line and your rear foot flat and parallel to your hips (see Figure 3.1). Exhale, bend your arms, move your chest to the wall, and shift your weight forward. Hold and relax for 25 seconds. Repeat on opposite leg.

Figure 3.1   Achilles tendon stretch.

HIP FLEXOR STRETCH

Stand upright with the legs straddled 2 feet apart. Flex your right knee and roll your left foot under so the knee and toes rest on the floor (see Figure 3.2). Place your hands on the floor. Exhale and slowly lean or push your left hip toward the floor. Hold and relax for 20 seconds. Repeat on opposite leg.

Figure 3.2   Hip flexor stretch.

LOWER LEG STRETCH

Sit upright on the floor with one leg straight and the other positioned so that its heel touches the opposite thigh. Exhale, bend forward at the waist, and grasp your ankle or foot (see Figure 3.3). Exhale and slowly turn your ankle inward. Hold and relax for 20 seconds. Repeat on opposite leg.

Figure 3.3   Lower leg stretch.

TRICEPS STRETCH

Flex one arm, raise it overhead next to your ear, and rest the hand on your shoulder blade. Grasp the elbow with the opposite hand (see Figure 3.4). Exhale and pull your elbow behind your head. Hold and relax for 10 seconds. Repeat with opposite arm.

Figure 3.4   Triceps stretch.

BACK STRETCH

Stand at arm's length from ledge positioned at shoulder height. While standing with legs shoulder-width apart, gently grasp ledge with fingers (see Figure 3.5). Bend at waist, keeping fingers on ledge to stretch your back. Hold and relax for 15 seconds.

BUILDING YOUR STRENGTH

Being strong is exciting. You'll see it in the way you look and feel it in the way you play. Opposing players, much to their dismay, will see it and feel it, too. Strength gives you confidence to go out and match up with any player—big or small.

Figure 3.5   Back stretch.

Strength is an acquired edge, and improving your strength starts in the weight room. Weight training tones and redefines your body. It gives you added strength in the large and small muscle groups. You'll discover muscles you didn't even know you had. Weight training also can help increase your flexibility. But you have to learn to train properly. By lifting weights using proper technique—such as lifting through the proper range of motion, not lifting too much or too fast, and breathing naturally—and committing yourself to a regular training program, you'll get a tremendous return on your investment and will begin seeing, and feeling, positive results in a relatively short time.

Experts have many different theories about weight training. Therefore, you have several choices. Do you use free weights (barbells and dumbbells), or weight machines (universal, Cybex, Nautilus machines), or plyometrics? Each has its good training points. Your preference and your individual needs will determine which program is best for you. Before you begin lifting weights, consult your coach for information about strength training. Your coach can help you find literature about strength training and can direct you to someone with additional strength training expertise, such as a fitness instructor at a weight training facility. Do not begin lifting without proper instruction! This could lead to injury or failure to meet your strength training potential.

Different Programs for Different Players

Athletes often say, "Give me a workout program." Sounds easy, but it's not. As we said before, there are many theories about how one should strength train. And players may have different goals they want to achieve from their strength training programs. We'll briefly examine the basics of strength training, giving you the main points. Use these points to get started. Be sure to consult with your coach or another strength training expert who can help you identify your goals and preferences and design the program that's best for you.

Determining Sets, Repetitions, and Weight.   The first step in designing your workout is to determine how much weight to lift (load or amount of resistance) and how many times to repeat the movement (repetitions and sets). A set involves performing a particular number of repetitions before stopping. We'll look at two ways to structure your repetitions, sets, and weight—the multiple and single set approaches.

The multiple approach to strength training suggests that you complete three sets of 5 to 8 repetitions for developing strength, and three sets of 9 to 15 for endurance. For example, when selecting your load for developing strength, select a weight that allows you to perform all sets at a point somewhere between five and eight repetitions. If you can perform more than eight repetitions, then your weight is too light. Likewise, if you can't reach five, you're lifting too much weight.

Another popular approach to strength training is the single set, or high intensity training (HIT). HIT suggests that you should lift an amount of weight that will permit you to perform one set of at least 8, but not more than 12, repetitions during the exercise. You then increase the amount you lift when you are able to perform 12 repetitions.

We recommend that you lift for strength during the off-season, lifting more weight for fewer repetitions. Most strength training experts agree that this is when you'll make the greatest strides in your strength development. During the season, lift less weight and more repetitions for more of a maintenance routine—you can stay toned and not lose strength. Heavy workouts in-season can lead to burnout or fatigue while playing.

Allowing Time Between Exercises.   Limit your workout to 12 to 14 exercises. Select a core group of about 10 exercises that will develop the five major muscle groups in your body (lower back and buttocks, legs, torso, arms, and abdominals). Then choose two to four additional exercises to specifically meet your particular needs or interests.

Time spent in the weight room should be short, 45 minutes or so, especially during the season. In the off-season, you can design a longer workout to add more strength. Limit the time between each exercise to less than 1 minute. Allowing time between workouts is also important. You might want to practice a split routine workout, exercising the upper body muscles one day, and the lower body muscles the next. (Exercise the abdominals each day.) This gives you a full day between workouts. If you want to exercise all of your muscles in one workout, an alternate-day regimen (Monday-Wednesday-Friday or Tuesday-Thursday-Saturday) might be best for you.

Weight Training Tips

The following suggestions are meant to help you get the most out of your strength training workout.

- Before you begin any workout be sure to warm up properly. Use the mirrors in the weight room. Take a good look at your body. Identify the areas in which you want to make gains.

- Get a buddy—someone who competes as you do or who is even more competitive. Compete with each other using the proper technique for each exercise.

- Throwing around heavy weights isn't the answer. Use the weight you can handle with proper technique. Check out some of the books or tapes on weight training and be sure to include your coach in your efforts. The more you understand, the better you'll be at it.

- Always drink fluids when you work out. Fluids cool your system and allow you to keep working hard without dehydrating. Water or sports drinks are equally effective.

- Always use weight-training gloves if you can. Gloves will help prevent sore hands or calluses that keep you from lifting or playing. Use a weight belt to protect your back from injuries due to having weight or stress on your lower back from various exercises. For example, squatting and dumbbell exercises that require bending at the waist place stress on your lower back.

• Record all weight, pool, and track workouts.

IMPROVING YOUR ENDURANCE

Endurance comes from many sources—running, weightlifting, and playing basketball. You'll probably notice improvement in your speed and endurance on the court after working on these three areas. The stronger you become, the better your muscles function. Increased speed and endurance are natural results. Some players are solid for 5, 10, even 20 minutes. But if you want to become the best player you can be, you must work to become solid for the entire game and beyond. The more endurance you have, the more mental discipline you will have. Decisions you face on the court will come easier because you won't be distracted by fatigue.

Basically, endurance is how many times you can repeat a certain function without getting tired. Exercise that improves endurance is commonly referred to as aerobic fitness or cardiovascular endurance. Aerobic activity, such as biking, cross-country skiing, dancing, hiking, rowing, running, skating, and swimming, stimulates your body's ability to sustain an activity for an extended period of time. It involves the ability of the heart, lungs, and circulatory system to supply oxygen to the muscles during exercise.

Running on the road or at the track is a tremendous way to gain cardiovascular endurance and challenge yourself mentally and physically in the process. Running provides a mental battle with conditions—wind, weather, being uncomfortable. It's all there; it's something to attack and conquer.

I suggest you look at the big picture: 4 months of off-season running, weightlifting, and basketball. Make sure not to go from no-base training to everything at once. Learning to build your conditioning in stages gives you the right steps to overall success. If you have worked out for a few weeks and you are tired, don't feel guilty about taking a day off here and there. It will allow your body to rest and recover.

I firmly believe in having a plan. Chart each day of running, weight training, and basketball playing. It will allow you to see progress, how you felt, and what improvement you made. Be detailed in recording each day's workouts. How far did you run? How did you feel? Was it easy or difficult? What were the weather conditions? You should strive for each workout to be more productive, even if it's one-half second better, or you did another repetition while lifting. Your chart lets you see your progress and pushes you to consistency.

BUILDING YOUR FOUNDATION

As you begin, think of training as a pyramid. The bottom of the pyramid is your base. This will be a 3- to 4-month process of building strength and endurance through longer running and heavier weight training. Figure 3.6 shows a sample 2-month chart to use as a guide. Your training should have you running 1 to 4 miles at the start. It's OK if your time is slow the first few times. Try to improve your time even if just by 1 second. Keep improving. As your conditioning improves, vary your running routine to include the track. Add speed training to your endurance training. You might run 3 days on the track, 2 days of 2.5 to 3 miles of long-distance running, and Saturday might be a day for a long, leisurely run of approximately 4 miles. When you're finished running, do your weight workout. This will add strength and endurance.

During the first several weeks of your training regimen, you're going to be tired and sore. Stay mentally tough. After a few weeks, you'll start feeling stronger. Your recovery time, aches, and pains will decrease. You will start to see progress. Push yourself mentally and physically to finish each training session. Soon, you will be to the point where running, lifting, and playing basketball several hours each day will feel great. You're now hitting the middle of the pyramid program.

You should run 1 to 4 miles during your 3-day-per-week program. You have to determine where you are with your conditioning. You might want to start at 1 mile and push yourself to increase your time and distance until you can feel that 4 miles is a solid distance for you to achieve.

After you have run hard, lifted hard, and played ball 3 days per week for approximately 5 weeks, take 1 week off to relax, to play ball, and to let your body recover and refuel.

Week	Sunday	Monday	Tuesday	Wednesday	Thursday	Friday	Saturday
1		Strength training 1 mile run Basketball		Strength training 1 mile run Basketball		Strength training 1 mile run Basketball	
2		Strength training 2.5 mile run Basketball		Strength training 2.5 mile run Basketball		Strength training 2.5 mile run Basketball	
3		Stength training 3 mile run Basketball		Strength training 3 mile run Basketball		Strength training 3 mile run Basketball	
4		Strength training 4 mile run Basketball		Strength training 4 mile run Basketball		Strength training 4 mile run Basketball	
5		Strength training 2 mile run Basketball		Strength training 3 mile run Basketball		Strength training 4 mile run Basketball	
6	Select days you want to play ball. Choose 3 days.						
7		1 mile run for time		Strength training 3 mile run Basketball		Strength training 3 mile run Basketball	Leisurely 4 mile run Basketball
8		2 mile run for time Strength training Basketball		2 mile run for time Strength training Basketball		Strength training 3 mile run Basketball	Leisurely 4 mile run Basketball

Figure 3.6 Sample weekly training chart.

On the first Monday after your days off, run 1 mile for time. Give it your all. Record your time. Wednesday, run and continue lifting weights and playing basketball. Do the same on Friday. On Saturday, run 4 miles at a leisurely pace.

For the next week, run 2 miles on Monday, Wednesday, and Friday. You should have a solid base of endurance, strength, and stamina after 8 weeks of training. The next step is to add speed and quickness. You should be playing basketball as much as you want— a minimum of 3 to 4 days per week.

As you may have guessed, it doesn't matter to your heart and lungs whether they are working hard because you are running, swimming, biking, or climbing stairs. You can take advantage of this to incorporate variety into your cardiovascular training and to minimize the potential for overuse-type injuries. If you have to run in your sport, then the majority of your cardiovascular training should come from running. You may be able to get into great shape using a stairclimber, stationary bike, rowing machine, upper body ergometer, or by swimming. But the only way to develop the skill of running is by running. You can use other cardiovascular tools to minimize the stress running can place on your joints, but you still must run if you are going to be effective.

Training Method Alternatives

These training methods are the actual tools that you will use to improve your athleticism. Your total program should include strength training, plyometrics, cardiovascular training (both aerobic and anaerobic), and extensive core work.

Weight training exercises/external resistance (ER) consists of leg and jump squats, leg presses, lunges, walking lunges, step ups, high step ups, pulldowns, pullovers, combo curls and presses, including bench presses. These exercises develop strength and power in the muscles emphasized.

Core work consists of abdominal circuit medicine ball throws, medicine ball rotations, twist and movement drills, and speed and agility movement drills. Core exercises work many muscles simultaneously.

A complete plyometric workout is beyond the scope of this book. You may want to consult another book, such as Donald Chu's *Jumping Into Plyometrics* (1992, Human Kinetics Publishers). The workout is not the whole key or the most important component. Consistency, intensity, and safety are the keys.

Workout Schedule

In this section, we'll suggest how you should schedule your off-season, preseason and in-season training regimen.

Off-Season.   This is where your strength training starts. The off-season gives you time to build muscle and add strength. Give yourself 1 day per week of strength exercise, 3 to 4 days per week of external resistance, 3 days of plyometrics, 4 days of distance running, and 4 days per week of core work.

As you progress from off-season to preseason, you will see a slight variation from building your foundation to increasing your speed and quickness.

Here are some tips:

- Use three different workouts per week.
- Focus on all body parts during each workout.
- Use one to three exercises per body part.
- Use 12 to 15 exercises per workout.
- For repetitions, do 10 to 15 for lower body; 8 to 12 for upper body.
- Keep the order of each exercise consistent.
- Work out for 30 to 40 minutes.

Preseason.   You will continue to do strength training as part of your overall workout. Give yourself 1 day of body work, only 3 days of external resistance, and 2 days of plyometrics. You are going to add sprinting for 3 days and reduce distance running to 1 day. You are now trying to add more speed and quickness to your training mix. Still, do your 4 days of core work. You always can work on that area. Use two different workouts per week and follow other off-season rules.

In-Season.   Your strength training is geared more toward maintenance rather than building strength. Give yourself 1 day of body work and 2 days of external resistance. You can see how your training regimen has been reduced from off-season to preseason and now to in-season. Also give yourself 1 day of plyometrics, only 1 day of distance running (a long, leisurely run), and 2 to 3 days of core work. Use two different workouts each week, with 7 to 10 exercises in each. Work out for 20 to 30 minutes.

Strength training overloads your muscles to achieve muscle growth. You must overload the muscle no matter what workout program you do, especially during the off-season and preseason. During the in-season focus on more reps and lighter weights. This is a quick, maintenance workout. Off-season and preseason workouts will use more weight to build strength and muscle. If you can complete more sets with proper technique, you should increase your weight. When you can rest for shorter amounts of time, this means you are getting stronger. Try to cut down your recovery time, but never eliminate it altogether. If you are willing to work out, make it worth your time and effort. Concentrate and don't get sloppy with technique.

Keep these tips in mind:

- The slower the movement, the greater the tension.
- The greater the tension, the harder the muscle works.
- The harder the muscle works, the stronger it becomes.
- The stronger the muscle, the stronger the joint.
- The greater the speed of movement, the less force production from the muscle.
- Preventing injuries means increased playing time.

Lady Magic Tips

▶ Always have proper supervision.

▶ Never try to do one rep max.

▶ Do basic exercises.

▶ Always use extreme caution.

ENDURANCE DRILLS

Plyometric training is specific work to improve jumping power accomplished by training the stretching and shortening actions of muscle contraction. During the stretching phase, a greater amount of elastic energy is stored in muscle. This elastic energy is then reused in the ensuing shortening muscle action to make it stronger. The key is to shorten the time it takes for the muscle to switch from the lengthening/yielding phase to the shortening/overcoming work phase. If not properly used, however, plyometrics can add a high risk of injury. The risk of injury occurs when the volume and frequency of the program is excessive. Therefore, it is important to resist the temptation to do more work than is outlined. Remember, plyometrics uses force to contract your muscles for a certain period of time, usually 10 to 20 seconds. By holding your muscles in a contracted position, you build strength and endurance.

The following are descriptions of the plyometric exercises that can be used:

TUCK JUMP

Jump in place, pull the knees to the chest while in the air. Use both legs.

RUBBER BAND JUMPS

Use a 48-inch by 1-inch rubber band for resistance.

JUMP UP

Jump up onto a box or a table that is mid-thigh to waist high (jump without using the arms, then jump with use of the arms)

SHUFFLE/SLIDE JUMPS

While facing the front of the backboard, jump and touch as high as possible on the right side of the backboard. Land and shuffle to the middle of the key, jump and touch the net, land and shuffle to the left, jump and touch as high as possible on the left side of the backboard. Repeat back to the right for a total of six jumps. This is one set.

SPRINT WORKOUT

This two-quarter workout should be done on weeks four and five of the conditioning schedule. It consists of 36 runs on a football field and will take approximately 20 minutes to complete (see Figure 3.7). Of those 20 minutes, 13 are rest time; thus you can put forth maximal effort on each sprint. For the second quarter, repeat the first quarter.

Football Field

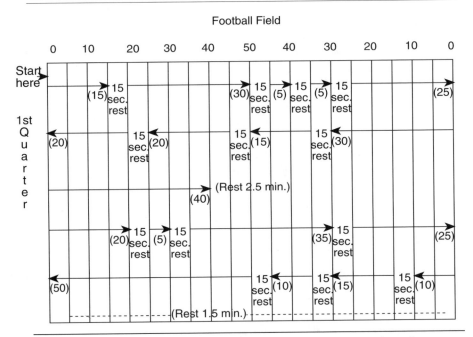

Figure 3.7   Sprint workout diagram. Numbers in parentheses indicate how many yards you have sprinted.

SLIDE DRILL

Stand midway between two imaginary lines 20 feet or more apart. Assume a defensive position with your knees bent, head up, and arms out. Slide back and forth and touch the imaginary lines with your feet, making sure that your feet do not touch each other as you slide. Continue the drill for 1 minute.

JUMP STOP DRILL

Stand at half court. Run and jump stop with your feet parallel to each other, knees bent, head and eyes up, and hand extended out. Maintain good body balance, with your weight evenly distributed between both feet. Continue this movement until you reach the baseline. Make three round-trips.

REVERSE PIVOT DRILL

Stand at half court. Run, jump stop, and execute a reverse pivot, lifting up your heels and pivoting on the balls of your feet. Continue this movement until you reach the baseline. Make three round-trips.

BACKDOOR MOVE DRILL

Stand at the baseline. Run to the foul-line extended area. Plant your outside foot and show your outside hand. Stay low to the ground, push off your inside foot while showing your inside hand, and look for a pass or layup.

V-CUT FOOTWORK DRILL

Stand at the sideline area extended from the block. Drive hard to the box and plant your outside foot. Push off your inside foot at a 45-degree angle, staying low as you drive hard off your foot. Extend your outside hand as if to look for a pass.

OTHER TRAINING ISSUES

There are other training issues in addition to flexibility, strength, and endurance. Good nutrition is very important to sound physical fitness, as is avoiding physically debilitating agents like drugs, alcohol, and tobacco. You need to be as sharp mentally as you are physically.

Good Nutrition

Dr. Robert Has, author of the best-seller *Eat to Win*, changed my eating habits forever. He taught me that you can recondition your body, as well as your tastes. When you improve your eating habits, you are helping your body, which will enable you to enhance your performance on the court. You will be able to play at a higher level for a longer time because of the excess energy you have.

A balanced diet should consist of 60 percent complex carbohydrates, 25 percent fat, and 15 percent protein. Three meals per day, with snacks when necessary, should take care of your food needs. To increase weight, add two or three snacks a day; to decrease weight, reduce your portions.

The way you treat your body is determined by how much respect you have for it. Athletes train hard to achieve results, but sometimes we overlook the importance of nutrition. You've got to eat right. Your body has only so much energy. Don't waste it by eating fats, salts, sugars, and oils. Those ingredients take away from your strength and energy levels.

The four major food groups consist of grain; fruits and vegetables; dairy products; and meat, poultry, and fish. You should consume each of the four groups every day for a balanced and nutritionally sound diet (see Figure 3.8). Grains and pasta are high in carbohydrates. Fruits and vegetables supply iron to your body. Dairy products give you calcium. Meat, poultry, and fish give your body proper protein.

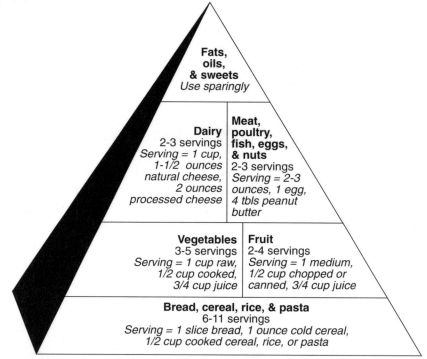

Figure 3.8 The food pyramid. *Note.* Data from the U.S. Department of Agriculture/U.S. Department of Health and Human Services.

If you consistently include these food groups in your diet, you will maintain energy storage, maintain the muscle tissue you have built up during your training and, most of all, reduce your body fat.

Here are some suggestions:

- Eat pasta rather than steak. Carbohydrates are easier than meat to break down and digest. Your body exerts energy to break down food. Vitamins and supplements give your body whatever it is missing nutritionally. For example, I dislike milk and obtain the calcium I need from vitamins.

- Carbohydrates, grains, fruits, and vegetables cover practically all the nutrition needs you will have. They should be the staples of your daily diet.

- Drink as much water as you can. Water prevents cramping and dehydration. Drinking water the day of competition can never replenish what you have sweated out. Store up on water the day before competition.

- Give yourself adequate time to eat your pregame meal. I recommend eating 3 to 4 hours before game time to properly digest your food. You don't want to play feeling heavy, nor do you want to be thinking that you're hungry.

Unsaturated vegetable oils and fats do not raise blood cholesterol, but they should be limited because they are high in calories. Generally, up to 6 to 8 teaspoons a day is acceptable. Desirable liquid vegetable oils are corn oil, cottonseed oil, olive oil, rapeseed (canola) oil, safflower oil, soybean oil, and sunflower oil. Peanut oil is less desirable but small amounts are acceptable. Margarine is a partially hydrogenated vegetable oil and is preferable to butter. Vegetable shortenings fall into the same category as margarine. Both contain quantities of transfatty acids—these are not naturally occurring and should not be taken in excess. Mayonnaise and salad dressings are often made from unsaturated fats, but they should be limited because of their high caloric content.

Breads, Cereals, Rice, and Pasta. These products are high in carbohydrates and protein. Most are low in fat. Therefore, they can be increased in the diet as substitutes for fatty foods. However, they contain calories and must not be eaten in excess. Cereals can be eaten as snacks as well as for breakfast. Combine large quantities of pasta, rice, legumes, and vegetables with smaller amounts of lean meat, fish, or poultry to derive complete protein sources with less fat and fewer calories.

Fruits and Vegetables. Fruits and vegetables should be a part of each meal. Both are rich in vitamins, fiber, and some minerals and contribute to achieving the recommended allowances of these nutrients. Certain green and yellow vegetables may reduce the risk for cancer. Fruits—and even vegetables—can be used for snacks and desserts.

Dairy Products.   Use skim milk or 1% instead of 2% or whole milk, which contains approximately 4% fat. Eat only small amounts of natural and processed cheeses. Substitute low-fat (2%) cottage cheese or synthetic cheeses produced from vegetable oils. Choose yogurt of the nonfat or low-fat type. Experiment with evaporated skim milk in recipes calling for heavy cream. Substitute low-fat yogurt or low-fat cottage cheese for sour cream in dips and salad dressings. Have at least two servings of very low-fat dairy products, such as two glasses of skim or 1% milk daily to help maintain calcium intake. Eat no more than three egg yolks per week. Egg yolks often are hidden in cooked and processed foods. Egg whites contain no cholesterol and they can be eaten often. Experiment with one to two egg whites instead of whole eggs in recipes, or use commercial egg substitutes that do not contain yolk.

Meats, Poultry, Fish, and Nuts.   Use lean cuts of beef, pork, and lamb. Lean cuts of beef include extra-lean ground beef, sirloin tip, round steak, rump roast, arm roast or center-cut ham, loin chops, and tenderloin. Trim all fat off the outside of meats before cooking. It is not necessary to severely reduce the amount of red meat you eat. Lean meat is rich in protein and contains a highly absorbable form of iron. Eat few high-fat processed meats, including bacon, bologna, salami, sausage, and hot dogs. Processed meats contain large quantities of "hidden" fat, and they are not rich in valuable nutrients. Poultry is a good source of protein. Fat should be reduced by removing skin and underlying fat layers. Chicken and turkey can be substituted for lean red meat in the diet, but they do not contain as much iron. Chicken and poultry should not be fried in fats rich in saturated fatty acids or covered with fat-rich sauces. Most shellfish contain less fat than meat and poultry. Some shellfish, including shrimp, are relatively high in cholesterol, but even these can be eaten occasionally within the recommended guidelines for cholesterol intake. Nuts tend to be high in fat, but the fat usually is unsaturated. The intake of nuts should be limited mainly to avoid excess calories. The same is true of peanut butter.

Cooking Methods.   Choose those methods that use little or no fat. They include steaming, baking, broiling, grilling, or stir-frying in small amounts of fat. Foods can be cooked in the microwave or in a nonstick pan without added fat. Limit fried foods and avoid frying in saturated fat. Soups and stews should be chilled after cooking and the congealed fat that forms on top after a few hours in the refrigerator should be skimmed off. When preparing meals, avoid the use of excessive sodium, which can contribute to high blood pressure in some people.

Eating Away From Home.   Order entrees, potatoes, and vegetables without sauces or butter. When meat exceeds the size of a deck of cards (3 to 4 ounces), part of it can be taken home for another meal. Choose vegetables or fruit salads, and ask for salad dressings to be served on the side. Use dressings sparingly. Limit high-fat toppings such as bacon, crumbled eggs, cheese, sunflower seeds, and olives—the latter two because they may be high in fat and salt. Ask for margarine instead of butter, and limit the amount of margarine used on bread and baked potatoes.

 ## One Fatal Mistake

In 1986, Len Bias, a college great from the University of Maryland, was headed for the big time: money and fame. He was the No. 1 draft choice of the Boston Celtics. Bias was being compared to Michael Jordan. He was a clean-cut guy who didn't party. After his return from Boston, he celebrated at school by trying cocaine. He used enough coke that by early morning, the country was shocked to hear of his death. Bias died of an overdose of cocaine. It's sad. He had it all: talent, skill, money, and a great family. Bias' death taught me and millions of players one thing: One mistake is too many.

Drugs, Alcohol, and Tobacco

I'm sure you remember times when people told you: "Don't do this." "That's bad for you." "You can ruin your life or die." Man, those are harsh words. But you wouldn't be at this level if you made bad choices. You're smart and there's enough information about drugs, alcohol, and tobacco for you to understand clearly what you want out of your career and life. Be selfish—don't let anyone pull you down or away from achieving your dreams. It's tough today. You face peer pressure and temptation. That's why I love basketball. It keeps you focused and limits your exposure to these temptations. When faced with a choice, your decisions are easy. Ask yourself, "Is this good for my career?" You're trying to make all-state and win the championship. Will this make it easier? I'm sure you'll agree. No! Stay strong.

Mental Aspects of Conditioning

Whenever you play basketball, there should be a part of you that is playing a mind game. Think how you might gain a small edge over your opponent. There will be times during games when you'll be drained. Although you are just about to run out of energy, never, ever let your opponents know that you're tired. If you need to catch your breath during a break in the action, turn your back to your opponent. Don't let them see that you're tired.

At the same time, if you see an opponent put her hands on her knees while trying to catch her breath, you know to take advantage of her weakness. Go at her the first opportunity you get. It's all part of the game we play on the basketball court.

Sending a Message

Your physical conditioning can send a message to your opponents that you mean business. Two months before the Olympic tryouts for the 1992 women's basketball squad, I turned up my training routine a notch. I was already in shape because of my pre-hab conditioning, but it was time to really get serious. Each morning at 7 a.m., I worked out at Creighton University with Mike Thibault, coach of the 1993 CBA champion Omaha Racers. He put me through drill after drill. Mike has coached with the Los Angeles Lakers and Chicago Bulls and he knows that basketball drills are not exactly exciting. I was "drilled" out after 2 months, but my basketball game was at its best. I trained 6 days a week—lifting weights, running, playing pickup games, and working on my skills.

When I reported for the tryouts, I sent a message to members of the selection committee. I wanted them to know that I was taking these tryouts seriously. I wasn't going to let myself be left off the team because I was out of shape. I walked onto the court confident— mentally and physically.

I didn't make the 1992 Olympic squad, which was disappointing. In a way, however, I accomplished my goal. I sent a message to the stars and future stars in women's basketball that being 30 doesn't mean your basketball career is over. If just one person, after seeing me play at age 33, said to herself, "I hope I can play like her when I'm 33," then I accomplished something.

PUTTING IT ALL TOGETHER

Use the summer months to play a lot and get into the weight room with a properly supervised workout. Add your track conditioning and be mindful of your diet. You will begin to see a change in yourself. As muscle definition begins, you will develop more confidence and self-esteem. If you see the changes, others will too.

When you walk into the first day of organized practice, it will be immediately clear that you went the extra distance. They might not know how you did it, but make no mistake, people will notice. This will speak volumes for your dedication and work ethic. Every coach wants a leader. Every teammate needs a role model. You be the one.

The Buddy System

I'm a strong believer in using the buddy system during physical training. It's OK to train by yourself, but when you train with someone else, you are pushed to your limits. A good partner can help take you to the point of fatigue. Buddy system training has a lot to do with ego, competitiveness, and peer pressure to give your best performance. Ego, when used correctly, can help you and your training partner. Ego pushes you to want to get better. However, ego shouldn't be misused. For example, don't lift more weight just to show off. Ego can also motivate you to train on those days when it would be easier to slack off. A solid training partner helps motivate you and makes sure you get a good effort out of the tough days.

Improving Your Skills

This is where your coach comes in. After the season, if your coach hasn't yet called you in for a face-to-face meeting, take the initiative and schedule one. Ask how you can improve. Ask your coach for drills to work on the areas that need improvement.

Your coach should know and identify your weak areas. Once you get the information you need, it's up to you to achieve the results. Playing in the off-season is important, but knowing what you should be working on will give you direction and focus. Then you can use your basketball workouts properly.

You can make great strides by doing the following:

- Know what areas need work.
- Know which drills to use.
- Determine how much time you can devote each day and then stick to it.
- Be efficient by being organized and focused.

Whether you are playing basketball, running, cycling, or lifting weights, your workout habits will let you know if you are successful.

10 Ways to Work

1. Have a plan.
2. Always think improvement.
3. Use the correct form.
4. Be mentally prepared.
5. Be physically prepared.
6. Have the right equipment.
7. Always stretch first.
8. Have a good attitude.
9. Always challenge yourself.
10. Never rest until you are the best.

For me, the off-season was great. Being dedicated to your mission of overall improvement and seeing areas of weakness turn into strengths should give you the attitude to work hard and want more. It won't happen overnight, but you will see gradual improvement. And a lot of gradual improvement will mean major steps in becoming a better overall player.

Lady Magic Tips

The off-season is one of the few times you won't have coaches around you giving you instruction. Enjoy the freedom of having your game in your hands. I recommend the following:

- ▶ Play in as many pickup games as possible.
- ▶ Play a lot of half-court games (one-on-one, two-on-two, three-on-three).
- ▶ Find some friends who have the same dreams as you and work out together.
- ▶ Be willing to make sacrifices if you want to be the best. It's a small price to pay.

If you want to drill on the court, here are a few of my favorites:

- ▶ Beat the All-American (see page 131).
- ▶ Two-player shooting to 50, shoot, rebound, pass. Run at the shooter with your hands up.
- ▶ Foul-shot golf (see page 126).
- ▶ Horse. Play by the traditional rules or make up your own.
- ▶ One-on-one.

Pushing Myself

In 1990, I asked my friend Dawn Marsh, former starting point guard for the University of Tennessee, to train me so I would be in top physical condition for the U.S. National Team tryouts. Marsh spent 6 weeks in Dallas, pushing me in the weight room, on the track, and at the gym. I knew that Marsh, coming from Pat Summitt's system, would be able to push me hard and focus on areas of weakness. She did that and more. I was extremely impressed with Marsh's organization. Each day was planned. I knew when and what was expected. My goal was to have immediate response from the selection committee—something like, "Wow, she must have worked hard to look that good." My body's appearance communicated hard work and effort to the selection committee although they had yet to see me in action during the tryouts.

Keep in mind that training should be fun and competitive. Treat your body right. Get plenty of rest so your body can recover from training. Your diet can be your edge; be selective how you eat. Stretching properly can prevent injury and give you a better chance to succeed. It's easy to train when you feel good. Complete the program each time. Ask yourself, "Am I feeling soreness or pain?" Soreness will go away, but if you feel pain, see a doctor or trainer. Stay focused. Improvement will come—sometimes quickly, sometimes slowly. Be patient, but be persistent. As your conditioning improves, find new challenges on the track, in the weight room, and on the court. Continue to strive for excellence. The opportunity is there for you to succeed; now you must take advantage of it.

Summary

Conditioning programs are designed to build your strength, stamina, and endurance from the ground up. If you have worked through the off-season, it's important to continue that pace throughout your preseason. Be mentally and physically strong. Your self-discipline will allow you to continue your journey to excellence.

Here are some things to remember:

- Commitment to mind and body starts with playing basketball, lifting weights, working out, and following a proper diet.
- Flexibility reduces the risk of injury.
- Pre-hab training helps you stay away from injuries and is your foundation for remaining in condition year-round.
- Building strength starts with weight training.
- Running and strength conditioning improve speed, quickness, and endurance.
- Off-season conditioning—your foundation—builds speed and strength.
- Preseason conditioning builds speed and quickness.
- In-season conditioning is basketball specific.
- Use alternative conditioning drills to keep your workout program from becoming boring.
- You are what you eat.
- The serious athlete must say no to drugs, alcohol, and tobacco.

CHAPTER
4

Becoming an
Offensive Threat

In order to develop into a fundamentally solid player, you must excel in many areas. One of the unique and exciting features of basketball is that all players handle the ball. No matter what position you play, you must dribble, pass, shoot, and rebound.

It doesn't matter if you're playing with your friends after school or on your high school team, you must be able to take care of the ball. You must become a threat to the defense. Can you dribble well with both hands? Can you read the defense and know when and where the opening is to attack? Do you make good decisions when you have the ball? Once you have the right moves, the defense is yours to beat. For example, if you have proper balance and know how to get the defense leaning with a simple jab or ball fake, you have won the first of many battles.

Coaches always have a place on their team for a player who can break down the defense, create mismatches, and ultimately score. It doesn't matter if you are a starter or a contributor off the bench. Scoring can spark your team, and finding ways for your team to score is the key.

In this chapter, we will emphasize improving and refining your offensive skills. We'll teach you some simple moves and will help you discover the ways to use them successfully. Basketball, in many ways, is like a chess match. You move; the defense counters. We'll help explore your options. We'll teach you to be mentally and physically challenging to your defenders. We'll show you ways to read the defense's reactions and then take your action. It's a game of cat and mouse. If you have the advantage, you'll keep the defense guessing. You know exactly where you want to go.

TRIPLE THREAT POSITIONING

Most coaches teach the "triple threat" position to prepare you to gain your first offensive advantage once you have the ball. You can use this position to become an offensive threat in three ways—passing, shooting, or driving to the basket. The option you choose depends on the defense and how your opponents are playing you. Remember, to take full advantage of this position you must be facing the basket once you have received the ball.

To get into the triple threat position (see Figure 4.1), stand in a comfortable position with your feet about shoulder-width apart.

Figure 4.1   Triple threat position.

Flex your knees and rock your weight slightly forward on the balls of your feet.

In the triple threat position, the higher you stand, the slower you are. Bring your center of gravity down and keep the ball in the proper shooting or passing position. Make yourself a threat by not allowing the defense to read your eyes. If you are looking at the floor, you certainly aren't looking to score or pass.

Being a Passing Threat

One aspect of being a solid player is having the ability to pass the ball and create scoring opportunities for your teammates. The more versatile you can be on offense, the more adjustments the defense will have to make to cover you.

From the triple threat position, make sure you can see what's happening on your team's end of the court. By facing the basket with the ball, you can see your cutters and judge who is in position to take the best shot.

Being a Shooting Threat

You've established yourself as a passing threat; now make sure that you're a scoring threat by staying in your scoring range. Know from where you shoot best. If you're not there, you have eliminated one of your options. If you're in your range, be prepared to read the defense. If it backs away, pull the trigger and get your shot off quickly.

Your shooting options from the triple threat position can be enhanced by being a driving threat.

Being a Driving Threat

If the defense is too tight and your opponent is in your face, use your third offensive option—drive to the basket and shoot or pass off to a teammate who's open for the shot. Keep your head up to see the whole floor. The defense will be off balance because they won't know if you're going to dribble, drive, pass, or shoot.

Putting the Triple Threat to Work

Once you make a decision to pass, shoot, or drive, you must execute your option. The following techniques will help put you in the best position for success.

Jab and Shoot.   The jab step is an offensive weapon that can create scoring opportunities. It begins with a ball fake at the defender—a hard, believable fake straight at her while you are in a triple threat position. The offensive player steps or jabs violently at the defense with her front foot, while keeping her pivot foot stationary. If the defense reacts and takes the fake by backing off, either explode up for a jump shot or go past the defense. If you choose to shoot, quickly release your shot to the basket. Remember to be in shooting range. Jab step about 1 foot in front of you. Then, you can quickly pull your jabbing foot back while being on balance.

Jab Step and Go.   With the jab and go, your pivot foot must remain on the floor until the dribble starts. Make your first step explosive because it is the most important one. You must go in some direction with your dribble to get away from the defense. This also helps you to read your defender's feet. Always attack the foot that is up. This forces defenders to open up as they drop step. Go straight at the foot as your defender opens up. Always keep your head up and look at the basket, not the floor.

Remember, if you jab step and go to your right, dribble the ball with your right hand. Use your left hand to protect the ball. If you jab and go left, switch the ball on the move to your left hand. Lefties should remember that their left foot should be slightly ahead. Their pivot foot is their right one.

Jab Step and Crossover.   This move is good to use when the defense is close. With the ball, jab step to the side of the defense. Then, step across and by the defense with your front foot. If you are right-handed, jab with the right foot. If you are left-handed, use the left foot. The defense will react and try to take away your strong side drive. Now, you can cross over in the opposite direction. You must protect the ball, taking it from the outside hand farthest from the defender. For example, if you cross over with the ball in your right hand, do not leave the ball open between you and the defense. Quickly switch the ball low from right to left using your right arm and body to protect the ball. The dribble begins before you pick up your pivot foot. Instead of going to the side the defense will open up, make your defenders drop step. It takes longer to drop than to slide. Attack the defense's weaknesses. Stay close to your defender's body so she cannot get an angle and catch up with you.

Rocker Jab Step.   From a triple threat position, the rocker jab step enables you to draw the defense to you after you have used your jab step at your defenders. You can get the defense moving back and forth, or side to side with this move. Stay in your triple threat position, but expand it. For example, keep your left foot as your pivot and jab at the defense with the right. Stutter step side to side. Rock back and forth—even putting your right foot behind you or crossing it in front of the left. If you catch the defense leaning and off balance, make your move because you have kept your dribble going.

Jump Stops. When a player lands on both feet at the same time, she is using a jump stop. Your legs should be shoulder-width apart for proper balance, and your knees should be bent slightly with your head over your knees.

The two-step jump stop is used when a player lands on one foot and the other follows. That second foot should land slightly ahead of the first so that you can be in a triple threat position. From that stance, you can shoot, pass, or dribble. With your feet in a staggered stance, you can use either as your pivot foot. Jump stops are most effective when you are driving the defense back. As you jump stop, your defenders are still moving backward. Jump stops will create space for you and release defensive pressure.

Hop Drive. A move we are seeing more today is a player driving hard to the basket and, as the defense closes off the drive, hopping with both feet past the defender or past two defenders.

Pivots. Pivots are valuable tools for changing direction. They allow you to break double teams. Don't be shy about establishing your space and position. Be physical, but not illegal.

Checkpoints

- ✓ Keep your head up. If you are looking down, the defense knows you are not a threat to score. See the whole floor and the basket.
- ✓ Protect the ball on your fake. Keep the ball close to your body on all ball fakes.
- ✓ Plant your lead foot—the one that starts the drive—as close to the defender's foot as you can. This takes away her angle to recover.
- ✓ You will find success attacking the front foot of the defense. Make her drop and open.
- ✓ Protect the ball on the drive. A simple rule is this: you, ball, defense. To get to the ball, the defense must go through your body, arms, and knees.
- ✓ Stay low. The lower you are, the more speed and quickness you have.
- ✓ Ball fakes and foot fakes, when done correctly, can freeze or make the defense lean in the wrong direction.

✓ Sell your fake. If your fake is believable, you'll have your defender constantly coming out of her stance.

✓ Play a lot of one-on-one with a one- or two-dribble limit. This will make you work on using your jab fakes in a game situation. You have to be quick and read defenses to make your move.

TRIPLE THREAT DRILLS

Practicing the following drills will help you become better at executing your offensive options during the game. Once you are comfortable with each drill, create goals for self-improvement, even if it's only performing the drill one more time through. Challenge yourself with the clock. For example, how many jumps and slides can you do in 60 seconds? Remember, always practice proper form. Don't sacrifice form for more repetitions or faster performance. A good way to rest is to take five foul shots between each drill. You'll improve your free throw shooting, as well.

ONE-ON-ONE JAB DRILL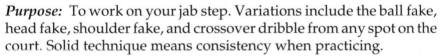

Purpose: To work on your jab step. Variations include the ball fake, head fake, shoulder fake, and crossover dribble from any spot on the court. Solid technique means consistency when practicing.

Procedure: Place basketballs in at least five spots around the perimeter of the court. Come from behind the ball in a low, balanced stance.

- Pick up the first ball and get in a triple threat position and jab at an imaginary defender. You should be about 20 feet from the basket.

- Make moves—jab and drive, jab and cross over, or jab and shoot. You have the option of the shot. Make a quick decision. If it's a jab and shoot, make your ball fake violent and rise up for the jumper.

- After completing that move, run to the next ball. Come at it in a balanced stance. Bend your knees, not your back. Pick up the ball, jab fake, and crossover dribble. Take the drive or shoot.

- Use the same continuation after your fake and crossover. Next time, use a different move. Always take the shot or layup to complete the drill.

- Finish jab fakes from all five spots. Take five foul shots while you're tired.

- Repeat this drill two times.

Lady Magic Tips

▶ Make believable jab steps and ball fakes even without a defender.

▶ Jab directly at the defense. This drill can be used with two players. Use the second player as a defender at each ball. After five spots are completed, shoot five foul shots and switch positions.

JAB STEP DRILL

Purpose: To make a believable jab step while attacking the defense. Then, go somewhere on your dribble. Dribble with a purpose. Strengthen your strong and weak hands.

Procedure: Get in a triple threat position. Place the ball on the floor. Pick it up on balance and jab at the defense.

- The first time through the drill, jab and take one quick dribble right, going somewhere off your dribble.

- Get back in your triple threat position, jab at the defense and take one quick crossover dribble left.

- Repeat each jab step and dribble three times in each direction.

- Do the same drill, adding two dribbles off the jab step. Take two dribbles to your right, then two dribbles left off the crossover. Repeat three times each way.

Lady Magic Tips

▶ Jab at the defense. Attack your defender, don't avoid her. Usually a six- to eight-inch jab step will keep her off balance.

▶ Right-handed offensive players should jab with their right foot; left-handed players with their left foot. This forces the defense to take away the strongside drive.

X-OUT ONE-ON-ONE DRILL

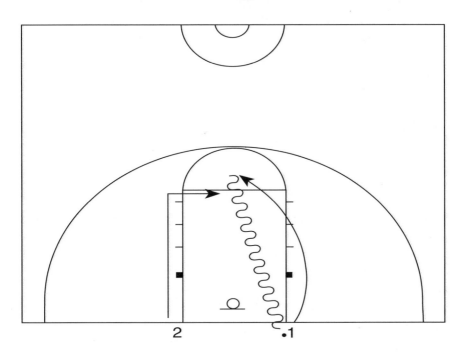

Purpose: To work on one-on-one moves off a triple threat position. This drill will improve your quickness, reaction, and ability to make split-second decisions while recognizing what the defense has given you.

Procedure: Player 1, the offensive player, is under the basket on the foul-lane line with the ball. Player 2 is the defender. The defender is on the opposite side of the basket on the foul-lane line.

- Player 1 rolls the ball to the middle of the foul line or beyond near the key area and sprints to pick it up. Player 2 sprints up the lane line, then slides across at the foul line elbow to defend against Player 1.
- Player 1 picks up the ball in a low, balanced position and pivots to face Player 2.
- Player 1, using assorted jab and ball fakes, makes Player 2 react.
- Player 1 and Player 2 compete one-on-one until Player 1 scores.

- Shoot five foul shots each when finished.
- The two players reverse positions and repeat the drill. Each player is the defender twice and the offensive player twice.

Lady Magic Tips

▶ Player 1 must roll the ball to the foul area, not bounce it.

▶ The offensive player should keep her head up and use a good, believable jab step at her defender.

▶ The offensive player should read how the defender is guarding her.

KNEE HIGH DRILL

Purpose: To increase the power and explosiveness in your running. By drawing your knees high, you create power. The more you do these drills, the better endurance and strength you will have in straight running and in transition.

Procedure: Start by standing in one place. Jump upward. Bring your knees up as high as you can.

- Place your arms by your side for balance. Use them for momentum and power as you drive your knees up.
- Jump for 30 seconds of alternate knee highs. Rest 30 seconds. Complete four sets of 30 seconds each.

CHANGE DRILL

Purpose: To condition and work on changing speeds and direction and to help you focus on your change of direction.

Procedure: Start on the baseline under the basket. Sprint straight down the court as hard as you can. Change direction instinctively. Stay low, planting your lead foot and pushing in the opposite direction.

- Start with 30-, 60-, and 90-second change drills. Rest between drills when necessary.
- You should be creative in structuring this drill. For example, you might want to sprint up and down the court several times without stopping, followed by several quick turns. Keep your running off balance. Try not to get into a rhythm.

- Complete three change drills. You can determine how long each one lasts (30, 60, or 90 seconds).

Lady Magic Tips

▸ Use your imagination and focus to keep changing your direction as if you were in a real game.

▸ Have a watch in your hand so you can monitor your time during this drill.

FOOTWORK

To be more effective on offense, you must work hard at improving your footwork and foot speed. The more efficient your footwork, the better your results. For example, you can use footwork to freeze your defender, then negate her speed by beating her to a spot on the floor.

The proper position for balance is to keep your head over your knees while leaning forward. This positioning also gives you more speed. Stay on the balls of your feet and try to be as light on your feet as possible. Relax and keep them moving. You'll notice that your center of gravity is lowered, thus allowing you to move more effectively and making it easier to change direction. If you are flat-footed or off balance, it will take longer and more energy to get going.

 A Good First Step

Former University of Nebraska all-American Karen Jennings has one of the best first steps I've ever seen. Karen is a 6-foot-3 post player. She has a tremendous outside game to go with her inside moves. She consistently took her opponents to the high post, caught a pass, and used simple jab fakes along with head and ball fakes. Boom! Her moves froze her opponents and she was gone.

Checkpoints

✓ Jumping rope increases speed, quickness, and endurance. It keeps you light on your feet.

✓ Sliding drills improve lateral quickness and strength.

✓ Short sprints increase leg muscle, strength, and explosiveness.

✓ Line jumps (front and side) increase speed and quickness going different directions.

✓ Change of direction (transition sprints) works on decreasing the time it takes to change direction and improves explosiveness.

✓ Knee highs focus on hip flex or muscles to respond more quickly when sprinting.

FOOTWORK DRILLS

Practicing the following drills will help you improve your movement and speed on the court. Once you are comfortable with each drill, create goals for self-improvement. Challenge yourself with the clock, for example. Remember, don't sacrifice form for more repetitions or faster performance. Take five foul shots following each drill to rest.

LANE SLIDE DRILL

Purpose: To increase your lateral speed, quickness, change of direction, and reaction time.

Procedure: Start on one side of the foul lane. Get in a good, balanced stance with your head up, knees bent, feet apart, and arms out in the passing lanes.

- Slide from one side to the other and back (up and back is one repetition). Stay low in your stance.

- Touch the lane line with your inside hand, then slide back in the opposite direction. Once again, touch the lane line with your inside hand.

- Do not cross your feet or bring them together. You will be off balance and slow. Use a crablike slide.

- Do this drill as fast as you can for 1 minute. Rest 1 minute. Complete three sets of 1 minute each.

BACKBOARD/NET TOUCH

Purpose: To strengthen your lower legs for quickness and explosive repetitive jumping. It's great for rebounding, too.

Procedure: Stand under the net or backboard.

- Jump 10 times off both feet with your right hand touching the net or backboard. Then jump 10 times using your left hand.
- A total of 20 touches equals one set. You can use a one-step takeoff.
- Rest 60 seconds. Repeat three times.

Lady Magic Tips

- ▶ Be explosive to the spot you are trying to touch.
- ▶ Use your arms, as well as your legs, to generate power.
- ▶ Come down and quickly go back up.

ONE-FOOT RUNNING JUMPS

Purpose: To combine sprinting, being on balance, pivoting, sprinting again, and jumping. All the transition moves you might have to make during a game are included in this drill.

Procedure: Start at the baseline under the basket, sprint to the foul line, and touch it with either hand.

- Lower your center of gravity as you approach or you'll be off balance.
- Pivot and sprint back to the backboard, jumping as high as you can off one foot. Touch the net or backboard.
- Repeat this exercise five times on each side for a total of 10 times—five with your left hand on your left side; five with your right hand on the right side.
- Rest 60 seconds after each repetition (three sets total).

Lady Magic Tips

- ▶ Work with a goal to touch some point (net, board) or jump as high as you can.
- ▶ Be quick on sprints.
- ▶ Be a high jumper (jump up), not a long jumper (jumping out).

Reaching New Heights

When I was 11 and growing up in New York, my favorite place to play was PS 10. The park had five courts, but one had an 8-foot rim. This became our dunk court. Our goal was to be the first to touch the rim and the first to dunk. I used an unusual way to increase my vertical jump—one that my mom didn't appreciate. Every time I left a room in our house, I'd jump and touch the top of the door. As I got bigger and stronger, my dirty little fingers went higher and higher until I could reach the ceiling. Finally, I could touch my whole palm on the ceiling. But success meant punishment. My mom didn't appreciate my progress. All the jumping and repetition really helped me dunk on that 8-foot goal. Later, as a 5-foot-8 high school senior, I could dunk on a regular rim. People didn't expect to see that from a girl.

JUMP ROPE TWO LEGS

Purpose: To increase endurance and foot speed. This exercise is a great conditioner when used at a solid pace.

Procedure: Warm up slowly for 3 minutes.

- Rope sprint 25 consecutive jumps. Rest 25 seconds. Five sets times 25 jumps (reps) equals one set. After completing one set, rest for 1 minute.
- Rope sprint 20 consecutive jumps. Rest 20 seconds. Six sets times 20 jumps equals one set.
- Rope sprint 15 consecutive jumps. Rest 15 seconds. Seven sets times 15 jumps equals one set.
- Rope sprint 10 consecutive jumps. Rest 10 seconds. Eight sets times 10 jumps equals one set.
- Warm down slowly for 3 minutes.

Lady Magic Tips

- ► Keep your body fairly straight for proper balance.
- ► Keep your knees flexed and eyes straight ahead.
- ► Stay on the balls of your feet.

▶ Have a good, solid pace and rhythm.

▶ Push yourself on the sprints; complete the number of jumps as quickly as possible.

▶ Use your forearms and wrists, not your arms, to create speed.

▶ To add variety to your workout, complete the drill using just one leg. Then complete the drill using the other.

JUMPING LINE DRILL

Purpose: To gain rapid improvement in jumping skills by practicing and executing jumping in all directions with maximum intensity.

Procedure: Stand sideways to any line on the court. Place your feet together. Stand on the balls of your feet and jump side to side using your arms for proper balance.

- Don't drag your feet on the slide. Jump over the line and clear it. You are working on movement as well as speed.

- Do three sets of line jumps, side to side. Each set lasts 30 seconds. Rest 60 seconds. Repeat three times with 1 minute rest in between.

- Do three sets of line jumps, front to back. Each set lasts 30 seconds. Rest 60 seconds. Repeat three times.

Lady Magic Tips

▶ Stay balanced. Use your arms for speed and momentum in each direction.

▶ Intensity is the key.

▶ Keep your knees and feet together.

▶ Try not to land with your knees locked.

Summary

Becoming an offensive threat can be challenging and fun. Through dedicating yourself to being more of a threat offensively, you work on areas that can lead you to overall improvement. You must work on

- triple threat positioning—passing, shooting, dribbling;
- triple threat options to enhance your offensive game; and
- triple threat drills to improve your footwork.

CHAPTER
5

Shooting the
Lights Out

Most players love to shoot. Fans, coaches, media, and teammates love to watch a player who can score almost at will. But it's never as easy as it looks. To be proficient in any part of the game—especially shooting—technique, concentration, and repetition are vital.

Few players have ever been proficient in sports without mastering the fundamentals. The truly great shooters have been unbelievable: Sheryl Swoopes, Jennifer Azzi and, maybe the purest shooter I ever saw or played against, Montclair State's Carol Blazejowski. All of these players had confidence and worked hard.

In this section, we will take you through the necessary fundamentals, concentrating exclusively on shooting, faking, offensive moves, a variety of shots, getting free for your shot, and a variety of drills to make your game better. Shooting isn't just doing it; it is thinking and visualizing yourself taking and making the shot.

I have seen and worked with some of the greatest shooting gurus, including Herb McGee and Howie Landa. None is better than Ace Hoffstein, the "Shot Doctor." He has graciously shared many of his techniques and drills for this book. Trust me; he has helped me and many others around the country.

GETTING READY

Preparation is one of the keys to becoming a great shooter. Being ready means your hands are up waiting for the pass. Your knees are flexed so when you do catch the ball, you can go right into your shot. Your feet are balanced and squared to the basket, ready to explode up into your shot. Your eyes are focused on the court. You see all your options before you shoot the ball.

The Hands

Always be prepared to catch the ball even if you're not open. Keep your hands up in front of your face or in front of your body. It takes time to move your hands up from your side to catch the ball. Spread your fingers apart and keep your fingers slightly flexed for "soft hands" (see Figure 5.1). Have your shooting hand open and ready to catch the ball. Your off hand is on the side of the ball. This allows you to have a quick release once you have received the pass.

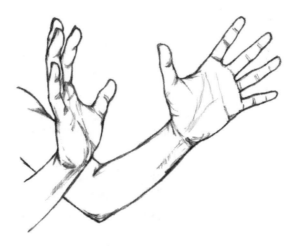

Figure 5.1 Hand position for catching the ball.

Once you receive the pass, your grip becomes the single most important feature of quality shooting. Start the process by spreading the fingers of your shooting hand wide apart. Next, when you place your fingers behind the ball, use the pads of your fingers. Don't use your palm. Apply pressure on the ball by grabbing it with your thumb and little finger. Then, place the middle three fingers on the ball in a gentle, but firm manner. To be assured of the greatest accuracy, point your middle finger at the valve on the ball and aim that finger at the rim. Place the ball in your hand with the seams across your hand. If you shoot the ball with the seams across, you can see if you have proper rotation on your shot.

Your nonshooting hand will help guide the ball straight at the target. Place your nonshooting hand on the side of the ball with your fingers pointing to the ceiling and your thumb toward your ear. Apply gentle pressure (see Figure 5.2). The real secret is for you to think of pushing your shooting hand (with the ball) through your guide hand (with your fingers pointing upward) and finish with your guide hand staying in the same spot. Your shooting hand is extended into a limp release by extending your wrist and elbow forward and outward, and your hand ending "down in the basket."

Footwork

As you learned in chapter 4, footwork is the key to balance and speed. Footwork is also important to your shooting game. Proper footwork

Figure 5.2   Proper shooting form.

enables you to be where you want and to be ready to shoot. Every great shooter has excellent balance prior to taking her shot. Her foundation comes from good footwork and legwork prior to the shot.

When preparing to shoot, your feet should be pointed to the basket, straight ahead, and at the middle of the rim (see Figure 5.3a). For good balance, your weight should be on the front foot to help keep you in a flexed and ready position. Your knees should be slightly flexed to allow for a deeper flexing movement of the legs to help generate an easy fluid upward motion (see Figure 5.3b).

Body Position

The best way to be ready to explode into your jumper is to catch the ball while you are already low in your shooting position. This way you can go straight up with the shot. Many players catch the ball while their body is straight up. Then they have to go down to gain

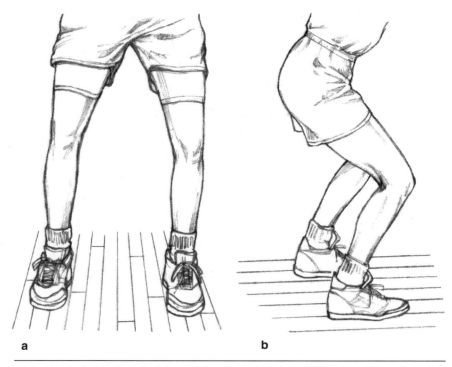

a   b

Figure 5.3   A right-handed shooter keeping the feet straight (a) and knees bent (b). If the shooter were left handed, the left foot would be slightly ahead of the right.

strength to make a jumper. Starting in a lower position permits a more efficient motion. (Remember, too, that a low center of gravity is better for speed and balance if you choose to drive instead of shoot from the triple threat position.)

As you prepare to shoot, square your shoulders to the basket and keep your head slightly forward. Your head is the heaviest part of your body. If it is leaning back, it will pull your shoulders back. Subsequently, your shot will be short. You want to be leaning into your shot, toward the basket and your defender, not away.

Arm Position

Make an L shape with your shooting arm with the underside of your arm parallel to the floor (see Figure 5.4). Do not use a V-shape arm formation with your elbow pointed toward the ground. Pretend you are a waitress with your hand being the tray and the basketball the food. Once you have achieved this "tray" position, you want your

Figure 5.4   Forming an L with your shooting arm.

long shooting finger and your shooting elbow pointed right at the middle of the rim. The fingers of your shooting hand generally are pointing to the ceiling.

When you are ready to launch the shot from your favorite "groove" or "pocket" area, you now know the quality spot from where you'll hit with consistency. It is extremely important to learn and know where your "shot spot" is. To maintain a good pocket routine, keep your shooting elbow out over your front, or shooting, foot. This will help your alignment and lead to an easy, effortless shot release.

Sighting

To prepare for your shot, you must learn how to "sight" or "aim." Take aim by staring and concentrating on the front rim. Don't follow the flight of the ball—more often than not you'll watch as you miss the shot. Always have your head up, whether you are shooting or not. If your head is up and you are seeing the floor, the defense doesn't know if you are going to take the shot, pass, or dribble. It also allows you to quickly shoot the ball because you see the rim.

The Finish

To check your finish, exaggerate pointing your shooting finger and shooting elbow (see Figure 5.5). Move your wrist and elbow in an outward and forward motion toward the rim. Release your shot so that you cannot see the back of your hand and try to put your hand "into the basket." Check the rotation of your shot by placing a piece of tape on the ball and counting the rotations of the ball

Exaggerate your follow-through. Shoot up, high above the rim, not forward. Shoot toward the basket. Shooting up will make sure your shot is not flat. With more arc, your shot will have a better chance to hit the rim or backboard, and fall through for two.

Figure 5.5   Proper hand and arm position for the finish.

Reading Your Shot

If you hold and shoot the basketball with correct form, you will be able to "read" your shot. Reading equals follow-through. If you are shooting and your shot is short, you need to add more arc and power. If your shot is too hard, you may need to use less leg strength. Alternatively, you might be pushing the ball. Think of how you are shooting to figure this out. If your form is correct and your shot is still too hard, you then should let up with your legs. If you are getting good leg strength into your shot, check your form. Has your L become a V? Maybe you are pushing the ball to the basket instead of shooting high above the rim. If your shot rebounds to the right, chances are your hand went to the right on your follow-through. By shooting the ball correctly and holding the ball with the seams, you can read the rotation of the ball and the direction the ball is moving. Once you are able to find the problem you can make the proper adjustment in your shot.

 Keep Trying

We all have games when we shoot well and games when we don't. It's how much you control the bad ones that makes you a complete player. Believe me, I've had games when the basket looked like a coffee cup and others when it looked like the ocean. Even though I may have been shooting poorly, I tried to read my shot and make the proper adjustment. Many times I was 5 for 20 in my college days but was able to come back at the end and hit the last three or four. Don't ever give in.

Checkpoints

- ✓ Square up to the basket. Keep your feet parallel, with one foot slightly ahead of the other. If you are right-handed, your right foot is up. If you're a lefty, your left foot is up.
- ✓ Your toes, knees, hips, elbow, shoulders, wrist, and follow-through should be facing the basket.
- ✓ If your shooting elbow is directly above your knee on the same side, you have proper form. If it's outside the knee, your elbow is not in close enough. Your form is incorrect.

✓ Lean into your shot. Be balanced.

✓ Follow through high above the rim.

✓ The seams should be across your palms.

PERFECTING YOUR TECHNIQUE

The more you work on your shooting technique, the better your chance for success. Good technique means less chance of mechanical breakdown in your shot. Less breakdown means successful shooting. This all goes back to repetition and practice. The more you practice with the correct form, the more likely it is that you will accomplish your goal of proper shooting technique. Here are some checkpoints for self-correction of your shots.

Short Shooting (front rim or air ball): Caused by leaping up for the shot and releasing the ball on the way down.

Correction: Shoot the shot following your upward jumping motion by releasing the ball as you are going up or at the peak of the jump. You must maintain a good L shot position and keep your guide hand in place. Finish with your hand in the basket.

Shooting Side to Side (right or left): Caused by poor hand position.

Correction: Recheck your hand position on the ball and keep your shooting hand in the middle of the ball. Point your elbow at the basket and finish your shot so you can't see the back of your shooting hand. Keep your guide hand firmly in place and push the shooting hand through the guide hand. When possible get to a wall and make an L with your shooting hand to feel the proper hand and arm position prior to the shot.

Long Shooting (back rim or backboard): Caused by going forward instead of straight up on the jumper or by hurrying the shot.

Correction: Release your shot with a higher arc, with your shooting arm fully extended, and with your hand in the hard finish position. Keep your eyes strictly on the goal, not on the flight of the ball.

SHOT SELECTION

Shot selection is pure discipline and knowing what is a good shot and what isn't. Why settle for a 22-footer when an 18-footer is better? You can control shot selection. Good shot selection means using your dribble to square up to the basket or using your footwork to get into the right position. By keeping your hands up, you will be able to concentrate on catching the ball and not pushing off your defender.

Shot Fake

The shot fake is one of the most underrated aspects of basketball. First, you must make the fake believable. This can be done in a variety of ways. Use whatever it takes—fake with your head, eyes, shoulders, body, arms, and feet. If you fake with the ball, be quick and keep your elbows close to your body. If the ball is extended too far out, chances are greater that the defense will slap it away.

A properly executed shot fake can create an easy shot or an open drive to the basket. When an offensive player fakes a shot to the basket, she must react to the defense. If the defense does not come out and defend the shot, she should take it. If the defense closes in on the offensive player and comes out of its defensive stance, she should step to either side and go by the defense.

Pump/Double Pump Shots

Pump-faking is a great way to get to the free throw line. It is an essential part of the game, especially when competing against opponents who are always trying to block your shot. The double pump move requires you to be strong, creative, and to adjust your body while taking a variety of shots. Only exceptional athletes can go up for a shot, be covered by the defense, and then change the shot in midair—all while concentrating on the follow-through to the basket.

Pump fake the ball as you get the defense to jump or react. For example, as you leave the ground to shoot, you draw the defense to you. When your defender comes close, double pump. Once your defender is in the air, you can draw contact and get to the free throw line. Remember, you must make the pump fake believable, as if you really are going up with the shot.

ASPECTS OF SHOOTING

The most important aspect of shooting is putting the ball in the basket. Because your shot opportunities may be available anywhere on the court, it's important that you have variety and creativity in your game. The great part of the game of basketball is that you never really know what your defenders will give you. You might want to take a jumper, but it's not there. You might have to penetrate and shoot a layup or a bank shot. The more shots in your arsenal, the better equipped you will be to score in any situation. Let's look at different types of shots you might have to take in a game or in practice.

Layups

The layup should be the first shot you master; it's a high-percentage shot. When shooting a layup, make sure you leap at a 45-degree angle to the basket. If you are starting from the right side, plant your left foot, then dip your inside leg (see Figure 5.6). This allows you to generate momentum going from a forward motion to an upward one as you move the ball up in unison with your shooting knee on the drive to the basket. Keep your head up and your eyes focused on the square above the basket. Your back and waist should be straight. Use your right (opposite) knee to explode up to the basket. Shoot the ball straight up. Follow through by extending your elbow, wrist, and fingers. Always keep two hands on the ball until you release it. Use your off hand to protect the ball. Don't worry about getting fouled. Finish the shot. Remember to jump up, not out. If you cannot go hard for layups on both sides, you do not have a complete game.

Power Layups.   The power layup is slightly different from the regular layup. Use both feet simultaneously, with a jump stop, and explode toward the basket (see Figure 5.7). Release the ball as you are airborne. A power layup keeps you in good rebounding position and allows you to maintain proper balance. Keep your eyes focused on the basket. This is a good move to draw fouls as you jump into the defense in order to create contact under the basket. Be sure to use your inside arm to protect the ball from your defenders.

Reverse Layups.   This layup is great going baseline or using the proper 45-degree angle while making your move to the basket. It puts the basket between you and the defense. Concentrate on the backboard as you float past it during the shot. As you start to go up with your shot, you need a little spin on the ball—not a lot or it will spin off the glass. It's a soft turn and flick of the wrist. As always, remember to work the reverse layup with either hand.

Figure 5.6   Shooting a layup.

Jump Shots

The one-handed jumper (see Figure 5.8) is the most efficient and most used outside shot. Like any shot, the ball is controlled with your fingertips; seams are parallel to the floor. You should always have the proper L position when shooting. Your head should go toward your target. Your knees are slightly flexed, ready to explode into your jump shot. As you are in the ready position to shoot, spring up off your toes and jump as high as you can. Release the ball near or at the top of your jump. Focus on the basket as you release your shot. Your follow-through hand and index finger should be pointed just above the rim. Remember to "finish hard" with your wrist. The lower you are when you catch the ball, the quicker you can jump up for the shot.

Figure 5.7   Shooting a power layup.

Add another dimension to your jump shot by mastering the fallaway jumper. The shot is exactly the same as a regular jumper except the jumping movement is different. In a game situation you might lean in slightly and then pivot away from the defense and the goal. Instead of jumping into your shot, you jump and fade backward. It's a tough shot for the defense to block because your backward momentum creates space between you and the defense.

Set Shot

The set shot usually is taken from long range when a player has plenty of time to set and shoot. It's still a very effective shot for many

Figure 5.8   Positioning for the one-handed jump shot.

players, especially against a zone. The one-handed set shot is today the preferred shooting style. It is similar to the jump shot with the exception of the actual jump. This shot can be tried whether you are stationary or moving. A shooter must find the open shot on the outside and be ready to shoot the uncontested set shot. The ball is shot more with the arms than with the legs.

Bank Shot

The glass and square above the rim give you good sight lines, making the bank shot a high-percentage shot. You can bank layups, short jumpers, or even outside shots. The ball should hit within the square. Avoid using too much spin on your shot. Your bank shot ideally should hit and drop through, barely touching the front of the rim.

Even on the fast break, use the glass. It softens your shot even when you are out of control. The key to the bank shot is knowing angles and where you are on the floor. A 45-degree angle is the best place from which to shoot the bank shot—a layup or a three-pointer.

Free Throws

How many games have been won or lost at the line? It happens at all levels—the pros, college, high school, and rec league. Developing a consistent, reliable foul shot can change your success and your team's success. With all the bumping and grinding you deal with during a game while trying to shoot over a defender, the free throw is a blessing. When you are at the line, no one is in your face playing D. You have worked hard to get to the line. Now take a deep breath, relax, and concentrate. Here are some things to remember:

- Take deep breaths; relax your muscles. Take a moment to catch your breath. You rarely go to the line rested.

- Repetition is important. Take a few dribbles prior to shooting to find a rhythm. Do the same routine before each foul shot.

- Use a consistent technique; each shot must be the same motion. Foul shooting is rhythm, routine, and mechanics. Stay balanced. Keep your elbow in; lean into your shot. Fix your eyes on the target and follow through.

- Line up properly. Most indoor courts have a nail placed in the middle of the foul line. Line up your foot with that nail. Line up with your right foot if you are right-handed; your left foot if you are left-handed.

- Think positively; you must believe in yourself and have confidence that you will make the shot. Confidence comes from success. Success comes from practicing your free throw shooting every day.

Checkpoints

✓ Pole/Ready—The proper foul shooting position evolves from what is called the pole/ready technique. Use a pole 6 to 7 feet in length. You and your teammates, one at a time, should assume your normal shooting position. Take the pole and place it vertically on the floor at the middle of your shooting foot. Have your hand in front of the pole and your buttocks behind it. Your knees should be slightly flexed so you will be in excellent "ready" position prior to your shot. Any time you miss a shot short (front rim or air ball) you should lean farther forward. You will seldom miss the second shot as a result of the "lean." If you miss a shot long (back rim) adjust your shot by using a higher arc. Again, you will seldom miss the second try.

✓ Elbow—Whenever you shoot free throws, maintain a good L position with your shooting arm and, more important, look down at your shooting foot and make sure your shooting elbow is over it. This is an excellent alignment factor and prevents your elbow from going out of the shooting line.

✓ Guide Hand—The wall drill can help you maintain a consistent straight shot. Go to a wall and, if you are a right-handed shooter, put your left shoulder against the wall and place your shooting hand across your body. Hold the ball up against the wall. Get a teammate to stand about 10 feet away, facing you. Push the ball along the wall toward your teammate by using your shooting hand. You will find that the ball will hug the wall when your shot is pushed. Develop this slogan: "If the wall is straight, the ball is straight." Now you should be ready to make your guide hand become your "wall," with your fingers pointing to the ceiling. Keep your guide hand (wall) in place, and push your shooting hand through the wall, which you have pointed toward the basket. Finish your shot by putting your hand in the basket so you can't see the back of your shooting hand.

Specialty Shots

Having a few specialty shots in your arsenal can give you a tremendous edge over your opponents. We'll describe three shots—the hook shot, tip-ins, and dunks—that require skill and a lot of practice. These shots won't be appropriate for all players; physical limitations might prevent you from performing them successfully.

Hook Shots.   The hook shot has been most successful for a few great players, including George Mikan, Kareem Abdul-Jabbar, and my former Old Dominion teammate, 6-foot-8 Anne Donovan. It is a great close-up shot. Even Magic Johnson, a guard, mastered what he called the "baby hook." When shooting a hook shot (see Figure 5.9), extend one leg and plant it in the direction you're going to hook the ball. Use your inside arm to create space and protect the ball. Hold the ball with the hand you will use to shoot with. Lift the ball to the basket with a full extension of your arm by your ear—all in one fluid motion. Flex your wrist and fingers. As you release the ball with a feathery touch to the basket, keep a wide base for proper balance. As you half turn (pivot), use your body to create the space needed to shoot over your defender. To be more effective, practice with both hands.

Figure 5.9   Shooting a hook shot.

Tip-Ins.   The tip-in is the part of the game that I practiced as a young girl in the school yards. We played "21," and the only way to score was by making your foul shots or tipping the ball in off a missed attempt. Only two tips were allowed on each missed free throw. Although girls and women don't yet play above the rim, you can still "tip" the ball into the basket. Practicing tip-ins helps you develop control, touch, and a mentality to always go for the ball—even if you cannot gain full control. The proper position for a tip-in is to have your body straight and knees flexed in a jumping position. Use your arms to help you accelerate up to the basket. Then, use your wrist and fingertips to guide the ball to the rim or backboard. As with all passing and dribbling, practice with both hands.

Dunks.   Yes, the dunk soon will be a part of women's basketball. So let's talk about it now. It's the most electrifying shot in the game. The dunk represents power and authority. It changes momentum. And it's the highest percentage shot in the game. There are a variety of dunk shots from the basic one-hander to the two-hand dunk. You can dunk off one foot or two. Successful dunking requires good timing on your jump as well as being able to palm or hold onto the ball long enough to power it home. Obviously, jump as high as you can. Clear the rim with the ball and with a downward wrist action, dunk it.

 Experience the Feeling

Although many women can't dunk on a 10-foot rim, that doesn't mean we shouldn't practice the shot. Each summer at my basketball camps, we have a slam-dunk contest for the little kids and the bigger girls. We lower the rims to 5 feet or so for the itty bitties and to 7 feet for the others. It's one of the highlights of camp. Kids get a chance to express themselves. Campers choose the winners. A lot of clapping by the campers means a pretty nasty dunk. For some it's the first time they've touched the rim. Their confidence gets a boost.

FORM AND TECHNIQUE DRILLS

The following drills focus on correct shooting form and technique. The drills give you checkpoints to see if you have accomplished correct form by working on ball rotation, strengthening your wrist, and being able to constantly hit your target. Repetition is important to improve form and increase confidence when shooting.

ONE-ARM SHOOTING

Purpose: To develop proper shooting form and technique. (There are checkpoints to make sure your mechanics are correct .) This drill will teach you to keep the same shot no matter where you are on the floor. What will change is the power from your legs and hips. I call this your "power base." This drill will also help your concentration, confidence, and development of a shooter's soft touch.

Procedure: Stand directly in front of the basket. Hold the ball with your shooting hand out in front of you, palm up. Slowly turn your wrist inward. This will drop your shoulder and put your arm in the proper L position. Place your opposite hand behind your back. The ball should be on your fingertips and approximately head high. Shoot the ball high, exaggerating your form and follow-through. Your fingers point up over to the top of the rim for high arch.

- Make five shots in a row from the same spot. Take one step back and repeat trying to make five in a row. Continue to repeat the drill until you have gotten to the top of the key. The farther you step back, the more you must keep your form. Use your power base to explode into your shot and lean in.

- Move to the block on the side of the foul lane, using a 45-degree angle on each side. Repeat the drill you just finished. The only difference is that now you're working on your one-arm bank shot. Lean in and follow through.

- Make five in a row, then take one step back each time until you hit the wing and are about 18 feet away.

Lady Magic Tips

▶ Proper form is the key. Make sure everything is lined up to the basket: feet, knees, hip, shoulder, arm, and follow-through.

▶ Always lean into your shot.

▶ Be relaxed when you shoot and in your "ready position." Your elbow in an L position, over your knee. Release the ball with a soft touch. Focus on your target, not the ball.

▶ Exaggerate your follow-through until your ball drops through the net.

ONE-HAND FLIP SHOT

Purpose: To discover your true shooting range using one-arm shooting with proper form.

Procedure: There are five areas to shoot from—in each corner where the sideline and the baseline meet, on either side of the foul line at a 45-degree angle, and from the top of the key down in a straight line to under the basket.

- At each of the five areas, start shooting 5 feet from the basket and back up and away from the basket in 3-foot intervals until your last shot is from 20 feet.
- Shoot at least three shots from each distance (18 at each area—a total of 90 shots for all five spots).
- Record your attempts and shots made.

Lady Magic Tips

▶ Always lean into your shot.

▶ The farther you are from the basket, the more you must use leg strength.

▶ Keep your shooting form in the L position.

CHAIR SHOOTING

Purpose: To exaggerate lifting the ball to the basket and learn to shoot the ball instead of throw it. Sitting in a chair forces you to keep your head up and focused on the target.

Procedure: Place a chair about 8 feet in front of the basket. Shoot 25 shots. Rest 1 minute. Repeat 25 more shots.

- Move the chair to bank-shot position at a 45-degree angle 8 feet from the basket. Take 25 shots. Rest 1 minute. Take 25 shots. Rest. Then move to the opposite side of the court and repeat the drill.

Lady Magic Tips

▶ Concentrate on a point over the rim. Focus on your target.

▶ Work on developing fingertip, wrist, and arm strength.

▶ Use the correct L position.

▶ Follow through hard, using a soft touch and backspin.

▶ When you are low in a chair, follow through extending your elbow.

FLOOR FORM SHOOTING

Purpose: To work on rotation/follow-through, developing a soft touch, and learning to read the spin of the ball by holding it across the seams. Lie on your back so you can check if your elbow is in, if your arm is in the L position and, most of all, if your ball has backspin.

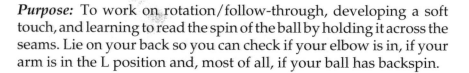

Procedure: Lying flat on your back, relax your shooting hand as you are holding the ball over your chest.

- Check your elbow alignment.
- Shoot the ball directly up into the air, completely extending your elbow, wrist, and fingers.
- The ball should come back into your hands.
- Shoot 25 form shots. Rest 1 minute. Take 25 more shots.

Lady Magic Tips

▶ Keep your elbow in place and your shooting hand relaxed.

▶ Create backspin.

WALL SHOOTING

Purpose: To simulate your shot using a strong finish (follow-through) with good rotation on the ball.

Procedure: Sitting on the floor, shoot the ball up high and accurately, while strengthening your wrist and working on consistency.

- Sit on the floor, facing a wall with the ball in your shooting hand.
- Mark spots on the wall and aim above the lowest mark on the wall with a nice easy wrist and elbow extension.
- Keep your fingers down. Repeat this above each spot until you have shown an exaggerated finish and good form.
- If you have a teammate, sit facing her about 4 to 5 feet away. Shoot the ball as high as you can to your teammate using good shooting form and rotation. You and your teammate should take about 20 shots until you both finish your shot simulation.

Lady Magic Tips

▶ Concentrate on proper form and follow-through on each shot.

▶ Keep your head up to follow the flight of the shot.

FREE THROW SHOOTING

Purpose: To develop good shooting habits each day.

Procedure: Take at least 100 free throws each day.

- Step up to the foul line and shoot two at a time. Step back off the line for a split second. Then, shoot two more free throws.

- Break up your shooting so you don't get in a groove. If you have access to another basket, shoot 25 at one end and 25 at the other. Then go back to the first basket and shoot another 25. Switch to the opposite end to finish your last 25 shots. This makes you refocus and get a look at a different basket.

Lady Magic Tips

▶ Take a deep breath before each shot to relax your muscles.

▶ Lean into the follow-through aimed high above the rim.

BLIND FORM SHOOTING

Purpose: To help you visualize what you should be doing mechanically on your free throws. You can concentrate on where the basket is and the form on your shot.

Procedure: Wear a blindfold or close your eyes as you are ready to shoot your free throws. Use the proper free throw form on your shot without the ball at first. This will simulate your shot and lead to good "form" shooting.

- Using the proper free throw mechanics, shoot the ball to the basket. Visualize exactly where the ball needs to be shot.

- Take 10 foul shots at a time—30 total.

Lady Magic Tip

▶ This is a fun drill to work on, but is beneficial and productive for you as well.

LAYUP DRILLS

Layups should be the highest percentage shot you take. If you take them, make them. Here are some different types of layups.

X-OUT SPEED LAYUP

Purpose: To develop your strong and weak hands, while improving your reverse dribble and off-the-speed dribble. This drill works on your quickness, timing, balance, and agility.

Procedure: In this drill you will shoot layups from both sides. Use your right hand on the right side and your left hand on the left side.

- Begin in a balanced stance at the foul-line elbow. Using a speed dribble, drive to the basket hard. As you approach the bucket, jump up, not out, and concentrate on the ball hitting the square above the rim.

- If you start on the left side, explode up off your right foot. If you start on the right side, use your left foot to plant and explode. Protect the ball with the opposite arm. After making the layup, catch the ball and speed dribble to the opposite foul-line elbow using your outside hand.

- As you approach the elbow, plant your inside leg and pull the ball (using the reverse dribble) back toward the bucket switching the ball to your outside hand.

- Alternate shooting your layups from the elbow each time. Make five on the left side and five on the right side. To challenge yourself, make as many as you can in 60 seconds.

- Take 10 foul shots, then repeat the drill three times.

Lady Magic Tips

- ▶ On the drive, dip your inside shoulder and knee to get your momentum going upward.

- ▶ Use the square for your sight. Extension of your elbow, wrist, and fingers all play a part in finishing the shot.

- ▶ Use game speed.

POWER LAYUP

Purpose: To work on balance and power as you go strong to the hoop. Many times a power layup is a great way to draw a foul.

Procedure: Place one chair at each foul-line elbow. Start outside the lane and flip the ball in front of you toward the hoop. Run and get the ball. Ball fake hard and go off two feet. Explode up to the basket.

- Get your rebound, dribble between the two chairs going to the opposite side. After you turn the corner around the chair, again flip the ball toward the hoop. Get it. Ball fake and go up strong for a power layup using both hands.

- Jump as high as you can on each shot.

- Make five on each side. To challenge yourself, see how many you can do in 60 seconds.

Lady Magic Tips

▶ Toss the ball toward the basket as if you were going in for a layup.

▶ Get there. Run the ball down. Be balanced. Make your ball fake believable.

▶ Go up strong, lean in, and jump as high as you can.

▶ After the rebound, when you are on the left side use a right-handed dribble and on the right side use a left-handed dribble to split the chairs. (The ball is always in your outside hand.)

REVERSE LAYUP

Purpose: To gain options around the hoop by using the backboard and rim as another form of protection from the defense. The reverse layup is a great shot to use in traffic. You should be able to shoot with either hand.

Procedure: Stand under the backboard with the ball, directly in line with the rim. Jump as you plant your right foot (inside leg) and shoot with your left hand using a flicking motion with your wrist. Spin the ball with your wrist inward, using the square above the rim as the target you would want to hit. Make 10 shots.

- Concentrate on each shot. Use your off arm to protect the ball. You are always shooting facing the entire court.

- Make 10 reverse layups on each side.

- Shoot 10 foul shots. Repeat the drill three times.

Lady Magic Tips

▶ Always keep your head up and jump as high as you can on the shot. As the ball comes down through the net, catch it and this time plant your left leg (inside leg) and shoot a reverse layup with your right hand.

▶ Start under the backboard so you have to use your wrist to spin the ball off the glass.

▶ Push yourself to game speed when comfortable.

▶ Follow through on all shots.

JUMP SHOT DRILLS

Learning to shoot on the move will improve your chances of making shots on the move in games. With practice, your shots off a fake or dribble will become one fluid motion.

X-OUT J

Procedure: Start with your outside foot on the block and your back to the baseline.

- Roll the ball past the foul line.
- Pick the ball up after it crosses the foul line, pivot, and face the basket. Shoot the jumper and follow your shot. (The ball shouldn't touch the floor after it goes through the net.)
- Make 10.

X-OUT SHOT FAKE J

Procedure: Start with your outside foot on the block and your back to the baseline.

- Roll the ball past the foul line.
- Pick the ball up after it crosses the foul line, but add a shot fake when you turn and face the basket. Take a dribble before you shoot the jumper.
- Make 10.

X-OUT COMBO FROM WING

Procedure: Start with your outside foot on the block and your back to the baseline.

- Roll the ball past the three-point line.
- Pick the ball up after it crosses the three-point line, pivot, and face the basket.
- Shot fake and dribble to the elbow or baseline for your jumper.
- Follow your shot. Make 10.

FALLAWAY JUMP SHOT

Purpose: Using the proper shooting form, this shot allows you to create space between you and the defender. This drill also develops the ability to be on balance and stay low prior to your shot.

Procedure: Start at the foul line extended (the T). You should be in a triple threat ready position. Make a hard drive to the basket and quickly plant your outside foot. As you go up for your shot, push back leaning away, instead of leaning in. Your release should be higher with more arch and a soft touch.

- Make sure your weight is on the pivot foot before pushing off it.
- Make 10 fallaway jumpers on the left side and 10 fallaway jumpers on the right side. Take 10 foul shots. Repeat three times.
- After your shot, rebound and dribble back to the extended foul line and continue the drill.

Lady Magic Tips

- ▶ Use the proper shooting form. The only change is that you're falling away instead of leaning in.
- ▶ Plant hard with your outside foot to drive the defense back.
- ▶ As the defenders retreat, fade back on your shot. That's where the space is created.
- ▶ Use high arch and follow through using a soft feathery touch.

BASELINE JUMPER OFF THE GLASS

Purpose: To help you see and feel where the defense is behind you. You will shoot on balance while turning baseline for a jumper off the glass. The drill will improve your ability to catch the ball off the jump stop and turn (pivot) baseline to face the defense in a ready position.

Procedure: Starting under the basket in front of the rim, toss the ball above the low block outside the lane. Catch the ball. Then, using your jump stop, check for the defense on either side by looking over your shoulder.

- Pivot with your inside foot and turn baseline, squaring up to the defense. You should be in a low triple threat position, driving the defense back.
- You can go straight up with the baseline jumper or use a few ball fakes. Then shoot. Aim for the near corner of the square above the rim.
- Use proper shooting technique.

- Rebound after your shot.

Lady Magic Tips

▶ Catch the ball and use a balanced jump shot.

▶ Use ball fakes to commit the defense.

▶ Shoot high and use the glass.

BANK SHOT DRILLS

Bank shots can improve your shooting because they help your sight lines. The square on the glass gives you a target to focus on. All layups should come off the glass, and angled jumpers as well.

TOSS AND SHOOT

Purpose: To work on tossing the ball and getting in the correct shooting and balanced position. This drill will help you focus on catching the ball in a low position as you turn to attack the defense. You should catch and shoot the ball in one quick motion.

Procedure: Use a 45-degree angle from both sides. Start under the basket and toss the ball out at a 45-degree angle to what you feel is your shooting range on the wing.

- As you approach the ball, jump stop, grab the ball, and turn with your body square to the basket. Stay on balance with your elbow in the L position and your shooting foot slightly forward.
- Rebound your shot and return under the basket to start again. Shoot for 1 minute. Record the number of shots made. Take 10 foul shots. Repeat this drill three times on each side.

Lady Magic Tips

▶ Stay behind the ball in ready position.

▶ Pivot around and square up to the basket in one motion.

▶ Your hands must be ready to shoot.

▶ When you shoot the bank shot or your jumper, aim for the square above the rim. Jump up and in slightly. Follow through hard, pointing toward the target.

▶ Look for the offensive rebound.

BANK SHOT OFF THE DRIBBLE

Purpose: To focus on your speed dribble with either hand and exploding into your shot.

Procedure: Start near the sideline, foul line extended. Toss the ball out in front, get it, and jump stop in a balanced position. In one motion, speed dribble to an area at a 45-degree angle.

- Stay within your shooting range. Stay low and be ready to rise up and shoot the bank shot.
- Concentrate on the top near corner of the box above the rim. Always follow through hard; exaggerate your follow-through.
- Follow your shot and change sides. On the left side, speed dribble with your left hand. On the right side, speed dribble with your right hand.

Lady Magic Tips

- ▶ Jump stop and receive the ball in one motion. Make your move for the speed dribble.
- ▶ Plant your inside foot and jump as high as you can.
- ▶ Stay focused on the rim.

BANK SHOT OFF SPIN DRIBBLE

Purpose: To work on getting your bank shot off after shaking the defense with a spin dribble (see chapter 7). It's another way to create a shot. You should work on ballhandling, focusing on the spin dribble with each hand being in proper position. Stay on balance. The drill will also condition you to think offensive rebounding.

Procedure: Start slightly back of the key area, using your left hand speed dribble to the foul-line elbow on the right side. As you approach the elbow, stay low, with your head up, and begin your spin to the outside.

- Switch the ball to your right hand (outside hand) using your left to protect the ball. Find your shooting range and pull up for a bank shot (45-degree angle).
- Jump slightly in and follow through to the square above the rim.
- Always follow your shot to work on offensive rebounding.

- Rebound and dribble back to the starting point. Make 10 bank shots off your spin dribble on each side. Take 10 foul shots. Repeat this drill three times.

Lady Magic Tips

- ▶ Don't leave the ball behind you on the spin. Pull it around, then switch hands.
- ▶ Spin with your head up so you can see the defense and the floor.
- ▶ Square up in a balanced position for your bank shot.

FREE THROW DRILLS

These drills are solely for repetition and concentration. The more free throws you shoot, the more confident you'll be at the line.

NAIL IT

Purpose: To develop good work habits, confidence, and concentration. It is important to relax and get into a good rhythm and routine. You can use this time to work on your mechanics.

Procedure: Step up to the free throw line. As you approach the foul line, look for the nail on the floor. It should be in the middle of the foul lane on most wooden floors. If not, center yourself in the middle of the free throw line, directly at the front of the rim.

- You should be shooting at least 100 foul shots a day. Break them into different sets—25 at one basket, then 25 at another. You can also shoot 20 one-and-ones. If you make the first shot, you shoot the second. Vary how you shoot your free throws, but remember to shoot 100.
- Make 20 straight. (If you're still improving at the line, you can lower the number. Always look to improve.)
- Shoot 10 one-and-ones.
- Make 20 straight.
- Shoot 5 one-and-ones.
- Make 20 straight.
- Shoot 5 one-and-ones.

Lady Magic Tips

▶ Step back from the foul line after two shots in a row. You'll never shoot more than two unless you are fouled while shooting a three-pointer, or if a technical foul is added to a foul.

▶ Use proper shooting form.

FOUL-SHOT GOLF

Purpose: To work on your foul shooting through repetition and concentration. This drill is a fun way to play alone or with others.

Procedure: Start at the foul line. You play 18 holes in this drill. You earn a "birdie" by hitting nothing but net. If it hits any part of the rim you haven't earned a birdie. You earn a "par" by just making the foul shot. You earn a "bogie" by missing your foul shot.

• You get three shots. If on your first shot you hit the rim, but make the shot, you earn par. Next shot you hit only net; you earn a birdie. Now your score is 1 under. You also hit net on your third shot. Now your score is 2 under. You have completed one round.

• You can start your next round, or if you are playing with others, it's their turn to shoot.

• When you have completed six rounds, 18 holes, the game is over. The player with the lowest score wins. If you are playing by yourself, challenge yourself by improving your score each time.

Lady Magic Tips

▶ Follow through with high arch and finish hard with your wrist straight to the basket.

▶ Concentrate on your target.

▶ Don't forget your score!

SPECIALTY DRILLS

These drills give you options. You never know when a hook shot might come in handy or you need to tip a shot to keep the ball alive. Work on them all when you have time.

MIKAN DRILL

Purpose: To work on planting your inside foot and using a semihook off the glass. The drill will help you to learn proper form, concentration, pivoting with each foot, shooting with each hand, keeping the ball up at all times once you get it out of the net, following the flight of the ball, and developing speed and quickness.

Procedure: Start directly in front of the rim. Plant your left foot to the right as if you are beginning a layup. Go up and attempt your semihook (layup) using your off hand to protect the ball. Use the glass on each shot.

- As the ball goes through the net, grab it and plant your right foot. Lean left and attempt a left-handed semihook. Keep alternating left to right.
- Make 10 shots on each side. Shoot 5 foul shots. Repeat this drill three times.
- To challenge yourself, see how many you can make in 60 seconds. Then take 10 foul shots. Repeat this procedure three times.

Lady Magic Tips

- ▶ Your head is always up. Don't drop the ball below your shoulders. Keep your elbows out. Plant your inside foot and explode up for the shot.
- ▶ Keep your head up and plant your inside foot.
- ▶ Follow through hard. Always use the glass.

TWO-HANDED HOOK SHOT

Purpose: To develop confidence and proper technique and to improve your strong- and weak-hand bank shot, using a crossover step. (Though mostly used by post players, this drill can be utilized by others as well.)

Procedure: Start sideways in front of the rim and hold the ball above your waist. Step with your inside leg. Going left, you will be shooting with your right hand.

- Use the crossover, step with your left foot at a 45-degree angle. You will pivot toward the basket. Your right knee comes up as you lean in to release the ball.
- Shoot high off the glass, aiming at the near corner of the square above the rim.

- Start with the ball close to your body near your hip. Bring the ball by your ear and the side of your head. As you extend your elbow, flex your wrist and fingers toward the basket, using your fingertips to release a soft shot with good rotation on the ball.
- As the shot goes up, rebound. Repeat the same drill from the other side.
- Continue alternating your hook shot from right to left, using the crossover step.
- Take 10 hook shots from each side. Take 10 foul shots. Repeat this drill three times.

Lady Magic Tips

▶ Start in the sideways position in front of the rim.

▶ Always use the crossover step; your inside leg is at a 45-degree angle.

▶ Aim high off the glass, using a soft, relaxed touch on the ball.

▶ Remember a missed shot is a pass to yourself. Rebound.

HOOK SHOT WITH A DROP STEP

Purpose: To work on reading where the defense might be and to improve footwork and offensive rebounding.

Procedure: Start slightly in front of the rim, your body sideways to the basket. Toss the ball outside the foul lane above the low block. Catch the ball with your back to the basket using a jump stop for balance.

- Check over each shoulder to see the imaginary defense. Then drop step baseline using your hook shot at a 45-degree angle. Repeat the drill until you have completed 5 baseline hook shots. After you catch the ball and jump stop, check over your left shoulder, drop step with your right foot and, using your left hand, shoot a hook shot in the lane. Take 5 shots.
- Alternate sides of the court after you complete 10 shots.
- Take 10 foul shots and repeat this drill four times.

Lady Magic Tips

▶ Start sideways in front of the basket.

▶ Drop step at a 45-degree angle.

- ▶ On the opposite side of the court, drop step baseline with your right foot and hook with your left hand. To the middle, drop step left foot and hook with your right hand.

- ▶ On the baseline hook, don't get caught too far under the backboard. Get a good angle (45 degrees).

- ▶ Rebound after each shot.

TIPPING

Purpose: To improve strength and endurance for rebounding. It's not always how high you jump; it's how quickly and how well you are positioned. This drill also will improve the strength in your hands and wrists.

Procedure: Stand on the left side of the backboard in front. Place the ball in your left hand. Keep your elbow in and wrist back. The ball should be shoulder high. Use only your left hand.

- • Shoot the ball high and controlled on the left side of the backboard. Keep tipping the ball up against the glass five times. On the fifth time, tip the ball in. Try not to catch the ball; tip it. You should be in a balanced position: legs shoulder-width apart, knees flexed, and ready to jump up to meet the ball in flight.

- • Switch to your right hand and repeat the drill.

- • Then, alternate hands. It's difficult and takes balance and coordination. Start on one side (left) and using your left hand, tip the ball over the rim to the right side of the backboard. You must slide over to the right side quickly to be in position to tip the ball with your right hand to the left side. Keep alternating sides for six tips—three on each side. The last tip goes in the basket.

- • Tipping certainly is an advanced drill. Use a wall instead of the backboard if that is more helpful.

Lady Magic Tips

- ▶ Keep the ball above your head when tipping. If it gets too low you lose control.

- ▶ Keep your fingers spread apart, flexed, and relaxed.

- ▶ When alternating the tip, slide side to side, quickly and on balance.

DUNKING

Purpose: To try something you might not have tried before and to work on your timing and jumping.

Procedure: Find an adjustable rim. Lower it to a height at which you can comfortably dunk.

- As you feel more relaxed and confident, raise the level.
- Try a one-handed dunk, a two-handed dunk, a reverse dunk. Do whatever you think you can do.
- Have fun.

Lady Magic Tips

▶ Don't hit your head on the rim—it ruins the fun.

▶ Jump as high as you can.

▶ If you have small hands, use "stick-em" or two hands.

DUCK-IN MOVE DRILL

Purpose: To get the pass to the post player in the paint. This drill will help you learn to position the post properly in the paint, create a passing lane, and thereby decrease the degree of difficulty for the pass. Players will learn to catch the ball under pressure and learn three offensive moves once they've received the pass. (The "duck-in" is a new term for "posting-up.")

Procedure: Player 1 has the ball and stands at the top of the key on the left side. Player 2, the offensive post, stands to the right of the lane. Player 3, the defensive player, stands in the lane.

- Player 2 brings her defender (Player 3) into the lane. She must break the broken circle to do this. If possible, she should line herself up so that she is in front of the rim.
- Player 3 stays with Player 2 and contests the passing lane.
- When Player 2 reaches the broken circle, she ducks in and steps over the leg of the defender, creating a lane for the pass. Player 2 now shows her free hand and calls for the ball which she should receive in the paint near the broken circle.
- Player 2 can now execute one of three offensive moves depending on how her defender reacts. If the defender is slow to react,

Player 2 executes a drop step, dribbles, and squares up for the layup. If the defender reacts and recovers, Player 2 takes one dribble toward the box, and executes a baby hook on the left side. If the defender recovers and positions herself between Player 2 and the basket, Player 2 drop steps, power dribbles, squares up, and uses a head-and-shoulders pump fake before going up for a short bank shot.

Lady Magic Tip

▶ If Player 2 uses a head-and-shoulders pump fake, she should not fake the ball up, but instead should fake it out of her chest to elevate the defender.

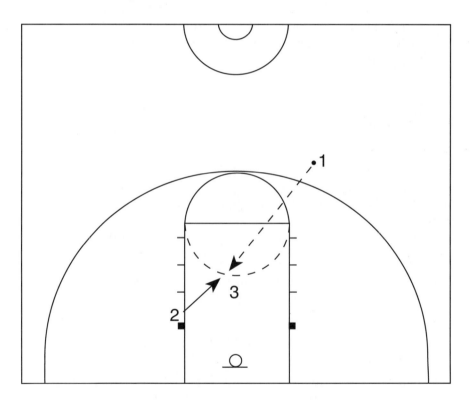

BEAT THE ALL-AMERICAN

Purpose: To build confidence and concentration on each shot and learn to be more selective on shots because a bad shot will cost you. In this drill you'll work on your offensive moves in a gamelike situation. Remember, it's you against the imaginary all-American—have fun.

Procedure: Start out shooting a foul shot. If you make it, you earn 1 point. If you miss, the pro receives 2 points. Ten points wins. Take any shot you want—layups aren't allowed.

- After the foul shot, you can shoot from any spot on the court. You must keep moving and you cannot shoot the same shot twice in a row from the same spot.

- Make sure you are in your range. Be positive and relaxed. This drill depends on great concentration for each shot.

- You also can play "Beat the All-American" from three-point range. This time, you shoot only from three-point range. If you make your shot, it's 2 points for you. If you miss, the pro gets 3 points. Play to 21 points.

Lady Magic Tips

- ▶ Shoot on the move—work on your concentration, shot selection, and form.

- ▶ Use all your moves and shots. Make it gamelike.

- ▶ Play to win.

RABBIT SHOOTING DRILL

Purpose: This program consists of 12 steps that will make you a better shooter. The workout is brief and must be done with intensity.

- Toss the ball to the three-point line. Get the ball and square up to the basket. Shoot and follow your shot. Time: 2 minutes. Goal: 20 to 25 shots.

- Shoot 10 foul shots. Record your score. Do not rest. Keep the shooting gamelike.

- Toss the ball to the three-point line. Get the ball and take one strong dribble. Square up to the basket. Shoot and follow your shot. Time: 2 minutes. Goal: 18 to 20 shots.

- Shoot 10 foul shots. Record your score. Do not rest.

- Toss the ball to the three-point line. Get the ball and take two strong dribbles. Square up to the basket. Shoot and follow your shot. Time: 2 minutes. Goal: 17 to 20 shots.

- Shoot 10 foul shots. Record your score. Do not rest.
- Toss the ball to the three-point line. Get the ball and square up to the basket. Shoot and follow your shot. Time: 2 minutes. Goal: 20 to 25 shots.
- Shoot 10 foul shots. Record your score. Do not rest.
- Toss the ball to the three-point line. Get the ball and take one strong dribble. Square up to the basket. Shoot and follow your shot. Time: 2 minutes. Goal: 18 to 20 shots.
- Shoot 10 foul shots. Record your score. Do not rest.
- Toss the ball to the three-point line. Get the ball and take two strong dribbles. Square up to the basket. Shoot and follow your shot. Time: 2 minutes. Goal: 17 to 20 shots.
- Shoot 10 foul shots. Record your score. Do not rest.

MULTIPLE PLAYER DRILLS

Doing drills with a partner can be fun, whether it's one-on-one or shooting drills. Play hard and concentrate.

FULL COURT ONE-ON-ONE

In the first game, pick up your player at half court. Work hard, box out, and run the floor. This is a great conditioning drill. First player to score 10 points wins. After a 10-minute rest, play a second game. Pick up your player at three-quarters of the court this time. First player to score 10 points wins. After another 10-minute rest period, play a third game. Pick up your player full court.

TWO-ON-TWO

Everyone should learn how to become a better team player. It starts with being efficient at one-on-one, then two-on-two. The two-player concept allows a coach to take a small group to work on specific techniques within a team concept. As a team player, you must be able to make your teammates better. Technique and precision are important in a team concept. Much like three-on-three, you learn timing and how to set picks. Most importantly, remember good teamwork.

THREE-ON-THREE

Three-on-three continues to be a popular playground game. Three-on-three tournaments have sprung up all over the country for players with every level of ability. In a half-court situation, three-on-three gives you the opportunity to be creative and not get cluttered in a limited area. This concept combines one-on-one and two-on-two. In this format, you have the chance to utilize your total game: passing, screening, cutting, defense, rebounding and, of course, scoring. With three-on-three, there is a lot of action off the ball. Timing is essential for creating scoring opportunities. The close confines of the three-on-three competition create a physical atmosphere. You must use all the fundamentals, including boxing out and setting good, solid screens.

TWO-PLAYER SHOOTING DRILL

Purpose: To simulate game shooting, moving, offensive rebounding, and passing.

Procedure: You are ready to shoot. The second player passes you the ball. Shoot from anywhere on the court.

- Rebound your shot and make a good pass to the other player, who has gone to a different spot on the court. Her hands are up and are showing you where she wants the pass.
- Run at that player with your hands up, defending the shooter with token defense.
- As the shooter rebounds her shot, spot up. You become the shooter looking for a pass.
- Continue the drill without stopping until a player scores 30 points.
- Execute this same drill taking shots from the three-point area.

Lady Magic Tips

▶ Concentrate on your shot.

▶ Make a good pass to the shooter.

▶ Go at game speed.

Nancy Lieberman-Cline's Shooting Workout

Incorporate the previous drills into the following shooting workout.

Warm-Up

- 10 shots each side low block—pivot and score
- 10 shots each side low block—±power move
- 20 seconds—toss and shoot, change directions

Perimeter Workout

- 2 ½-minute shooting drill—5 spots, 10 shots
- 10 bank shots each side off pass (half court and full speed)
- 5 free throws
- 2 ½-minute shooting drill off penetration (use chair—reach the spot on your first step)
- 5 free throws
- 10 bank shots each side off penetration (half court and full speed)
- 5 free throws
- 2-minute jump shot off toss (turn over right and left—alternate)
- 5 free throws
- 2-minute jump shot off dribble (top of key)
- 5 free throws
- Free throw line across for 2 minutes (receive ball from wing—off pass and off dribble)
- 5 three throws
- Creative shooting drill for 2 minutes using one-on-one moves (with defense when possible)
- 5 free throws
- 2 ½-minute shooting drill off the pass
- 5 free throws
- Transition shots off penetration (be creative) from the point
- 10 free throws

- Weakside cut to elbow from wing—10 each side off pass
- 5 free throws
- Weakside cut to elbow from the wing—10 each side off penetration
- 5 free throws
- Offensive boards toss—10 each side and vary your shots
- Make 5 free throws in a row
- 2 ½-minute shooting with penetration
- Make 10 free throws in a row

Summary

Shooting is always fun and the thing players do the most. So why not shoot the ball with proper technique and form? Remember the following points:

- Proper body, hand, arm, head, and foot position are necessary for proper shooting form.
- Use the checkpoints to be sure you're ready for success.
- You have many types of shots to master. It takes practice and proper form.
- Nancy Lieberman-Cline's shooting workouts can make you a better shooter.

CHAPTER
6

Getting Open and Being a Threat Without the Ball

To be a complete player on offense, you must be able to move effectively without the ball to get open. This means you must see the floor, find the open spots, and be ready to receive the pass from your teammate.

Cutting and moving without the ball is an art. It takes precision, not just speed and quickness. You must set up your opponent with constant movement. If you stand in one place waiting for the ball, you aren't likely to get it. Cutting to the perimeter, however, will put you in position to score or drive to the basket. The toughest player to guard is the one who's constantly on the move.

In this chapter, I'll show you ways to establish your position. It takes hard work, determination, patience, and intelligence. By using fakes, screens, picks, and cuts, you can free yourself to get to the position you want.

SETTING SCREENS

A good screen will enable your teammate to get free for a potential scoring opportunity. With so much happening on the court—motion offenses, the flex, and spread offenses— setting a simple screen is no longer the only way to be effective on the court.

The proper way to set a screen is to jump stop, have a good wide base, and place your arms against your chest. You must set up in a stationary position to block the defender from the offensive player who is trying to get open.

When setting a screen, make contact. Don't let the defense slide over you. Be big, balanced, and square up to your opponent who is being screened. Catch the defender in the middle of your body. Screens will be much more effective if your teammate sets up the defense with a move in the opposite direction followed by a hard cut off your screen.

The player with the ball must be patient and allow other players to screen for one another. She must cut as close to you as possible so the defensive player does not slip between. If the ball handler is on the outside, she'll find the open shot. If she's on the inside, she'll roll hard to the hoop. Always be alert and look for a return pass; if the ball handler drives, she may pass up the shot and pass to you for the score. Next we'll give you tips on following the ball after you set a screen.

Roll to the Ball

After you set a screen, continue to roll to the side the ball handler is traveling. See how the defense plays the screen. If you are in front of your defender after the screen, roll to the basket. You have the lane and the defense is behind you. If the defense has played the screen smartly and sagged into the lane, you might stay high and look for a return pass for your shot. You can't predetermine the situation. You have to "read" your options. If the screen is solid, it will make the defense switch. You could potentially have a mismatch. If the defense has jumped to the ball handler and gotten over the screen, keep rolling. You might receive a quick pass as you go to the basket. You might be able to set a second screen if your teammate can set up the defense. Always have your hands ready to catch the pass. Try to keep the defense on your back. Use your body to shield a defender trying to front you. Be a big, wide target.

Screen and Roll/Pick and Roll

If the defense is not alert, a blind pick can be quite effective for your team and a bit painful for your opponent. The idea behind the screen and roll, and the pick and roll, is to provide a teammate with an open shot. It is difficult for defenders to both guard their opponents and watch for other offensive players getting in their way. This creates confusion and communication problems for the defense. Any split-second delay could create the desired shot by the offense.

To execute this option, move to either side of the defensive player who is guarding the ball handler and jump stop to gain good balance (see Figure 6.1a). Remember, when setting the screen, you must be stationary with your feet spread shoulder-width apart for proper balance. Place your arms across your chest to avoid being called for illegal use of hands.

The ball handler must then step foot to foot with you as she begins to rub the defensive player into the screen (see Figure 6.1b). The ball handler continues to dribble with her head up to watch for you as she rolls to the basket. As the ball handler goes by you, use a reverse pivot and roll toward the basket (see Figure 6.1c). The ball handler reads the defense to determine whether to shoot, drive, or pass the ball. The success of this maneuver depends on the defender's reaction to the pick and roll. Remember, when setting a screen, always keep your eyes on the ball handler and be prepared to catch a quick pass.

Figure 6.1   Set the screen (a), pivot with the ballhandler (b), and roll to the basket (c).

Step Outs

By "reading" the defense, you might see that the pick and roll isn't your best option. Let's say you have set the screen for your teammate, and her defender has gotten over the screen, but is still trailing the play. Your defender might hedge out to slow the ball handler from turning the corner. Normally, you would pick and roll. But you see the defense clogging up the middle. Why go into traffic? Step away from the defense but stay in shooting range. Be ready for the return pass. Take the shot if you're open.

CUTS AND ANGLES

Basketball is a game of angles, from how you slide to shaking the defense off a drive. The key is to use fakes and deception to get the defense leaning in the opposite direction. Change of speed, change of direction, and straight-line cuts are the best ways for the offensive player to free herself from the defense. Here are a few tips for using angles:

- Make your cuts sharp and precise. Plant hard with the foot you will be pushing off with. Explode in the other direction.
- Stay low and balanced.
- Cut as close to the defender as you can. It takes away her recovery step (the angle she needs to recover).
- Set your opponent up. When making a cut off a pick, decoy your opponent, then make the hard cut.
- Always slide with your outside leg in the direction you are going. Do not cross your feet or bring them together.
- For speed and balance, your head should always lead in the direction you want to go.

Flash/Body Cut

This is a very effective inside cut when you are coming from the perimeter to the inside and back to the perimeter. Step right at your defender. As you lean toward the defender, she will back away. Now, make a hard flash cut/body cut near the perimeter to receive the ball. Be sure to have your hands up as you make your cut (see Figure 6.2).

Figure 6.2 Flash/body cut.

Pivot and Cut

This is a great way to establish good inside position in the low-post area. Step right at your defender. Plant your foot and drive her back. Quickly make your cut into the lane to receive the pass. Always have your hands up to receive the ball.

Step and Cut

This is a great change-of-direction cut. Your first step is really a decoy to pull the defense in the opposite direction. Then, cut in the other direction away from the defense to receive the pass. Always have your hands up and ready to receive the pass. The most important thing is to plant your foot and make a believable fake or cut to lure the defense. Then, make your move to the open spot.

V-Cut

The V-cut (Figure 6.3) is the most common way for an offensive player to get open and receive the ball outside. For example, if the wing player is denied an entry pass by the defense, she makes a sharp cut toward the basket. This drives the defense back. As the defender is backpedaling, the wing player stops, pivots, and sprints back to the original spot where she wanted to receive the ball.

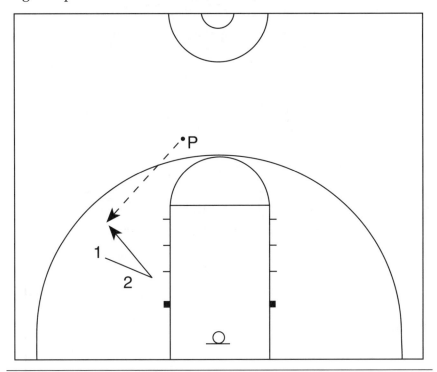

Figure 6.3   V-cut. P = pass, 1 = offensive wing, 2 = defender.

L-Cut

The L-cut is another option in getting open. You might be stacked on the block, trying to get into your offense. Come straight up the lane line and, at the foul line, cut hard to the outside L (see Figure 6.4). Make sharp cuts, not ones that are rounded off.

Backdoor Cut

When executing a backdoor cut (Figure 6.5), start by making short fakes on the wing to get open—similar to the V-cut. The defense is

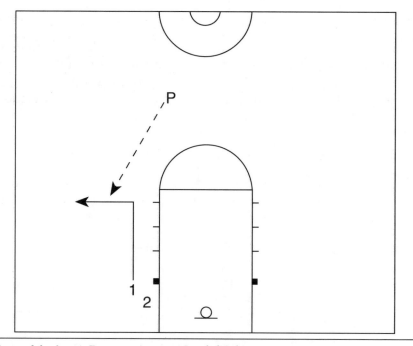

Figure 6.4　L-cut. P = pass, 1 = you, 2 = defender.

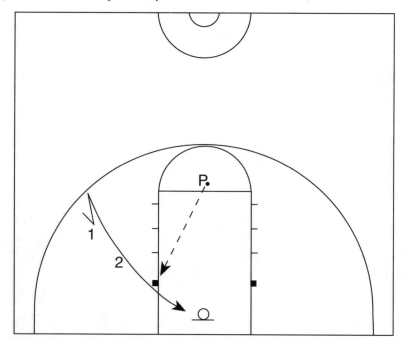

Figure 6.5　Backdoor cut. P = pass, 1 = you, 2 = defender.

trying to deny the entry pass to the wing. If the defender is pulled off balance, pivot and break hard to the basket. When going backdoor, expect a pass from your teammate. It could be a bounce pass, chest pass, or even a lob. Use the glass for a layup. It's best to go in at a 45-degree angle. You can use the square above the rim as a focal point for your shot.

Give-and-Go

The give-and-go (Figure 6.6) has been used in basketball for years. It is a simple play where the ball handler passes to an open player and cuts in front of the defender to the basket or an open area. This play is most successful when the defender is watching only her player or when she is watching the ball and loses sight of her player. Good offensive players will exploit that type of defensive breakdown by using change of speed, change of direction, and sharp cuts.

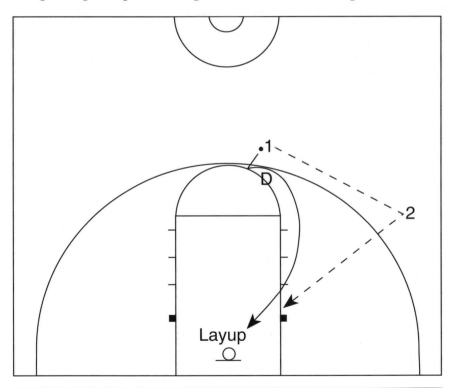

Figure 6.6   Give-and-go. 1 = offensive player, 2 = offensive teammate, D = defender. The dotted line is the direction of the pass; the solid line is the offensive cut.

SPLITTING THE POST

Many times offenses get bogged down because the defense is doing a great job of denying the wings. The point guard will call a high-post play to relieve the pressure. In a single-guard front, the point then can run off the post for a give-and-go, and the post can start the offensive play. In a two-guard front, the ball often will be passed to the high post to increase movement, and the guards will scissors cut.

Splitting the post is one of many three-on-three concepts available in a half-court offense. The basic set is two guards and a center. The passer, usually a guard, makes the first cut off the center and rubs her defender to the outside of the court. The other guard makes the second cut off the high post to the opposite side of the court. (See Figure 6.7). The high post needs to be alert and watch how the defense reacts. Then, the post needs to decide which cutter is open. If neither is open, the high post must look to shoot or drive to the basket. This gives you a chance to find the best option available for scoring.

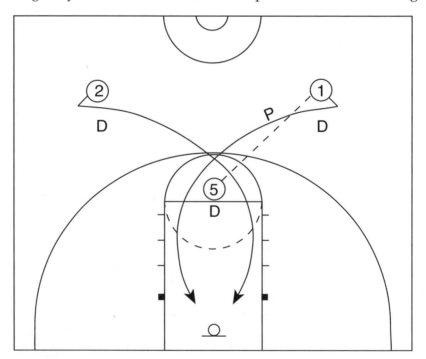

Figure 6.7   Splitting the post. 1 = point guard, 2 = shooting guard, 5 = post, D = defender. The dotted line is the direction of the pass; the solid line is the offensive cut.

When you have a lot of cutting and movement in your offense, remember to keep the floor spread out and balanced. If too many players are on one side, it's easier for the defense to guard them. Spread out the defense with proper spacing.

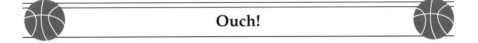

Ouch!

In 1992, I was in the ESPN studio watching the final eight teams try to qualify for the women's basketball Final Four. During the Virginia-Vanderbilt game, I noticed that every time Donna Harris from Vandy made her cut from the wing across the lane, Virginia center Heather Burge bumped her. Harris, after several hits, decided to take a different route. It took her out of her range, and she was never a factor in the game. I had hoped, as she cut through, she would use a fake or change of pace to get by Burge. She didn't and it affected Vandy's offense.

ON THE BREAK

Great athletes love this part of the game. A well-executed fast break is thrilling. It takes a lot of team effort, though, to be successful. You need to be sure of the following: who rebounds, who fills the lanes, who is the floor leader, and who takes the shot. The following is a breakdown of the responsibilities of each position and tips for getting open to score off the break. Figure 6.8 shows typical positioning for a fast break.

The Post

Most of the time, except for a steal, the fast break starts with a rebound. Running teams must remember to box out and hit the boards. Get the outlet pass out quickly. Keep the ball high so it's not stolen or deflected. If you're in traffic, take a quick step. Power dribble away from the defense.

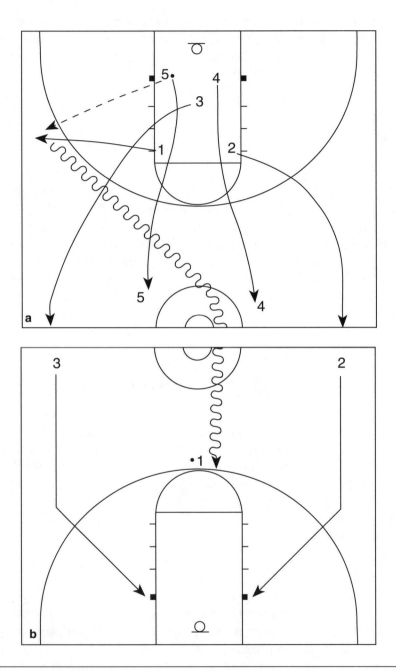

Figure 6.8 (a) Getting into position for a fast break. 1 = point guard, 2 = shooting guard, 3 = small forward, 4 = power forward, 5 = post. The dotted line is the pass, the crooked line is the path of the dribbler, and the solid line is the path of the offensive player. (b) Finishing the fast break in the front court.

It's now important to run the floor and trail the play. Try to beat your opponent down the floor. You must establish position for

- going to the glass and securing offensive rebounds, and
- setting picks if the break isn't there and you go into your secondary offense.

Forwards/Wings

First box out. Then, it's horse-racing time. Get out on the wings and fly. Use your speed and quickness. Stay 2 or 3 feet inside the sideline. This will eliminate stepping out of bounds or getting too close and cutting down the ball handler's passing angle. As you hit the opposite foul line, make that sharp 45-degree-angle cut to the hoop. Remember these pointers:

- Box out first and get the rebound. You can't run without the ball.
- Call for the ball. You should get the ball from your point guard early enough to make your move. Remember to use the strategies that you've learned to get open.
- If you haven't received the ball, make your cut 45 degrees to the basket. Be ready to receive the pass.
- Read the defense. Do you have a layup or should you pull up for a short or long jumper?
- Draw the defense. If you don't have the shot, make the defense commit. Then, find your open teammate.

Point Guards

You are the brains behind the fast break. What do you see? Do you have the advantage (the numbers)? Should you push it or pull it back out and set up? Seeing the floor and making the correct decision is important. Go to the ball. You must come to the ball and help your rebounder out. If you fade away, the defense will step up and steal the outlet pass. Remember these pointers:

- Keep your head up. See the floor and the defense. The defense might try to pick up a charge if your head is down.
- Pass the ball. Passing is quicker than dribbling. If a teammate

who can handle the ball well is open, get the ball up the floor.

- Stay in the middle of the floor. The defense will try to force you to a side to eliminate your options. Don't help your defenders by shading that way too early.

- Keep track of the numbers. This is what the fast break is all about: advantage. Do you have a three-on-one, a three-on-two? If it's in your favor, attack. Make the defense commit. Then, find the open player. Remember, the defense is hustling back. Be quick and know who's coming from behind.

- Avoid forcing the numbers. This means you need to know how many opponents are down the floor ahead of you. With 10 players on the floor, 5 are your teammates. If you have the numbers in your favor, say two-on-one or three-on-one, you have an advantage. If you don't have the advantage, back the ball out and get into your team's half-court offense. Take the break only when it's there.

- Look off your pass. Use your fakes, looking off the defense. You have the advantage. Keep it; don't telegraph which direction you are going to pass. By looking off your pass, the defense might be fooled into thinking you are passing in the other direction.

- Consider taking the shot. Pass to the wing. Step in and toward the ball. Be ready to shoot if you're open on the return pass.

- Penetrate. Attack the defense. Force the defense to guard you. Dish off to a teammate if you are not open to the hoop.

Shooting Guards

Quickness and the ability to stick your shot are essential for shooting guards. When your point guard penetrates and draws the defense, you must find the open place on the court for your shot. You also can use your quickness to slash and penetrate to the basket. If you are on a moving team, the minute your teammate gets the rebound it's your job to get in the outside lane and run the floor in transition.

- Be ready to receive a pass from a penetrating player on your team.

- Find the open spot on the floor where the defender vacated.

- Shooting guards can be good rebounders offensively. Go hard to the glass.
- Hitting your shot will open up your drive because the defense will have to play you tighter.
- Run hard, stay wide, and make your cut to the bucket at a 45-degree angle from the foul line extended.
- When you get the ball going to the basket, concentrate and finish the shot.
- Shooting guards can be good passers. Work on that skill.

Summary

Many times we think "I have to have the ball in my hands for my team to score." That's not necessarily true. Moving without the ball will create many scoring opportunities for you and your team if you know how to get open. This chapter addressed these key areas:

- Moving without the ball and getting open
- Types of fakes you can use
- Setting screens, using angles and cuts to get open
- Inside and outside cuts for post and perimeter players
- Splitting the post and establishing position
- Running the fast break—guards, forwards, and post players

CHAPTER
7

Dribbling–What's Your Handle?

Holly Warlick
Courtesy of the University of Tennessee

What a fun way to play the game: you come down the court, sense how you are being played by the defense, get your defender leaning, and you're gone. She's shaking her head, wondering what happened. Imagine that you are so comfortable and confident with your ballhandling that you never need to look down to see where the ball is. What an advantage. You can direct the action, see the mismatches, and create scoring opportunities.

Have you ever thought, "I could have gotten by her if I could have dribbled with my left hand"? If you can go left and right equally well, you will be much tougher to guard. Can you take your opponent off the penetration for the bucket when the defense steps up to help out? Were your eyes up and did you see the court? Did you hit your teammate with the sweet pass? When you have mastered ballhandling, you've given yourself the ability to be a great individual and team player. Besides, you'll be fun to watch.

Before you can execute the dribbles we will be talking about, you must be able to protect the basketball at all times (see Figure 7.1). Stay low, keep your head up, and see the defense. Use your off hand and arm to shield the ball from the defense. A good rule of thumb is to

a   b

Figure 7.1 Protecting the ball with a right-handed (a) and left-handed (b) dribble.

position your body between the defense and the ball. This means your body, arm, or leg is always between you and the defense. Remember, use your arm only to protect the ball. Don't swing it at your opponent. The referees will call you for that.

DRIBBLING OPTIONS

Your ability to dribble can have a great impact on your team's ability to run its offense. Expanding your ballhandling options can enhance your team's ability to bring the ball up the court, open you up for a shot, or help you get the ball to a teammate for the score. In the next section, we'll talk about the seven most common types of dribbles.

Speed Dribble

The speed dribble is used to advance the ball as quickly as possible. It is a higher dribble so you can push the ball out in front of you at a comfortable speed. The ball handler uses more of a running style as the ball is pushed out in front of her body at the waist to mid-chest area. Controlling the ball is most important. Find a speed at which you can maintain control. Your head must be up so you can see where the defenders and your teammates are on the court.

Hesitation Dribble

The hesitation dribble, a combination of control and different speed dribbles, is used to freeze your defender. Changing speeds keeps the defender off balance and guessing about your next move. The hesitation dribble forces your defender to react. A quick stutter step might open an opportunity for you to drive by your defender. If the defender backs away and anticipates your drive, you have just created the space needed for a jump shot. The hesitation is a great dribble to use in attacking your defender. When you combine the hesitation with a head fake, your defender might believe you are shooting and rise out of her defensive stance. When she starts to rise, stay low and accelerate past her to either side.

This dribble kept me in the men's United States Basketball League for 2 years. Since the male players were bigger and quicker, I had to attack first. Keeping the defense off balance allowed me to get the ball up the floor without having to turn my back to the action or possibly be double-teamed.

Crossover Dribble

The crossover dribble is used when you are facing your defender. It takes you from one direction to the next. To be effective against the defense, the crossover dribble should be low. Dribble by switching or bouncing the ball from one hand to the other, keeping the ball low and under the defender's hands. Make sure your opposite hand is out protecting the ball from the defense. Get the defense leaning one way. Then, using a forward angle, cross over, and explode in the opposite direction.

Proper footwork is necessary once you have accomplished the crossover dribble. You must take your crossover foot and place it as close as possible to the defender's foot. The other leg allows you to push your change in direction with power. This will help you create a favorable angle to the basket. A favorable angle is a straight line to the basket. For example, if the ball is in your right hand, you want the defender leaning to that side. You quickly cross over, staying low and protecting the ball. As you cross the ball from right to left, your right foot follows. Place your foot directly next to your defender, switch the ball to your left hand, and use your right arm and body to protect the ball. You will be able to go straight past your defender. Do not look at the ball on your crossover; doing so gives the defense time to slide and recover. If you go straight past the defender, she will be forced to stay behind you because you have the angle on her. Remember to always keep your head up. See the floor.

Spin/Reverse Dribble

If used properly, the spin/reverse dribble (see Figure 7.2) can be extremely helpful. As the ball handler, change direction by planting your inside foot (the foot closest to the defender). Attempt to split the defender's leg with your planted foot, pivoting quickly as you turn back toward the defender. As you reverse pivot, the ball changes hands and your body changes direction.

Do not leave the ball behind you as you spin. Your defender will try to knock the ball away or steal it. Always keep the ball protected by your body as you spin. Spin as close to the defender as you can to gain the best angle to move up the floor or toward the basket. You must keep your head up because it is easy for defenses to trap off a spin dribble. If you are aware of everyone on the floor, you can spin or pass the ball as you see the trap developing. Remember that defenses will try to force you to spin on the sideline, using it as a third defensive player. Stay away from the sideline as much as possible.

Step-Off Dribble

A step-off is a backward dribble used to help you move away from your defender. The step backward helps create space between you and the defense. It also gives you a better passing lane and a better angle to your teammates, especially to the post area. The maneuver is simple, but effective. When you are dribbling backward, protect the ball with your opposite hand.

Behind-the-Back Dribble

As you refine your skills and gain confidence in your ballhandling, the behind-the-back dribble is one you should add to your repertoire. Contrary to what some may say, the behind-the-back dribble can be a valuable option. When used properly, the behind-the-back dribble can help you gain an advantage on your opponent.

If you are dribbling the ball with your right hand—with the defense in front of you—lean slightly to your right making the defense believe you are headed in that direction. Immediately put the ball behind your back, pushing it all the way to your left side. The dribble behind your back must occur when your right foot is forward. As the ball is pushed forward to your left hand, the left foot moves forward so that it is out of the way. Your left hand controls the ball and your dribble continues. Your right arm now protects the ball.

Between-the-Legs Dribble

If you are being guarded closely by your defender and cannot cross over, the between-the-legs dribble is a great technique to use. Similar to the behind-the-back dribble, this dribble is a useful option because it allows you to change direction while moving.

Figure 7.2   Executing the spin dribble.

(continued)

Figure 7.2   *(continued)*

Forward.   When going to the right, dribble the ball with your right hand. Keep your weight on your right foot as you bounce the ball forward between your legs to your left hand. Use your opposite arm, your body, and your leg to protect the ball as you change direction. Explode as you push off to gain advantage on the defender.

Backward.   Dribbling between your legs allows you to move in a backward motion while changing direction. Plant your right foot when dribbling to the right side. Pull the ball backward between your legs while your dribble continues. The ball now is in your left hand. Use your right hand, arm, and body to shield the defense as it recovers. Also, this backward dribble enables the ball handler to start another offensive series if her teammates are tightly guarded. You can back off and allow your teammates to reposition themselves.

BALLHANDLING DRILLS

Before you practice your dribbling skills, warm up with the following drills. They will quickly get blood flowing to your fingers, hands, and wrists and will improve your ballhandling skills.

BALL SLAP

Purpose: To warm up your hands, quickly getting blood flowing to your fingers, hands, and wrists. By warming up, it will be easy to grab a pass, rebound, and dribble.

Procedure: Hold a basketball in one hand. Slap the ball hard with the opposite hand. Keep moving the ball from right to left while constantly slapping the ball. Slap the ball 10 times with each hand.

Lady Magic Tip

► Stand up straight when doing this exercise.

BALL AROUND WAIST

Purpose: To work on your hand speed and coordination. In this drill, you are pushing yourself against a clock to improve your speed.

Procedure: Take the ball around your waist, then around both legs, back around your waist, and then around your legs again. Do this 10 times and use a clock to time how many rotations you can complete in 30 seconds.

- Reverse the ball and again count how many rotations you can complete in 30 seconds.
- Rotate the ball around your waist, then around just your left leg for 30 seconds, then around your right leg for 30 seconds.

Lady Magic Tips

► Keep your head up.
► It's OK if you lose the ball. It means you are pushing yourself to the limit.

FULL-BODY CIRCLES

Purpose: To improve your ability to dribble with either hand, develop confidence, and condition your arms for speed and endurance.

Procedure: Put the ball above your head, with your hands straight up. Using your fingertips, tap the ball back and forth 20 times. Keep your fingers spread out on the ball.

- Quickly move the ball clockwise around your head 10 times. Then reverse the direction and move the ball around your neck another 10 times. Do the same around your waist.

- Quickly move the ball around one leg. Keep your knees bent, leaning in the direction of that leg. Your knees should be comfortably apart for balance and space. Go 10 times around one leg, then reverse direction 10 times. Switch legs and repeat drill.

- Figure eight. Stay low and balanced. Lean in the direction you are putting the ball around. Go 10 times in one direction, then reverse the figure eight for another 10 times.

Lady Magic Tips

▶ Stay in a balanced stance with your feet and knees flexed.

▶ Keep your hands cupped, not stiff.

▶ Always follow through and control the ball.

▶ As you feel more comfortable and confident, increase your speed. Challenge yourself.

AROUND ONE LEG

Purpose: To build strength in your wrists and hands as well as work on your speed and coordination. Make sure you do not use your arms. Concentrate on using your wrists and hands.

Procedure: Your body should be slightly bent with your legs apart for balance. Keep your head up and do not look at the ball. Bend slightly at your waist and bend your knees. Rotate the ball around your left leg as fast as you can for 30 seconds, then reverse the direction for 30 seconds. Do the same around your right leg for 30 seconds. Repeat this drill four times—twice around each leg.

Lady Magic Tips

▶ Remember to bend your knees, not only your waist.

▶ Keep your eyes up and not looking at the ball.

ONE-BALL DRIBBLING DRILLS

The following drills will help you work on proper ballhandling techniques, protecting the ball with your off hand, and improving your weak hand and overall confidence. In this six-step drill, you will work on your strong hand, on your weak hand, and on protecting the ball. Always start with the ball in your weak hand.

CRAB DRIBBLE

Procedure: Start in the basic balanced stance with your knees bent, your head up, and your feet shoulder-width apart. Start with the ball in your weak hand. Turn slightly from the defense and use your off hand, leg, and body as a shield. Change your pace of dribble every 10 dribbles, from waist high to a below-the-knee dribble (1 minute with each hand).

LINE DRILLS

Procedure: Stand behind a line on the court and move the ball side to side with one hand. Keep your head up and stay in a balanced stance (1 minute with each hand). Concentrate on moving the ball with your dribble.

SIDELINE DRIBBLE

Procedure: Find a line and stand next to it. This time, dribble the ball on your side, pushing and pulling it front to back. Move it in front and in back of the line on the court. Switch hands (1 minute with each hand).

FIGURE EIGHT

Purpose: To improve change of direction and moving the ball against the defense.

Procedure: Keeping the ball low to the ground, use your fingertips to dribble the ball back to front and through the middle of your legs. Change your hands each time as the ball goes through your legs. Keep following the figure eight motion (1 minute).

Variations:

- Kneel on One Knee: If your right knee is down, start with the ball in your right hand and dribble around to the left side. As the ball is directly behind your foot, use your left hand to meet the ball and continue the dribble on your left side. Then push the ball with your left hand through your legs and start again (1 minute). Then switch knees and repeat the drill in the opposite direction (1 minute).

- Sitting: As you are sitting on the floor, your knees should be slightly bent. Keep your head up. Dribble for 1 minute with your left hand, then dribble the ball under your knees with your left hand. Dribble low and fast for 1 minute on your right side. (Repeat two times for 1 minute on each side.)

- Control Dribble: Take three hard dribbles up the floor. On your last dribble, pick up the ball. Take three hard backward dribbles. Stop with your knees bent and in a proper balanced stance. Take three hard dribbles with the ball in your right hand as you shuffle to your left. Pick up the ball. Take three hard dribbles with your left hand as you shuffle to the right.

Lady Magic Tips

▶ Develop good balance and the ability to dribble with your head up.

HIGH DRIBBLES (RICOCHET)

Purpose: To work on your coordination, speed, and ability to catch the ball.

Procedure: Bounce the ball with two hands from the front through your legs to the back. Quickly move both your hands behind you to catch the ball as it comes through your legs.

- Start slowly at first. As you get your timing down, start bouncing the ball harder and faster.

- After the ball goes through your legs, take the ball around your waist to the front. Repeat this 10 times.

Lady Magic Tips

▶ Bounce the ball through your legs at an angle so it doesn't come straight up.

▶ Keep your legs slightly more than shoulder-width apart.

▶ Keep your head straight. Don't look at the ball.

SHOOTING OFF THE DRIBBLE

Purpose: To develop patience and skill when shooting from the seven most common dribbles you'll use in a game: speed, hesitation, crossover, spin/reverse, step-off, behind-the-back, and between-the-legs. The drill will help you learn to pull up on balance and use the correct form for the jumper.

Procedure: Place a chair in the middle of the foul line. Start between half court and the key area with the basketball. Speed dribble toward the chair. Start to slow down as you approach the key area. Use the straight dribble, then pull up for a foul-line jumper. On the shot, look for the offensive rebound. Dribble back to your starting point. Speed dribble to the opposite side of the chair, pull up, and shoot the jumper. Dribble back to the start and repeat—this time using your crossover dribble. Pull up for the jumper. Rebound.

- Repeat the same drill using all the dribbles mentioned—one time to each side.
- After all five dribbles have been completed to each side, take 10 one-and-one foul shots.

Lady Magic Tips

▶ When you are attacking the defense, it's important that you read your defenders and your options.

▶ Stay low as you approach the chairs. Keep your head up.

▶ Your explosive dribble at the chair should take you near the lane for a short jumper. Don't circle your cuts and fade for long shots.

▶ Protect the ball with your off hand. When on the left side of the floor use your left hand; on the right side use your right hand.

FULL-COURT DRIBBLING DRILLS

I strongly recommend that you do the following drills wearing gloves. Any kind of work gloves will do. You'll find them at any hardware store. If you can dribble the basketball with gloves, after you take them off you will have a great feel for the ball. You will control the ball better because it will feel smaller and more comfortable in your hands. Start with the full-court warm-up drills. Then move to the succeeding drills to work on numerous types of dribbles.

WARM-UP

Purpose: To improve skills when dribbling full court in a game. Work on keeping low to the ground, getting up and down the court, keeping your head up on the dribble, and seeing the entire court.

Procedure:

- Crab Dribble: You are bent over in a crablike position. Run full court with the ball while putting the ball through your legs as you are running. Work on speed, coordination, and balance. Keep the ball moving swiftly through your legs.

- Full-Court Zig-Zag: This drill will work on your change of direction. Start on the endline, stay low, dribble to the sideline, plant, pivot, cross over, and head in the opposite direction. Take three dribbles and change direction. Explode in that direction. Go full court up and back two times. Remember while changing directions to have some bounce (stay light on your feet) as you push off in the opposite direction.

- Crossover Dribble: Throw the ball off the backboard and go after it as if it were a rebound. Come down on balance, pivot, and be in a triple threat position, facing the entire court. Foot fake in one direction, then zig-zag down court, exploding in the opposite direction as you crossover dribble. Go up and back one time.

- Jump Stop: Follow the same procedure as the crossover dribble. As you go down court, jump stop on balance at the foul line, at half court, and, at the opposite foul line, pull up for a jumper. Do the same thing coming back. Go up and back one time.

- Spin Dribble: Follow the same procedure as the crossover dribble. Zig-zag down court. At each line, spin dribble, plant your upside foot, and spin in the opposite direction. Move the ball and protect it with your opposite hand. Stay low. Keep your head up. Go up and back one time.

- Behind-the-Back Dribble: Follow the same procedure as the crossover dribble, except dribble in a straight line down court. At each line, dribble behind your back, pushing the ball out to your side. Protect the ball with your opposite hand. Keep your eyes up to see any defender coming or teammates who are open.

- Between-the-Legs Dribble: Follow the same procedure as the behind-the-back dribble. Put the ball through your legs front to back, plant, and change direction at each line. Go up and back one time.

Lady Magic Tips

- ▶ Go full speed in all drills.
- ▶ Stay low and balanced as you dribble full court.

▶ Keep your head and eyes up to get a full view of the court.

▶ Protect the ball on all dribbles.

CONE DRIBBLING

Purpose: To work on proper technique, sharp cuts, and change of direction by using cones to simulate a defender.

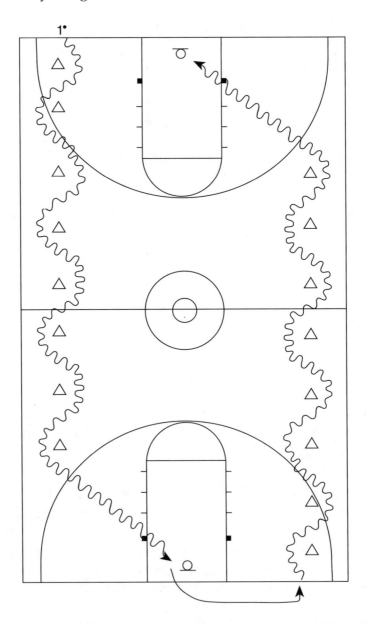

Procedure: Set cones every 5 feet from one baseline to the opposite foul line extended. Do each dribble under control and as fast as you can. After your last dribble, make a layup with the right hand going down, then with the left hand coming back.

- Crossover Dribble: Dribble full speed at the first cone. As you approach it, plant your outside foot and change direction as you use a low crossover dribble. Keep the ball waist high as you approach the second cone. Plant with your outside foot and cross over. Continue until you reach the last cone, then make a hard cut to the basket for a layup.

- Spin Dribble: Dribble full speed at the first cone. As you approach it, lower your body and plant your inside foot. Start on the right side, spin in a clockwise direction. Be sure to move the ball from your outside hand on the spin to your left hand, using your body and off hand to protect the ball. Keep your head up to see the defense. Continue to spin at each cone, alternating hands until you approach the last cone. Go in for the layup.

- Behind-the-Back Dribble: Dribble full speed to the first cone. As you approach the cone, your body should be forward in front of the ball. Quickly pull the ball with your wrist, fingers, then arm around your back to change direction. The ball should be waist high. As the ball changes direction, use your off hand and body to shield it. Proceed to the next cone and repeat, alternating your behind-the-back dribble from left to right and right to left.

Lady Magic Tip

▶ Complete each drill twice going full speed at all times.

COMBINATION DRILL

Purpose: To add an assortment of gamelike moves, ballhandling, and shooting to the drill. This simulates gamelike conditions. Work on the layup, power dribble, bank shot, corner shot, and foul-line jumper.

Procedure: Start at the baseline. Speed dribble using your left hand on the left side of the court to the foul line. Then, when you are at the foul line, spin dribble going toward half court. Crossover dribble at half court; stutter step or use the inside out dribble at the foul-line extended. Using a 45-degree angle, make your cut to the basket for the layup. Up and back is one set. Take five foul shots, then go from the right side using the same dribbles and layup.

- Complete the same drill, driving for a 2-foot power layup.
- Complete the same drill, this time pulling up for a bank shot from the wing area.
- Complete the same drill, this time taking your last dribble hard to the corner for a baseline jumper.
- Complete the same drill, this time using a crossover dribble to pull up at the foul line for a jumper.

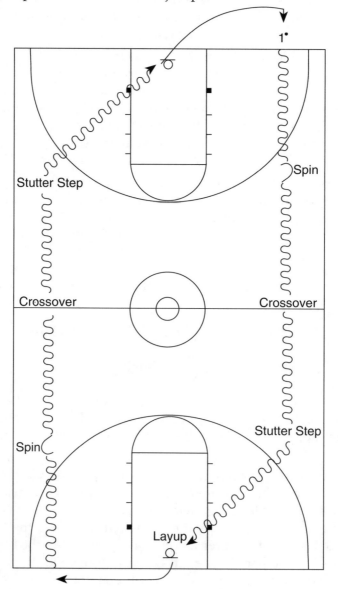

Lady Magic Tips

► Use game speed and intensity.

► Keep the ball waist high, protecting the ball with your off hand.

► Make explosive cuts to the basket for layups or jumpers.

► Make your last dribble a hard one so the ball comes up quicker for your shot.

WEAK-HAND DRILL

Purpose: To work on your weak hand through repetition and various dribbles. Improvement will give you more confidence and options on the court.

Procedure: Start on the left side of the court under the basket. (Let's assume your left hand is the weaker hand.)

• Start with the speed dribble full court and make a layup on the left side.

• Rebound your shot and dribble again full court with the speed dribble for a layup. Continue this drill for 60 seconds. Take 10 foul shots while resting. Begin the drill again.

• Push yourself and record how many layups you've made in 60 seconds. Always try to increase the number as you get better conditioned and confident with your weak hand.

• Do five sets of 60 seconds each with 10 foul shots in between.

Lady Magic Tips

► Always use your weak hand to improve it.

► Dribble the ball waist high. Don't throw the ball out and chase it. Dribble it with control.

DRIBBLING TWO BALLS

Purpose: To use high dribbles in the open court while pushing the ball up the floor. The drill will help your timing, strengthen both hands, and develop the confidence to know you can dribble with either hand.

Procedure: Walk with two balls, dribbling full court. Then, run the full court with two balls, dribbling together, alternating dribbles.

Variations:

- Dribble two balls out in front of you and move them side to side.

- While standing in place, dribble with both balls on your left side. Place your opposite arm across your body. Then dribble with the balls on your right side. Your knees should be slightly bent.

Lady Magic Tips

▶ Keep your head and eyes up.

▶ Stay under control by alternating dribbles.

ADDITIONAL DRIBBLING DRILLS

Here are some other ballhandling drills you should incorporate into your practice routine. You'll be amazed at the results.

RHYTHM DRIBBLES

Purpose: To improve your timing, coordination, and hand speed.

Procedure: Bend forward slightly from your waist and flex your knees. Your legs should be shoulder-width or more apart. Drop the ball in front between your legs. Take the ball completely around your right leg, then drop the ball between your legs. Rotate the ball around your left leg, then all the way around your right leg.

- Do two rhythm dribbles (ball bounces between legs) and three total ball rotations around your right leg one time, left leg one time, right leg one time.

- Go slow, listen to the beat—the rhythm of the ball—and your hand slapping on the ball. As you improve, use a quicker pace.

Lady Magic Tips

▶ Work on hearing the ball, as well as on timing, coordination, and hand speed.

▶ Keep your head up and your eyes looking straight ahead.

▶ Bend at the knees for proper balance.

ZIG-ZAG

Procedure: Place eight chairs in a zig-zag formation on the court.

Zig-zag (crossover) dribble through the chairs as fast as you can under control. Pull up and shoot a jumper at the opposite foul line. Come back and do the same at the other end.

Lady Magic Tips

- ▶ Stay low and protect the ball on each crossover dribble.
- ▶ Keep your head and eyes up. Try not to knock over the chairs, which you should imagine are defenders on the court.

INSIDE OUT

Purpose: To get the defender leaning one way, while you take her and go another direction.

Procedure: Using eight chairs, similar to the chair drill, act like you are about to crossover dribble. As you lean in with the ball to cross over, you quickly pull it from the inside of the chair to the outside. As you dip your shoulder to go inside, the defense should lean in that direction. Now, go to the outside as quickly as you can.

- Do this drill up and down the court with your right hand, then back with your left.
- Place chairs down the middle of the court. You can pull up and shoot a jumper at the foul line or fan out on your last dribble and take a wing shot.

Lady Magic Tips

- ▶ Stay low and balanced. Keep your head up.
- ▶ Make your inside fake believable.
- ▶ Protect the ball—always.

STEAL GAME

Purpose: To concentrate on your dribble while being distracted.

Procedure: Two players work against each other while dribbling in a tight area. Each player must protect her ball, while she tries to steal or knock the other player's ball away from her.

- Stay in one half court or foul-line (key) area.
- Protect the ball with your off hand as you try to dribble and deflect the other's ball or steal it.

- Force the other player out of the circle. If you steal or deflect her ball, you win.
- Switch hands after the drill is over. Then start again.

Lady Magic Tips

▶ Stay low and protect your ball. Keep your eyes up.

▶ Use both hands during this drill.

▶ Be aggressive. Try to deflect or steal the other player's ball.

TWO-MINUTE TAG

Purpose: To be aware of many players around you. You have to be alert, move the ball, and protect it with your body and arm.

Procedure: Use half court with four or more players. Everyone has a ball. Everyone dribbles left-handed for 2 minutes.

- One person is "it." That person chases the others, trying to tag someone. Whoever gets tagged then tries to tag someone else.
- Do this drill for 2 minutes with everyone using her right hand.

Lady Magic Tips

▶ As always, stay low, balanced, and protect the ball.

▶ Be alert so you are not tagged out. Keep moving.

LOW DRIBBLES

Purpose: To work both hands dribbling the ball as low as you can with your head up. The confidence you gain by being able to handle the ball with either hand will come in handy in game or practice situations.

Procedure: Dribble two balls in front of you, one in your left hand and one in your right. Dribble very low in front with each hand for 30 seconds. Stay low, bend your knees, and lower your back to simulate a sitting position.

- Use your fingertips, not your palm, to keep your dribble alive. Repeat four times for 30 seconds. Each time count how many dribbles you complete in 30 seconds. Push yourself to increase the number.

Variations:

- With two balls out in front of you, dribble to half court and back with a low dribble.

- Alternate the two balls in front of you, dribble to half court and back with a low dribble.

- Low dribble with two balls, one ball on each side. Stay low, keep your head up and eyes focused in front of you. Concentrate. Do the drill for 30 seconds, rest for 30. Do this drill four times.

- Low dribble around one leg. Stay low, bend your knees, lower your back, and keep your feet spread more than shoulder-width apart. With your left hand, start your low dribble around your left leg for 30 seconds. Use your fingertips to push and then pull back the ball on the dribble around your leg. Start by going counterclockwise for 30 seconds, then rest for 30 seconds. Switch hands and legs to the right side. Do this drill four times, two drills per leg. Then do the drill four times going clockwise on each leg for 30 seconds.

Lady Magic Tips

▶ Stay low, bend your knees, and stay balanced.

▶ Keep your eyes up at all times.

▶ Work your wrists and fingers as you dribble each ball.

TYPEWRITER

Purpose: To strengthen each of your fingers, your hands, and your arms. The drill will build your confidence with both hands as each finger becomes stronger when handling the ball.

Procedure: Place a ball in each hand. Crouch and dribble the ball like a typewriter, with one finger at a time, using both hands simultaneously.

- Start with your thumb, then work your index finger, middle finger, ring finger, and finally your pinkie. Dribble the ball 10 times low with each hand and then with each finger 10 times.

- Dribble the ball as hard and as controlled as possible to develop strength in each finger. After you feel comfortable, speed up. Keep your dribble low, about ankle high. Do this drill two times up and down (thumb to pinkie), then switch hands.

Lady Magic Tips

▶ Bend down low. You are working to strengthen your fingers.

▶ Push yourself when you get tired.

▶ Don't look at the ball.

HIGH DRIBBLE WARM-UP

Purpose: To work on timing, controlling the rhythm of your dribble, and strengthening your fingers, wrists, and forearms. This drill will get your blood flowing and get your hands and body warm and ready to execute other drills.

Procedure: Dribble the ball through your legs as you walk to half court. Keep putting the ball back and forth through your legs. Walk naturally. Go up and back one time.

- Use the same drill, but put the ball through your legs back to front instead. Walk up to half court and back one time. Dribble backward, placing the ball through your legs slowly and naturally. Remember to bounce the ball front to back. Walk up to half court and back one time.

- Skip, dribbling the ball through your legs front to back. Skip up to half court and back one time. Skip backward while dribbling the ball through your legs front to back. Skip up to half court and back one time.

- Dribble behind your back. Lean back slightly with your knees bent. Bounce the ball from side to side, one dribble per side and waist high behind your back. Look ahead. See the ball in the corner of your eye. Walk slowly full court one time. Dribble behind your back while walking backward. Walk slowly full court bouncing the ball with a good angle in the center of your legs behind you. Lean to the side of your dribble.

- Dribble behind your back with one dribble. Take one step to the left and bounce the ball with your left hand for one dribble. Push the ball behind you to the opposite side (right) and lean in that direction. Then take one dribble with your right hand as you take one step to the right. Repeat this for a total of 20 times.

- Scissors jump while dribbling the ball through your legs. Think of yourself as jumping rope down the court. The ball should be dribbled back and forth between your legs in the front. Repeat until you reach the other end of the floor. Scissors jump backward while dribbling the ball through your legs. The ball should be dribbled back and forth between your legs from the back. Repeat until you reach the other end of the floor.

- Dribble a ball low with both hands using your fingertips. Stay low and on balance while flexing your knees. Lower your hips until you are in a sitting position. This drill will help improve your hand speed and increase your fingertip control.

Lady Magic Tips

▶ Keep your dribble knee to waist high.

▶ Concentrate on each warm-up.

▶ Keep your head up. Try not to look at the ball.

▶ Feel the timing as you move.

▶ Keep the ball on your fingertips, not your palm.

HIGH DRIBBLE WRAPAROUND

Purpose: To build hand and arm speed while developing coordination, timing, and your ability to catch the ball as it goes through your legs.

Procedure: Stand upright with your knees slightly bent. Wrap the ball from the front around your waist to the back and bounce the ball waist high between your legs.

- As it goes through to the front, catch the ball with the same hand you wrapped around with.
- Alternate each side, 30 seconds each. Rest 30 seconds. Complete four sets total, two per side.

Lady Magic Tips

▶ Concentrate.

▶ Push yourself as you wrap the ball around your waist.

▶ Catch the ball with one hand—the hand you start with.

HIGH DRIBBLE BEHIND THE BACK

Purpose: To build confidence and improve coordination and ball control by not looking at the ball. This drill will help you learn how to dribble behind your back as an added option.

Procedure: Stand upright with your knees slightly bent. Take one dribble to the left side with your left hand. Push (bounce) the ball behind your back to the right side. Then, with your right hand catch the ball on the dribble, take a dribble with your right hand, and push it back to your left side.

- Keep your feet shoulder-width apart for balance. Repeat this drill 10 times on each side for a total of 20 dribbles behind your back. Do two sets of 20 behind-the-back dribbles.
- Lean into the direction of your dribble.

Lady Magic Tips

▶ Be balanced.

▶ Push the ball at a good angle so the ball comes up waist high on your opposite side.

▶ Your first dribble is more of a rhythm dribble, as you get ready to push (bounce) the ball to the other side.

JUMP DRIBBLES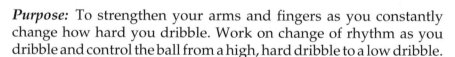

Purpose: To strengthen your arms and fingers as you constantly change how hard you dribble. Work on change of rhythm as you dribble and control the ball from a high, hard dribble to a low dribble.

Procedure: Place a ball in each hand and jump as you dribble them as high as you can. Then jump medium high while keeping the balls at waist level. Next jump slightly while bringing the balls to a low dribble. Alternate high dribble to medium, medium to low.

Lady Magic Tips

▶ Jump as high as you can off both legs.

▶ Control each ball simultaneously.

▶ Keep your head up.

LOW DRIBBLE FIGURE EIGHT

Purpose: To work on feel and the touch you have while dribbling the ball and to improve your ability to move the ball when it's low to the ground.

Procedure: Spread your legs slightly more than shoulder-width apart. Bend your knees and lower your back. Start with the ball in your right hand and dribble low with your fingertips around to the outside front of your right leg. Then dribble around the outside.

- Push the ball between your legs out to the front of your left leg and continue to fingertip dribble around your left leg to the outside. Dribble around and push the ball through your legs to the front. Lean in the direction you are dribbling. As you get comfortable, do this 10 times.

- See how many figure eights you can do in 30 seconds. Then reverse the ball and go in the opposite direction for 30 seconds.

Variation: Get into the same position as in the figure eight. Lean in the direction that you are dribbling. Using your left leg, dribble a circle around that leg 10 times clockwise, then 10 times counterclockwise. Rest 30 seconds and repeat the drill, this time using your right leg. As you improve, challenge yourself with a clock. See how many repetitions you can complete in 30 seconds. Push yourself to the limit. Time how fast you can go.

Lady Magic Tips

▶ Stay low. Keep your head up and eyes focused in front. Do not look at the ball.

▶ Use your fingertips to push and pull the ball around your legs.

▶ Relax your hands and fingers. The ball will be easier to control.

SPIDER DRIBBLE

Purpose: To increase your hand speed and coordination while dribbling the ball quickly in one spot between your legs.

Procedure: Stay low with your legs spread approximately shoulder-width apart. Drop the ball in front of you in the same spot. Touch the top of the ball two times in front and two times from behind. Keep the ball knee high as you move your hands from front to back.

- Dribble the ball on top quickly—once with your right hand, once with your left. Swing your arms around to the front. Keep the dribble alive with your hands on top of the ball—right, then left.

- Keep this up for 30 seconds. Keep the ball low and dribble hard. You must remain loose and relaxed for this drill to be effective. This is a superb drill for improving hand speed and coordination.

Lady Magic Tips

▶ Don't get frustrated and rush—that will cause mistakes.

▶ Keep your knees flexed.

LOW LINE DRIBBLE

Purpose: To work on dribbling the ball low to the ground while protecting it.

Procedure: Place one ball in each hand out in front of you. Find any line on the court. Stay low and dribble with one hand across that line. Using the line you will be able to see if, in fact, you are moving the ball enough with both hands. Practice going somewhere while dribbling. Do this 15 times with your left hand and 15 times with your right. Complete two sets of each.

Variations:

- Low Line Dribble (side): Place one ball in each hand to your sides. Stay low and balanced. Find another line on the court and set up beside it. You will do the same dribble but with one ball on each side. Move the ball up and down by the side of your foot. If you are dribbling with your right hand, use a line near your right foot. Do the same on your opposite side. Do this 15 times with your left hand and 15 times with your right. Complete two sets of each. Again, this drill allows you to move the ball as you dribble, pushing it out and pulling it back. Do not forget to challenge yourself against the clock. How many drills can you complete in 30 seconds?

- Low Crossover Dribble: Start with the ball in your right hand and cross over low in front of you. Use the line to make sure you moved the ball on your crossover to the left side. Constantly cross the ball from side to side using both hands. Do 50 crossover dribbles, 25 each way. Then push it and see how many you can complete in 1 minute.

Lady Magic Tips

▶ Make sure when dribbling with your left hand that you move the ball left to right.

▶ Move it around instead of staying in one place.

▶ Stay low when you dribble, keep your head up, and protect the ball with your off hand.

▶ Use your fingertips to dribble the ball. Don't use your palm.

MACHINE GUN DRIBBLE LOW

Purpose: To develop hand-speed, quickness, and touch.

Procedure: Stay low and balanced. Using both hands at the same time, dribble the ball as low and as hard as you can. Make sure your hands are on top of the ball. The lower you can keep the ball alive and the quicker you can dribble it with both hands, the more speed and strength you will build in your wrists and arms. Do this four times for 30 seconds each.

Lady Magic Tips

- ▶ Push yourself during this drill to improve coordination.
- ▶ Keep your head up and don't look at the ball.
- ▶ Think rhythm, not speed.
- ▶ Stay very low to the ground.
- ▶ Use your fingertips, keeping them round, not stiff.

Summary

No matter what position you play on the court, you will be a greater asset to your team if you can dribble the basketball effectively. Work on the basic dribbles until they become a solid part of your game. Then take the creative dribble and give your game even more weapons against the defense. This chapter takes you through the following areas:

- ▶ Dribbles—speed, hesitation, crossover, spin/reverse, step-off, behind-the-back, between-the-legs.
- ▶ Ballhandling warm-up.
- ▶ Ballhandling drills—half court and full court, one ball and two ball, low dribbles, high dribbles, and no dribbles.

CHAPTER
8

Passing and Catching
Turnover Free

There is no greater and more exciting display of teamwork than a player passing the ball correctly and with style. The women's game is full of great passers: Virginia's Dawn Staley, along with Stephanie White, Monica Foote, and Teresa Edwards. The list goes on and on. Each has a different style, but the results are the same.

Old Dominion University highlighted passing in the late 1970s and 1980s. We were an exciting team. We were solid passers. We made each other look good on the floor. Today, Colorado, Tennessee, Texas, Stanford, and Connecticut have terrific teams—as do many others—and the pass is a part of their success.

PASSING FUNDAMENTALS

At every level of the game, you should know the basic passes. It's important to know why you're using a certain pass, what its purpose is, and what the result will be. Passing is the thinking player's part of the game. If you know what pass to make in a given situation, you are eliminating potential turnovers. As you improve your passing skills and increase your understanding of situations, you will see the floor in a totally different way.

Even though you may know how to break down the defense through passing, you will be even more effective when you have the necessary skills to create scoring opportunities for your teammates. As a passer, you have the power to make your teammates look great or terrible by how and where you deliver a pass. I can't think of a more motivating or exciting play in basketball than making an incredible pass that scores 2 points and gets the fans and your teammates fired up.

Passing skills can be one of the best parts of your game. Passing can help you bring your teammates' level of play up and confuse defenses. Understanding the game and having the correct skills has nothing to do with how big or small you are. You need passing lanes against bigger and quicker players and you need space.

Faking With the Ball

The simplest way to create a passing lane is by using a ball fake—an effective tool that often is overlooked. You do not have to be fast but you must be believable and able to read how the defense is playing you. If you are tightly guarded, use ball fakes to back the defense off. If your defender moves, you have created your passing lane. For example, if you want to throw a bounce pass, fake high with an overhead pass. This will cause the defense to react to prevent the overhead pass. While your defenders are reacting and putting their hands up, use the bounce pass.

You have to make your fakes believable, which often means you have to overexaggerate. Don't telegraph where you are going to pass the ball. Just because you know you want to pass to the wing doesn't mean the defense has to know this. Be deceptive. Look off the defense in the opposite direction—which takes practice, confidence, and trust in your teammates—and protect the ball (see Figure 8.1).

Figure 8.1   Protecting the ball while looking to pass to a teammate.

You will be surprised by your success the first time you attempt a key pass and look off the defense. The easiest areas to get a pass by a defender are on either side of her head, under her arm, or close by her body. It is difficult for a defender to react to a pass in those areas.

If your defender isn't playing you tightly, other passing lanes to your teammates will be open: wing passes, entry passes to the post, and guard to guard passes.

By using ball fakes effectively, you can freeze a player for a split second and accomplish your task as a point guard. Until you and your teammates spend quality time on the court together, "no look" passes off someone's hands, head, or nose can be common. It may take time for teammates to avoid being faked by your fakes.

Timing

Timing is crucial to good passing. For example, sometimes you'll want so badly to get the ball to your teammates that you'll force the pass. Read the situation. Let the defense make its move. Let your defenders cheat. You might find other players open. For example, you want to make a lob pass to your post under the bucket, but you have a teammate making a baseline cut. Take your time. Let the area clear out. Then, make the pass. You will be surprised at how effectively you can pass when you add a little patience to your game.

Know Your Personnel

Know what your teammates like and don't like. Can she catch a bounce pass and score? Does she have great hands or hands of stone? Does she go get the ball? Find out. You may be making passes to the wrong player in the wrong situation. If you have a great one-on-one teammate, give up the ball early so she can do her thing. If you get the ball to her late down the court, you may be taking away some of her options. Don't give the ball to your low post way out on the wing. Give it to her down on the block where she can do damage.

The same can be said for forwards and post players. Study how your teammates pass at different positions. You never want to be fooled by a pass from your teammate. Every player has her own style and timing of how she likes to pass. If you receive these passes, pay attention. You never know when a pass is coming your way.

Pass With Both Hands

If you're on the left side of the floor, pass with your left hand. If you're on the right side, pass with your right. I always stress options. The defense is trying to limit you. Don't help your defenders.

Pride in Passing

Put the ball in your teammate's hands away from the defender's arm. Bounce the ball in so that it comes up to your teammate's waist and all she has to do is shoot. Pass to the hand she is showing. Use a ball fake so you have space to make the play. Lead her to the bucket for the score. Talk to your teammates. Passers are leaders. Be positive. Show confidence in whoever is on the court.

Communicate

This is what passing really is. The essence is letting your teammate know what to expect. If she knows the options, she will be prepared. Communication comes in many forms: a head fake, eye contact, or a signal with your hands. That's all nonverbal communication. Today's crowds are noisy. Sometimes you can barely hear the coach in the huddle. That's why all players need to be aware of who has the ball and what scheme is being called.

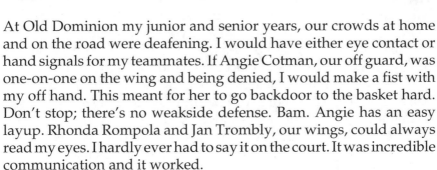

Keeping in Touch

At Old Dominion my junior and senior years, our crowds at home and on the road were deafening. I would have either eye contact or hand signals for my teammates. If Angie Cotman, our off guard, was one-on-one on the wing and being denied, I would make a fist with my off hand. This meant for her to go backdoor to the basket hard. Don't stop; there's no weakside defense. Bam. Angie has an easy layup. Rhonda Rompola and Jan Trombly, our wings, could always read my eyes. I hardly ever had to say it on the court. It was incredible communication and it worked.

PASSING OPTIONS

While on offense, you have many options, including a variety of passes. Master all of them and you'll become a more difficult player to stop.

Chest Pass

A chest pass is one of the most fundamental passes in basketball. The ball is supported at chest level, primarily by your fingertips on both hands. Your thumbs should be behind the ball with your hands and fingertips spread out toward the sides. Position your elbows close to your body. Place your feet in a triple threat position with your weight on your back foot. Shift your weight forward as you step into the pass. Extend your arms and rotate your thumbs downward.

For more speed and distance, place emphasis on shifting your body weight quickly and snapping your wrists as your thumbs rotate toward the floor. Follow through to your target and get your weight behind the pass (see Figure 8.2). Don't float your pass. Snap it and get it to your receiver. Use the chest pass in the right situation. It's a good, solid short pass that gets the ball from you to the receiver as quickly as possible. It can be used in long situations, but not often. If there's a fast break, use it if your teammate is uncontested. Long chest passes slow your break since they tend to float.

Bounce Pass

The bounce pass (Figure 8.3) is often used on the fast break or in a half-court offense by perimeter players to get the ball inside. Put some zip on this pass. Get the pass to your teammate quickly.

One or two hands may be used to successfully execute the bounce pass. Either way, the passer places her hands or hand behind the ball, extends her arms, and releases the ball in a downward fashion. The ball should strike the floor about two thirds of the way to the receiver so that it can be caught at waist level. Bounce passes can be used to deliver the ball under and away from your defender's hands. In most cases, this type of pass should be made when the defensive player is one pass away from the ball. A bounce pass through traffic is difficult. Be smart how you use bounce passes.

The bounce pass is like the chest pass in many ways. It works well in the half court getting the ball to the post and on backdoor cuts. Most defenders' hands are in the passing lanes, so lay a bounce pass under the arm of the defender. The closer the pass is to the body, the harder it is for the defender to react. Before they know it, your teammate has the ball. Like the chest pass, you can use it for distance, but make sure you pick your spots and put some power behind the pass.

Figure 8.2   Chest pass follow-through.

Figure 8.3   The bounce pass.

One-Handed Bounce Pass

Passing with one hand (Figure 8.4) is more difficult than passing with two—especially if you are being pressured by a defender. It also is more difficult to disguise this type of pass or to stop it once you have begun throwing it. A good ball fake will clear the defense from your passing lane. When throwing this type of pass, step with your inside leg in the direction of your pass. If you do not use the crossover step, take a short backswing so you can camouflage your pass. Don't allow the defense to read which pass you are using. You can be stationary when throwing this pass or you can throw it coming off the dribble.

Using this type of pass helped when I played in men's leagues. The defense didn't know whether I was keeping my dribble or passing. It gave me a split-second advantage. I was able to bounce pass off my dribble. I know from experience that if you are being guarded by a quick player like Tyrone "Muggsy" Bogues, you need time.

In the women's game, quick and speedy players can be found on most teams. So being able to disguise your passing and keep the defense off balance is a key.

Figure 8.4   The one-handed bounce pass.

Baseball Pass

A baseball pass frequently is used by a team that runs. This one-handed pass allows the passer to advance the ball a long distance.

The baseball pass begins with a staggered stance and the ball held primarily in one hand. Initially, the ball is supported by your nonpassing hand. As your weight is shifted backward, the ball then is guided by both hands just behind the shoulder of your throwing side (see Figure 8.5). On the throw, your passing hand extends in a forward and upward motion. The ball is released as your arm straightens. Step into your pass. Practice with both hands. This is a great pass to use when the defense is caught up court or napping.

Figure 8.5   Preparing to make a baseball pass.

Overhead Pass

The overhead pass (Figure 8.6) can be executed with speed and accuracy over a long distance, which is why it is quickly becoming one of the more popular passes used today. It may be used to make an outlet pass to begin a fast break or as a skip pass to swing the ball from one side of the floor to the other.

The ball should be held just above your head with your hands and fingers spread on each side. Do not move the ball behind your head. It can easily be stolen from behind. The palm of each hand should be cupped as the ball is firmly supported by your fingertips. Your elbows are turned to the outside of your body. As you position your feet in a staggered stance, your weight should shift from your rear to

Figure 8.6   An overhead pass.

forward foot as the ball moves from the top of your head forward. Release the ball out in front of your head as your fingers and wrist snap toward the receiver. Remember to follow through to your target. On this pass, be big and physical. Make yourself a threat on the court. Being big means taking up space. Your arms are out. You have a wide stance. Control the rebound so you can make the overhead pass. Many times this is the pass you make off a rebound in traffic. Stay big, balanced, and pivot around to keep your defenders away. Swing the ball violently from side to side as you move the ball. This is a legal move. However, you shouldn't try to hit or hurt anyone; just establish your area as you hold the ball. Move the ball. Don't swing your elbows at anyone. It will open up space for you to make the pass. Remember, your area is like your house. Don't let anyone in!

Hand-Off Pass

Many offenses rely on a simple hand-off pass from the point to the wing, from guard to guard, or from a guard into the high-post area (Figure 8.7). This pass is used when a player cuts closely by a teammate who hands off the ball. As you turn to hand off the ball to

Figure 8.7 A hand-off pass.

your teammate, be sure that you turn your body to shield it from the defense. The ball should be handed off waist high and into your teammate's hands. If you are handing the ball off, be aware if everyone goes with the ball. Roll to the hoop or open spot on the floor. Read the situation. Make sure as you hand off the ball to set the pick. Be squared up to the defender sliding with your teammate. Set a solid screen on the defender. Don't let her slide by.

Lob Pass

Known as the "alley oop," this pass works well in fast-break situations leading to offensive plays. The pass is the same as the two-handed overhead pass, except you add a little arch to it (Figure 8.8). You also can make the lob pass from the waist, if you aren't being

Figure 8.8   A lob pass.

guarded and have enough time. It's not easy to make a proper lob pass on the run. It takes good timing. The lob is also a great pass to enter to the low post.

A lob pass takes touch and you must be able to read where and how the defense is guarding your teammate. You do not want this pass to be thrown in a straight line, nor do you want it to be a high pop fly. Give the pass some arch. Remember, touch is vital. This pass was a key to Old Dominion winning two national titles. With 6-foot-5 Inge Nissen and 6-foot-8 Anne Donovan in the middle, the lob pass led to many easy baskets. They, of course, had to set up the defense by getting solid inside position between the backboard and the defense. They leaned on the defense to create space as the lob was in the air. It's important that your teammate gives you a target to shoot for— one or two hands up in the air.

Behind-the-Back Pass

Just like dribbling behind your back, a behind-the-back pass (Figure 8.9) can be a valuable asset in your game. It also can be a difficult pass to control because you are passing with one arm. With the ball placed

Figure 8.9 A behind-the-back pass.

in the palm of your passing hand, swing your arm in a circular motion and follow through around your back. It is important to snap your wrist in the direction of the intended receiver. This also can be a crowd-pleaser when successfully thrown in the right situation.

Tip Pass

With a tip pass, you never truly catch the ball. As you receive the ball, you merely tip it or guide it in a certain direction toward your teammate (Figure 8.10). You may even use this type of pass to tip the ball to yourself to gain control. It's smart and effective.

Figure 8.10   A tip pass.

Off-the-Dribble Pass

The better and more proficient you become, the more you can use the off-the-dribble pass (Figure 8.11). You can make it in any direction. It's a great pass for guards because they handle the ball so much. The pass is made as you are dribbling the ball by quickly moving your dribbling hand from the top of the ball to the back. Instead of taking the next dribble, you push it forward, flicking your wrist to pass to your intended receiver. Having a quick pass is a tremendous advantage. You have passed the ball before the defense realizes it's gone. There's no telegraphing the pass when it's done correctly.

Figure 8.11   Passing off the dribble.

RECEIVING THE PASS

Passing and catching go hand in hand, so to speak. Always keep your eye on the ball and keep your hands up and ready to catch the ball. Great passers are tricky. Whether the ball is caught often depends on the type of pass thrown and the position of the defense. All passes above the waist should be caught with your fingers up. All passes below the waist should be caught with your fingers down.

Always control the ball with your fingertips. It's difficult to catch the ball in your palms. Your fingers give with the ball when it arrives. Keep your fingers spread and relaxed.

Meet the ball. Make your fake, then come back to meet the pass. By moving toward the ball, you reduce turnover possibilities. The only times you don't move to the ball are when you are cutting to the basket or making an adjustment to receive the ball.

You worked hard to get the ball, now protect it. Use your arms, legs, and body. Where and how did you receive the ball? How is the defense playing you? Face the hoop. Use your pivoting, faking, passing, shooting, or dribbling to get by the defense.

PASSING DRILLS

You can become an expert passer with a little dedication and some patience. Use these drills to help you become better at hitting your teammates for the easy shot or getting the ball downcourt on the move.

RAPID-FIRE DRILL

Purpose: To develop three basic types of passes: the two-handed chest pass, overhead outlet pass, and baseball pass. The drill will also help you learn to catch a hard pass and make a quick release. It will strengthen your hands and wrists and develop hand-eye coordination.

Procedure: Using tape or chalk, mark an area on the ball you are targeting. If you have a "toss back" available, use it. Stand about 2 feet from the wall. Make a hard chest pass against the wall. It should be a rapid-fire pass. As you make each quick, hard chest pass, take one step back, until eventually you are 10 feet away.

- It should take you 10 passes to get 10 feet back.
- Continue back toward the wall taking 10 steps as you make your chest pass.
- Repeat this drill with the overhead pass and the baseball pass. On the latter, start by using your left hand. Finish with your right hand.

Lady Magic Tips

► Use correct fundamentals for each pass.

► Step into your passes. Be balanced.

► Focus on your target.

► Look off your pass. Try not to telegraph it, even in a drill. It will become a habit.

TWO-BALL RAPID FIRE

Purpose: To work on your quick release while not looking at the receiver. You'll learn to see all five players in front of you and learn to catch the ball quickly while passing.

Procedure: Have five players stand in front of you about 5 to 6 feet away. Your teammates are one arm's distance from each other. You have one ball and one of the five other players also has a ball. As you pass quickly to one of the players, the other ball will be passed back to you. If you happen to be looking in the direction of your pass expect to get beaned by the other ball. Make as many chest passes as you can in 1 minute. Then, rotate so everyone becomes the lone passer. Each player should have 3 minutes total of passing.

Lady Magic Tips

► Use a quick release and keep your focus straight ahead. Make your pass as quickly as you can. Quick passes build speed.

► Keep your hands up and be ready to receive the pass.

MONKEY IN THE MIDDLE

Purpose: To give you a target with your teammate and create pressure with the defense—the player in the middle. This three-person drill adds gamelike pressure and harassment by the defense. You can work on bounce passes, overhead passes, right- or left-handed hook passes, and reverse pivot passes.

Procedure: Stand about 15 feet across from the other player. The "monkey" is in the middle. You have the ball; the defender should be contesting your pass and harassing you. Using one of the appropriate passes (reverse pivot, hook pass, overhead, etc.), try to pass to your teammate. On the flight of the ball, the defense should be sprinting over to cover the new passer.

- Do not pass the ball until the defense has arrived.
- After 1 minute or a deflection, rotate positions.
- Everyone should get three chances to be on the outside as a passer.
- If the defense deflects or steals your pass, you're in the middle playing defense. If there is not a steal or deflection in 1 minute, rotate and change positions.

Lady Magic Tips

▶ Remember to use a ball fake and look off your pass.

▶ Use quick passes and be sure to protect the ball.

▶ Don't telegraph your pass.

▶ Stay on balance.

TOSS BACK/WALL PASSING CIRCUIT

Purpose: To improve your ability to make a variety of passes quicker, with power and accuracy. This drill will improve your strong hand and strengthen your weaker hand.

Procedure: Stand 10 feet from the wall or toss back. Pass and catch the ball as quickly as you can, using the chest pass, bounce pass, overhead pass, baseball pass, and behind-the-back pass. Make 25 passes of each. Take a 1 minute break after you have completed all five passes 25 times each. Repeat each set of five three times.

Lady Magic Tips

▶ Concentrate on the spot where you want your pass to head.

▶ Keep your hands up and be ready for a return pass.

PASSING ON THE MOVE

Purpose: To teach confidence, timing, quickness, power, and accuracy while passing on the move.

Procedure: Put tape (your target) on a wall. Then, place tape on one spot on the floor and on another spot 12 feet from the first. Start by standing on the tape on the floor. Pass the ball at an angle to the target on the wall. Slide to the other piece of tape and catch the ball. Then make another pass to the tape on the wall and slide in the other direction to catch the ball. Use a chest pass for this drill and take short quick lateral slides without crossing your feet. Follow through to your target with the proper angle that will get the ball to the opposite side. Do this drill for 30 seconds. Rest for 30 seconds. Repeat three times.

Lady Magic Tips

▶ Start out in a balanced stance—feet shoulder-width apart.

▶ Use a proper chest pass. Remember the fundamentals—keep elbows in, lean into the pass, follow through with good rotation on the ball, keep your thumbs down and palms out.

▶ Have your hands ready to catch the pass.

Summary

With so much emphasis on scoring and defense, passing and catching don't receive the attention they deserve. To reduce turnovers and have a better chance to win, you must work on the fundamentals of passing and catching. You should work on the following:

• Faking with the ball.

• Timing your pass.

• Knowing your personnel.

• Using both hands to pass. If you can use both, more options will be open to you.

• Communicating.

• Different types of passes.

• Receiving the ball.

• Passing drills.

CHAPTER
9

Becoming a
Defensive Stopper

Anne Donovan
Courtesy of Old Dominion University

Great teams play great defense—great overall players play great defense. If you play tough defense, it's just another way to stand out on your team. It can inspire teammates to the same commitment to win on the defensive end. Just think how much easier it will be to win if your defense can create points for you and your team.

Many times you will see a team with less talent win games because its defense causes turnovers, plays smart, forces you into taking poor percentage shots, and boxes out and rebounds well.

As the saying goes, offense sells tickets, defense wins championships. Besides, defense takes mental toughness, desire, and spirit. It's you against your opponent. The challenge is there! Make your opponents work for every possession and every point.

DEFENSIVE SKILLS

Let's take a simple test. When coaches ask whether you are a complete defensive player, they're looking for 10 qualities of a defensive stopper. Can you answer *yes* to the following questions?

1. Are you coachable and defense minded?
2. Do you have the necessary attributes—mental toughness, hustle, heart, and desire?
3. Do you get good positioning on the floor—on the ball and off? Do you see the ball on the weak side?
4. Do you have the correct defensive stance?
5. Do you jump well?
6. Do you have quick hands and feet?
7. Do you communicate with your teammates?
8. How smart are you? Do you understand how to play defense?
9. Can you play a variety of defenses?
10. Are you a good transition player? Can you switch quickly from offense to defense and vice versa?

These are the basic areas to work on to be a great defensive player. If you can answer *yes* to these questions, you will be great and so can your team. The following seven principles will help you answer *yes* to questions 3 through 7. They should increase your defensive awareness and make you more coachable. They also can help you overcome any shortcomings caused by your genetics. Training for questions 8 through 10 comes later in the chapter.

Body Positioning

The better defensive position you are in, the better the results. Keep your center of gravity low (see Figure 9.1). The lower you are to the ground, the quicker you will be. Even if your opponent fakes or changes direction, you can recover. You must condition yourself to stay low and balanced.

Figure 9.1   Keeping a low center of gravity.

Checkpoints

- ✓ Position yourself where you can see your opponent and the ball.
- ✓ Overplay the baseline at all times to protect it.
- ✓ Turn your opponent into the middle where you have help.

✓ Position yourself so your body forces your opponent to go where you want her to go.

Knee Position

Your stance is the foundation of good defense. Flex your knees as if you are sitting on a chair with your head over your knees for balance. Do not bend your back to achieve this position. If you do, it will pull you off balance. Here are some points to remember:

- Turn slightly sideways to your opponent.
- Never get your head and shoulders in front of your waist.
- Your weight is on your rear foot because you must be ready to go back at all times.
- Try to create mistakes rather than steal the ball. The defense is given more balls than it ever steals.

Power Base, Hips, and Back

You'll generate power if you stay low and explode up. Keeping a balanced, low power base will lead to explosive starts. The stronger your hips and back are, the better your positioning will be. Keep your knees flexed and back fairly straight, and keep your hips down.

Arms and Hands

Deflections and steals often are the result of proper arm and hand placement. Your arms should be slightly flexed for balance with your palms open toward the ball for steals. Your hands are always out in the passing lanes. If your opponent begins to shoot, put a hand up to contest the shot. If you're guarding a left-handed shooter, get your right hand up and vice versa. This way you never cross your body and get off balance.

Proper footwork is important, but active hands can allow the defense to apply immediate pressure on the ball. Be intimidating and harass the ball handler by using your hands. Your palms should be up if you try to steal the ball. Steal it as the dribble is coming up, not going down. The ball is slower on the way up. Also, try not to reach down to steal. This takes away your balance and commits you defensively.

Head and Eyes

Your head is the heaviest part of your body. Keep it over your knees. If it is too far forward, you will be off balance. If it is too far back, you will be on your heels. Your head should always be up, and your eyes focused on the waist of your opponent, not on the ball. Great ball handlers have great moves so try not to get faked out by the movement of the ball. A ball handler isn't going anywhere without her hips. You want to watch for the direction her hips are moving.

Communication

In competition, there are many things that can distract you: the noisy crowd, loud announcers, other players, lack of concentration, and referees. In spite of all this, you must continually communicate with your teammates. This is especially true on defense. By shouting "help," "screen," "ball," "dead," etc., you can help a teammate know what's coming at her or what's happening on the court. Communicate to your teammates that the blind screen is coming, or anything else you notice on the floor. On the basketball court, talk is not cheap. It is priceless. It can mean the difference between winning and losing.

Footwork

Good footwork is as important when you're on defense as it is when you're on offense. Always keep your feet moving. If your feet are stationary, your footwork is not energy efficient. It takes more time and energy to go from stopping to starting than it does to continue movement. Use your momentum to quickly change position or direction. A defensive player should be cautious while making adjustments. Slide to get to your destination; don't run. Find the angle to beat your opponent to a spot. Of course, there are always exceptions; if your opponent has blown by you in the open court, sprint to the other end. Find the area she's going to and attempt to cut her off. Don't cross your feet or bring them together. Once you do, you have lost the proper defensive edge. You are then off balance.

Before you attempt to play solid player-to-player defense, you need to know how to do it correctly. To achieve good defensive play, footwork is essential. The lower you are, the quicker and more explosive you will be. You will be able to change directions more efficiently. Do not bend at the waist. Flex your knees, keep your rear end low and keep your arms out in the passing lanes. Stay active and pressure the ball. Keep your feet shoulder-width apart with your head over your knees so your weight is equally distributed on both feet for proper balance. Don't get caught flat-footed.

As you begin to play defense, you need options to attack, contain, or recover from your opponent's moves. The footwork methods to work on are step and catch, attack step, drop step, and retreat step.

Step and Catch.   As you are guarding the ballhandler, she will make a move in either direction. You must be in your low and ready defensive position. Using your outside leg, slide at an angle to a spot where the ballhandler is heading. Never bring your feet together. As you approach the spot, turn the ballhandler in the other direction.

Attack Step.   The offense is always attacking you. With foot fakes, you can be the aggressor. It's almost as if you are fencing—one foot is slightly ahead of the other. The hand on the side of that foot should be extended toward the offensive player. Make her use a retreat dribble. If you attack your opponent, it makes her think and take time to react. Push off your back foot and, in a balanced position, go at the ball handler. Stay low and be on balance. You can take a one-step fake or a two-step attack fake at the ball. If done properly, you can make the ball handler pick up and kill her dribble. When you do get her to pick up the dribble, yell "dead, dead." This lets your teammates know the ball is dead. They can help you deny all passes.

Drop Step.   This is more of a recovery step if the offensive player beats you. The offensive player is probably in a triple threat position. Boom. She jab fakes at you and your front foot is up. By pivoting off your back foot, then opening or swinging your front leg in the direction of her drive, you can slide to an area to recover.

Retreat Step.   The offense is always trying to attack and break down the defense. When the offensive player is in her triple threat position, you must be low and in good defensive position. If an offensive player goes left or right, you can use the retreat step to push off and slide in that direction. The best way to generate the power is by pushing off with your front foot in that direction and taking a retreat step with your back foot. Then, quickly slide with your front foot. Now, you are back in a balanced stance.

Dos and Don'ts of Defense

Dos—On Ball

- Stay low and balanced. Keep your feet shoulder-width apart. Keep your hands active in the passing lane.
- Step and catch as you slide, hawking the ball.
- Dictate and try to control where the dribble is going. Pressure and contain the ball.
- Keep your head on the ball. This way you are always in front of the ball.
- Focus on the offensive player's hips.
- Your palms should always be open and your thumbs up.

Dos—Off Ball

- Focus on the passer's eyes. They don't lie.
- See the ball and the player by using peripheral vision.
- Keep your hand in the passing lane, your knees flexed. Stay one arm's length from the player.
- On cuts backdoor, open in the lane. See the ball and feel the player cutting behind you.
- Use a fencer's attack and retreat steps.
- See all screens; read and react.

Don'ts—On Ball

- Don't cross your feet. You'll be off balance.
- Don't bounce slide.
- Don't get beat down the floor.
- Don't let the ballhandler go side to side to run the offense.
- Don't get nailed by a pick—see it and get over or through it.

Don'ts—Off Ball

- Don't turn your head to see only the ball or only a player.
- Don't lunge at passes. You will be off balance and get beat.
- Don't have your back to the top of the key when your player is cutting backdoor. See the ball.
- Don't forget to box out.
- Don't get caught too far over if you are weakside help.
- Don't get picked off and fail to communicate that you need help.

TEAM DEFENSE

Defense is hard work and playing it as a team is a tough but important challenge. Our six top reasons for learning to play good defense are:

- The defense will be consistent night after night while the offense often plays up and down.
- Having to practice against a tough defense will make your offense better.
- A good defense helps build mental toughness that will help you win close games.
- A good defense helps defeat a team mentally. It creates doubt in your opponents' minds about their ability to score and win.
- In a losing game, you won't get beaten badly enough to be humiliated.
- You will never get so far behind that you can't catch up.

In order to play good team defense, you must understand your responsibilities. In the next section, we'll outline the responsibilities of each position.

Point Guard

The point is the communicator between coach and players. Usually the quickest player on the floor, the point guard dictates tempo and pressure on both ends of the floor. She is the focal person on pressuring the ball handler. If you are a defensive point guard, you should have an attitude to disrupt your opponent. Some of the greatest point guards in women's basketball have been Marianne Stanley, who won two national championships at Immaculata College in the early '70s, Dawn Staley from the University of Virginia, Kim Mulkey of Louisiana Tech, and Holly Warlick of the University of Texas. They not only were great floor leaders, but also great passers and communicators. Their presence on the court was like having coaches on the floor for their teammates. Players respond to point guards who have a take-over attitude. A point guard must have self-confidence to gain the respect of the other players on the floor.

Shooting Guard

At the No. 2 spot, you have different responsibilities than the point guard. You probably will guard your opponent's best shooter. Your speed and quickness should be an asset. You have to be tough on defense. You will be fighting hard through screens as your opponent tries to shake free. See the screens, anticipate, and get help from your teammates. Most of all, get there! After the shot, box out and rebound. As much as you want to fly on the break, do first things first. Get the board! Then, it's time to be offensive-minded. There have been many great shooting guards in the women's game: Cynthia Cooper, a two-time Olympian; Teresa Edwards, a three-time Olympian and widely regarded for years as the best player in the world; Sheryl Swoopes of Texas Tech; Katie Smith of Ohio State; Charlotte Smith of North Carolina; Ann Meyers of UCLA—the list goes on and on. They were great players and major assets to their teams.

Small Forward

The No. 3 spot is where the greyhounds live. You must be an exceptional athlete—big, strong, and fast. Depending on the matchups, you could guard your opponent's best shooter. Use your quickness to harass the offense. If you are guarding a perimeter player, use your speed; if you're down in the post, use a combination of strength and quickness. Fight for position because if you work the offensive boards, you will pick up a ton of points off missed shots. Lynette Woodard of Kansas, Cheryl Miller of USC, Medena Dixon of Old

Dominion, and Clarissa Davis, Andrea Lloyd, and Bridgette Gordon, all of Texas, were the prototype small forwards. They could get up and down the floor, rebound, shoot, and play defense.

Power Forward

You should be big and physical. You must run the floor well. Your mobility will help you guard the high post and also get down in the trenches with the low post. Be willing to help your teammates by shutting down the lane. Picking up a charge means you saw the play, reacted, and got the job done. You have to be an aggressive, fearless rebounder. You can start your own fast break if you clean the glass and get the ball out to a guard. Some of the best that I saw at this position were Pat Roberts of Tennessee, Carolyn Bush-Roddy of Wayland Baptist College, and Lisa Leslie of USC. Leslie could play the power position or post. Inge Nissen from Old Dominion, at 6-foot-5, played power forward while 6-foot-8 Anne Donovan played the post. Katrina McClain might be the best of the bunch. She's a two-time Olympian. She's big, strong, quick, relentless on both boards, can score in the half-court offense, and can run the floor like a guard.

Post

As the No. 5 player, you must be the enforcer. You set the tone on defense and in rebounding. Remember, your home is the painted area and nobody comes in your house without an invitation. You must be physical and willing to fight for inside position, as well as help out on all drives to the basket. Be smart. You don't have to block everything, just contest everything! You have to own the boards and be an intimidator in a variety of ways. Hall of Famer Lucy Harris of Delta State University was strong, intimidating, could block shots, and score at will from the inside. Inge Nissen could take an opponent off the dribble, shoot from 18 feet out, and pass and block shots. On the other hand, Anne Donovan, a three-time Olympian, just basically would throw an opponent's shot off its course. No matter how good the move was to get to the basket, she would take the opponent's spirit away and force teams to change their offense to the outside game. The women's game over the years has had some dominating post players and its share of the finesse type of post player.

Checkpoints

✓ Double-teamers should allow at least 3 feet between themselves. Keep your arms raised and play in the passing lanes. Approach cautiously to prevent the offensive player from splitting you with a dribble.

✓ Keep constant pressure on all offensive players at all times. When only one pass away from the ball, extend your ball-side arm out in the passing lane to keep your opponent from receiving a pass. Make her cut behind you, not in front.

✓ Watch both your opponent and the ball after she passes off, but don't lose her. She is your responsibility until your team has possession.

✓ Do not bat the ball under the defensive basket. Catch all balls coming off the board and pass to outlet zones as quickly as possible.

✓ Force your opponent to take long, hurried shots. Contest every shot with a hand in the shooter's face.

✓ A good defensive player will never let her opponent go where she wants to go without a struggle. Jump in front of her, draw charging fouls, and force her from her normal pattern.

✓ Once your opponent passes off, loosen up on her immediately and sink toward the ball. Never let your opponent pass and break toward the ball. Position yourself quickly so the pass back to your opponent has to be made over you.

✓ Use a boxer's step or lateral shift on defense. Never cross your legs on defense. When you are getting beat on a drive, resort to a running stride until you recover and return to your boxer step.

✓ If you are assigned a poor scorer, try to help your teammates anytime it is possible. Sink inside a great deal on the post player and play for interceptions more than usual. Bluff your opponent when she has the ball and fall back quickly for an interception.

✓ If you are caught with your back to the ball, throw up one arm in front of your opponent and extend the other arm in the direction of the ball. You may deflect a pass.

✓ Don't ever jump unless you are sure the ball is being shot. Shooters will try to fake you up to get you in the air. Once you leave the floor the only thing you can do is block the shot or contest the shot.

✓ If you are guarding a player who is two passes away from the ball, you can sink or sluff more than you can if she is only one pass away.

✓ Play a post high, almost in front of her when she doesn't have the ball. Make her go behind you as she crosses the lane. Never let her come over the top and receive a pass. You are then helpless.

✓ Regardless of how easy a shot may appear, always get yourself in position to rebound in case it misses. Never take a basket for granted. Your teammates will miss more often than you think.

✓ Study your opponent closely during the early part of the game. Pick out her weaknesses and her strong points. Play her accordingly. If she only can go right, force her to go left. If she isn't a good shooter, play her for the drive.

PLAYER-TO-PLAYER DEFENSE

Great defense can turn on a crowd and inspire your team. The best defense is an aggressive, harassing type, especially if you are trying to force teams into mistakes and turnovers. Other types of defenses work, such as zones and trapping. It depends on the team's strategy and how your coach decides to play a particular team.

Aggressiveness demands hard work, reading situations, determination, and pride. Good teams and players keep an enormous amount of pressure on the ball from the start to the end of the game. That style of pressure can wear down opponents mentally and physically. Many opponents get frustrated and then you have them—they'll turn the ball over, miss their shots, and lose their spirit. But, remember, there is a difference between playing solid, aggressive defense and making mistakes and committing unnecessary fouls.

Basketball is broken into two kinds of defenses—player-to-player, where you guard an opponent individually, and zone, where you cover an area of the court, forcing teams away from penetration and into a perimeter game. In this section, we'll concentrate on the skills you need to become a terrific player-to-player defender.

The first point to remember about player-to-player defense is to position yourself an arm's length away from your opponent with your knees bent as you take a triple threat position. Remember to keep your feet shoulder-width apart. Do not bend at the waist. Keep your head over your knees and do not stand flat-footed.

As the ball handler is dribbling, you should be directly in front of her—unless you are overplaying and forcing the ballhandling on her weak side or to one side of the floor. Your head should be over the ball; wherever the ball is, that's where your head should be. That technique keeps you centered on the ball.

Watch and study your opponents on film or in pregame warm-ups. Know if they are good ball handlers and quick, good passers. If they are quicker than you, back off a step and play good position defense, forcing them to a particular area of the floor.

Use everything you can to distract the defense. If the ball handler shoots, put your hand in her face. Stay low with one hand up and the other hand in the passing lane. Keep yourself on the ball. Follow the ball with your hands as it is being passed. Your job is to distract the ball handler with constant pressure.

If the ball handler passes to a wing or the post, always jump in the direction of the pass. Get in front of the cutter, make her go behind you, and deny the return pass. If the ball handler shoots, get a hand in her face. Turn toward the shooter, reverse pivot, and box her off the boards. There are three main aspects of player-to-player defense:

- Containing the ball handler. Keep the offense from the basket.

- Channeling or focusing the ball handler to one side of the court to limit her options.

- Going one-on-one (player to player) with the ball handler.

Advantages of Player-to-Player Defense

Today, most coaches employ player-to-player defense for ball pressure and more aggressiveness on defense and to force a quicker tempo. Coaches will dictate what type of defense is used depending on the talent and ability of their opponents. Player-to-player defense is great against teams that don't shoot well from the outside. It forces more passing and movement. Good player-to-player defense can force the offense to use up the shot clock and force shots with little time on the clock. Zones can be effective as well, but you are encouraging the outside shot and taking away the dribble penetration.

Weaknesses of Player-to-Player Defense

This is a high-intensity defense. You are depending on each other to contain and attack the offense. Teams that have great ball handlers can break down a good defensive team with penetration and can draw the defense by shooting or passing off. This type of defense also extends the floor so there are more gaps for teams to cut into. It takes players away from the boards. To play pressure player-to-player, you and your teammates have to be superbly conditioned.

Other Aspects of Player-to-Player Defense

To have a well-rounded defensive game you have to understand why you are being asked to play a certain way. Know how to play the passing lanes on the ball, how and when to switch, how you need to get over a screen. It's all part of understanding how to play defense.

Overplaying the Pass.　Overplaying a pass is one way defensive players get an edge. If you have done a solid job of forcing the ball handler to pick up her dribble or overplaying her to one side, you must now read her remaining options. Get in the passing lane by keeping your arms up and ready (see Figure 9.2). You can deflect a lot

Figure 9.2　Denying the passing lanes by overplaying the pass.

of passes and prevent the offensive player from passing to the open spot on the floor. Overplaying can be risky in terms of forcing turnovers. It can be used as a surprise tactic. You'll reduce the risk if you have made the ball handler pick up her dribble first. Never give your opponent an easy passing lane. Make her work to get a good pass off.

Off-the-Ball Defense.   I always found off-the-ball defense to be fun and challenging. It's a pressure defense, but it's a different type of pressure. It's cat and mouse. You're reading the ball handler and seeing the player you are guarding at the same time (see Figure 9.3). Are you going to allow her to get the ball? Heck no! And if she does, it will be in an area where she's not ready to shoot. The key here is simple: See the ball, see the player. If you do that, you're in control.

Figure 9.3   Keeping an eye on the ball and your player with off-ball defense.

One Pass Away—Denial Defense Wing.   If you are using player-to-player defense and putting considerable pressure on the ball handler, your teammates should be denying one pass away if the ball is on the strong side. Denial positions add pressure for the ball handler trying to pass to a teammate. Position yourself back to the ball, arms extended, and denying the pass to the receiver. Your opposite arm should be extended behind the passing lane. You want to be as big as possible. You should be an arm's length from the receiver with your head positioned over the shoulder on the side of your front foot. This foot should be positioned between the feet of the receiver. As your arm on the same side is extended into the passing lane, keep your head over the shoulder. Look straight ahead. You should be able to see both the ball and the offensive player by using your peripheral vision. As the receiver fakes toward the ball, use the defensive slide to cover your opponent. Stay on balance and do not lunge for the ball. Do not bring your feet together.

Always be flexible. You know the receiver is going to try to fake you. Read the situation. Should the offensive player receive the ball, quickly retreat back to your on-the-ball defensive position. If you are doing a great job denying and the receiver goes backdoor, quickly open your position to the ball by reverse pivoting with your outside foot. Keep your arms in the passing lanes and slightly feel your opponent as she cuts through the free throw area. Make sure you always see the ball. If the ball is not passed inside and the receiver goes to the opposite wing, continue in a one-pass-away denial position. Let the offensive player know she is going to have to work hard for the ball. You'll be surprised how many players aren't willing to work for it. Even a good player, if pressured by good denial defense, can be taken right out of the flow of the game.

The close out on the wing can be very effective if you are on proper balance. Stay low as you run toward the receiver as she catches the ball. Slow down into a balanced jump stop. Keep your hands active and in the passing lane. Keep your head up and feet shoulder-width apart. Now you can force the receiver to the inside baseline side. If you are standing straight up the receiver can go by you.

Two Pass Away.   Two-passes-away defense requires an altogether different mentality. If you play it right, your team will be successful. If you gamble often, it puts added pressure on your teammates to cover for you. The weak side is weak because, in many cases, it is the last line of defense if the ball is moved quickly by the offense.

If you are the weak-side player, read the passer's eyes. Many times the passer won't look off her pass and you can step in for the steal. If the ball is reversed quickly to the weak side, you can get there and play good defense until your teammates have rotated into position.

There are several ways the defense can play an opponent two passes away. If the ball is on one side and you are on the weak side, you should be in an open stance, seeing the ball and your opponent. Use peripheral vision so you can see both. If you turn your head either way, you will lose sight of the ball or your opponent. Also, be prepared to defend the lob pass or skip pass over the top of the defense. Make sure you position yourself properly on the weak side with one hand toward the player and one hand toward the ball. Shade over to the ball side, splitting the rim. You can drop off your opponent the farther she is from the ball. Cheat ball side or help side. Help means just that: help defend against any cutters. If an opponent is cutting through the lane, make her change her route by stepping in front of her. Take away dribble penetration if a teammate needs help by sliding over and forcing the ball handler to pick up her dribble. Also, be willing to pick up the charge by rotating over. Boxing out on the weak side boards is a must.

Players who help must be aware of ball movement and where their opponent is so that they can adjust accordingly. In addition, it is important that a weakside player talk and call the screens. You are in a perfect position to see the play develop so it is your responsibility to communicate with your teammates.

Defense Against Screens.   The worst thing in basketball is having a screen set on you—whether you see it coming or not. A blind pick hurts. You should constantly be looking left, right, and checking where the offensive players are. The key to getting through screens is making your move before your opponents set the screen.

When you are playing tight defense, be aware of screens that the offense will set to free a teammate. There are various options you can use to get through or over a screen. Switching can be very difficult for offenses to work against. The key is communicating with one another. Know the personnel. If the opponent you are guarding is a great shooter, get over the top of the screen. See the screen coming, belly up to the offensive player, and stay between her and the screener. This is also referred to as jumping to the ball. Slide through the screen (see Figure 9.4). You must communicate with your teammates on this as they allow you to go between them and over the screener. If the player you are guarding isn't a great shooter, you can slide behind the screener and your teammate. For this option to work, you must have help or hedging from your teammate. When your teammate hedges, she is stepping out and forcing the ball handler to go wide, preventing her from turning the corner to go to the basket. By your teammate forcing her wide, you can recover from the screen and slide over to guard the ball handler again.

Most importantly, yell "screen" or "pick" to your teammate. Let her know left side or right side. In my opinion, the worst situation in basketball is being screened by a blind pick and getting nailed when a teammate could have warned you.

Figure 9.4   Getting over the screen.

Switching.   Your first option should be to slide over the screen and stick with your player. Sometimes, the screens are solid and you have to switch with a teammate to help you out. After you have either gotten over the screen or slid through, try to get back to your player as soon as possible. If you can't get over the screen you must communicate this to your teammate. It usually sounds like this: "SWITCH! HELP!" Switch means you stay with that player; help means you will pick your player back up after you get over the screen and can recover. Switching can be very difficult for offenses to work against. The key is communicating with one another.

Some coaches will tell players to automatically switch on all screens 18 to 20 feet away or those close to the basket. The key is to do it. You must be committed to calling the switch and doing it. Sometimes, a player will think, "I can get through it." They don't switch and they get beat.

Screen on the Ball.   Good defensive players can put a lot of pressure on the screener if they are alert and active. Check both sides and listen for your teammates to call out screen. If you sense a screen coming, jump to the player who has the ball and get as tight as you can to the ball handler so you can fight over the screen. The more active you are, the more likely you will be able to draw the screener out of position or even get an illegal screen called by the officials. This over-the-top technique in a nonswitching situation calls for your teammate guarding the screener to hedge out as the ball handler attempts to turn the corner around the pick. This gives you the chance to recover and catch up to the ball. Once your teammate has hedged, she jumps back to defending the screener. If the screener rolls to the basket, get between the ball and the screener. Make the offense lob pass over the top. It's a tough one to make. If you are guarding the ball, do not commit yourself until the ball handler starts her dribble or the screen is set.

Screen Off the Ball.   If you are off the ball, you should be opened up and able to see who is cutting and screening. You should not be screened two passes away. You have the ability to anticipate a screen coming by being in a sagging position. Slide through the screen. Make sure you communicate with your teammates. Find your opponent and recover to defend her. You will know if you can or cannot get through or over a screen. This is when a decision to switch must be made. Situations change quickly during a game. That's why communication is key to being successful.

Guarding the Post.   Because many teams try to get the ball inside to score, defending the post is one of the most challenging aspects of half-court defense. If the post player has good position, the defender must constantly be moving and reading where the ball is. This will determine how to effectively defend the low-post player. Your options are playing in front of the post, behind the post, or three-quarters denial—either baseline side or inside. Guarding the post takes pride, intelligence, and the ability to be physical.

Fronting the Post. This means getting in front of the post player with your hands up high and making yourself big and active. You are encouraging the passer to make a pinpoint lob over her defender, who should be applying ball pressure. You are in the passing lane and should expect weakside help on the lob pass. If there is no weakside help, the offense gains the better offensive rebounding position.

Playing Behind the Post.   If you are playing behind the post, you allow the post player to receive the entry pass. As she turns to shoot or make a move, take a step back and play straight-up defense with your arms up to defend the shot. If the post puts the ball on the floor, the guards should be dropping. You have inside position; when the shot goes up, box out and the rebound is yours.

Three-Quarters Denial Defense.　This is all part of different looks you are giving the post. If your opponent is on the low post, three-fourths her baseline side, with your outside hand in the passing lane as you are splitting her side (see Figure 9.5). Force your opponents toward your help, which will come from the weakside guard. This type of defense makes the post appear not to be open. If you are getting ball pressure from your guard, it's a tough entry pass to make.

If the post player has gone to the high post and the ball is up, you can deny high side, which is again a different look. You should have help weak side under the goal. If the ball is passed to the wing, jump to the ball in front of the post on the flight of the ball. This way, as the post goes back down low, you already are in baseline three-quarters denial defense.

Figure 9.5　Denying the post with three-quarters defense.

TRANSITION DEFENSE

Run, run, run. Uptempo is what today's coaches want. The key is having better and quicker athletes who are able to play the transition game. You might be a great running team but you must know how to get back against a team with similar style. Transition is simply reacting quickly to and from offense to defense. This is where real conditioning pays off. It takes a lot of precious energy to turn and sprint as a team, get back to set your defense, slow down the ball, or force the ball handler to pick up her dribble. That effort allows your teammates to recover down the floor. When you have stopped the ball, recover and find your player or help out a teammate if someone is open. In person-to-person, you find the open player. In a zone, go to your assigned area. In both cases, hustle and communicate with each other. Some basic rules for transition defense include:

- In transition, turn and sprint. Always know where the ball is.
- Try to contain or stop the ball handler from advancing.
- Get the ball out of the middle of the court. Force the ball handler to commit to a side.
- Play defense in half court, whether it is player-to-player or zone. Get back and into your defense.
- Nothing beats communication. Talk to each other.

DEFENSIVE DRILLS

There's no better way to improve defense than by using your feet, not your hands. These drills will help you increase your foot speed in different directions.

LANE SLIDES

Purpose: To improve foot speed, balance, and defensive sliding.

Procedure: Start on one side of the foul lane in proper defensive position. Slide from one side to the other, back and forth. Stay down in your defensive position. Try not to raise up. Touch the lane line with the outside hand and slide in the other direction—once again using your outside hand to touch the lane line.

Lady Magic Tips

▶ Stay low, keep your head up, and stay in proper defensive stance. You'll be quicker and more effective in the drill.

▶ Think "step and catch" when you are sliding. Don't bounce. Step with your outside leg and catch up with your inside leg.

▶ Do not cross your feet or bring them together. If your feet are together you'll be off balance and slow.

TRIANGLE SLIDE

Purpose: To develop all three areas of defensive movement: lateral slides, close out and attack, and retreat steps. The drill will improve quick drop steps and balance.

Procedure: Start at point A (top of the triangle) in a defensive stance, one hand in the shooter's face, and one hand in the passing lane. Slide laterally to point B, open to the corner, lateral slide to point C denying the low post. Close out to point A, quickly and on balance.

- Touch point A and change direction, retreat slide back to point C, open to point B, and close out to point B. Then, lateral slide from point B to point A.

- Repeat this drill three times. Take 30 seconds for each rep. Rest 60 seconds.

- Always start your next repetition at a different point so you are using your lateral slide. Close out and retreat steps in all areas.

Lady Magic Tips

▶ Stay low and in your proper defensive stance.

▶ Think ball pressure. Slide quickly to win. On the closeout, you are running at the imaginary player with the ball. As you approach, slow up and be balanced.

▶ Use short, quick steps. Keep your head steady and knees flexed.

▶ Change directions quickly.

▶ Always lead with outside leg when making your defensive slide.

DIAGONAL SLIDE

Purpose: To develop defensive quickness with balance in a diagonal slide backward, to improve your ability to change direction quickly, and to work on transition for offense and defense.

Procedure: Start at the baseline, face under the basket, and use the low block and foul-lane area for this drill. Stay low and in your proper balanced defensive stance. Start on the left block and, with your right foot, slide back at a 45-degree angle.

- Use short, quick retreat steps. Stay on the balls of your feet as you move in a diagonal direction. Slide to the opposite lane line. Touch the line with your feet.

- Quickly drop step with your left foot and pivot with your right. Slide to the other side of the lane. Make three lane slides at a diagonal angle until you reach the foul-line elbow.

- Slide across the foul line facing half court to the opposite side. Then, repeat the three diagonal slides backward until you reach the low block. See if you can complete the slides up and down in 30 seconds. Rest 60 seconds, then repeat this drill three times.

Lady Magic Tips

► Use short, quick retreat steps, stay on balance, and never cross your feet.

► Push off with your inside leg and always use your outside leg to slide in that direction.

► Always work hard in all defensive drills. Keep an attitude of pride. This is a great one-on-one drill.

MIRROR DRILL

Purpose: To work on sliding, running, attacking, and retreat steps; and to work on quick footfire and ball fakes. (You can do this drill with a teammate as a mirror or use your own imagination.)

Procedure: Start in the middle of the court in the proper defensive stance. If you have a partner to mirror, do what she does. Start by using a quick stutter step or foot-fire drill. Then, slide in all directions, retreat, attack, close out.

- Add a ball fake as you are doing the footfire or stutter step. If you are doing this drill alone, fine. It's a great time to use your imagination and determination on defense.

- Do this sliding drill the first time hard for 2 minutes each day. Add 1 minute until you can slide continuously for 20 minutes. That's right—one half of a game.

- This is a great conditioner and can be a lot of fun with a partner. You can take turns mirroring each other. Split the total time with each other.

Lady Magic Tips

- ► Stay in your stance and on balance. Don't cross your feet when you are sliding at angles. Remember to stay low.

- ► On attack or closeouts, put your hand to the ball to contend the shot. Your hands are always in the passing lane.

- ► Slide quickly in all directions on all change of directions. Drop step quickly with either foot.

- ► On footfire or stutter steps, keep your feet moving quickly as you fake at the ball. Make it believable.

- ► Concentrate as you get tired. Have pride. Don't get sloppy. Do all drills with 100 percent intensity.

TUBE SLIDE

Purpose: To increase strength and improve footwork technique so that you can learn to stay down in the proper defensive stance and slide without crossing your feet.

Procedure: Using an old inner tube or a piece of plastic, tie the ends together to make a circle—anywhere from 2 to 4 inches wide and about 24 inches long. Slip the tube around your legs, above your ankles. You should feel the tube tightly on your ankles about shoulder-width apart. Start at the foul line (either side) and get into proper defensive position. Slide to the opposite side of the line. Keep the tube tight as you slide across the lane. This will keep your concentration on the tube being tight and not bringing your feet together. Return to the other side using the same technique. To build your conditioning and strength, do this drill for 10 minutes.

Lady Magic Tips

- ► Do this drill slowly to enable you to feel the pull of the tube on your legs.

- ► You will improve your speed, strength, and conditioning. You'll have overall improved footwork.

HALF-COURT SHUFFLE AND SLIDE

Purpose: To work on many areas of player-to-player defense and conditioning.

Procedure: Start under the basket and face the baseline. Shuffle backward to the middle of the foul line. Be sure you're in the proper defensive position. Slide right until you reach the sideline. Shuffle backward to half court. Slide across half court to the opposite side. Shuffle backward to the foul-line extended area. Slide across to the foul line and finish the drill by shuffling backward until you are out of bounds. Do this drill continuously for 5 minutes.

Lady Magic Tips

▶ Use proper stance, don't cross your feet. Stay on balance.

▶ Keep your hands in the passing lane. Keep your head up and straight.

BLOCK-TO-BLOCK MEDICINE BALL

Purpose: To condition and develop your strength and quickness when sliding in either direction.

Procedure: Start at the left foul-lane block with a medicine ball. Face the sideline in the proper defensive position. Pick up the medicine ball, holding it waist high. Slide left until you reach the foul line. Put the ball down and quickly slide to the right and back to the block without the ball. Touch the block with your outside hand and slide back to the medicine ball.

• Pick it up and slide across the foul line facing half court. When you reach the opposite lane line put the ball down and slide right. Slide back across the foul line until you reach the lane line. Touch it with your outside hand. Then, slide back the other way to the medicine ball.

• Pick it up and slide down the lane line facing the sideline. When you reach the low block, put the ball down and slide back to the right, touching the foul line and then sliding back to the ball.

• Do this drill six times, three in each direction.

Lady Magic Tips

▶ Stay low and balanced. You will have more speed and quickness.

▶ Work hard on the change of direction once you have put the medicine ball down.

▶ Place the medicine ball on the court. Don't drop it or throw it.

LANE SLIDE AND CLOSEOUT DRILL

Purpose: To work on all different types of slides and be ready to guard the shooter. When on defense, you often have to slide against your opponent. Sometimes, you have to slide against her and sometimes you have to quickly close out (attack or contain) the player with the ball. Without lunging or being off balance, close out (sprint) under control and on balance and be ready to guard the shooter.

Procedure: Start under the basket on the left side facing the foul line. Close out to the foul line with one hand up to the shooter and one in the passing lane. As you approach the foul line, start to slow up. Touch the foul lane with your foot and backpedal to the baseline with your hands above your head.

- Again, close out to the foul line, pivot this time (turn), and sprint to the backboard. As you approach it, touch the backboard with two hands if you can. (If not, touch the net.)

- Close out to the foul line, sprinting up the foul lane. Retreat step and diagonal slide, back and forth, across the lane to the baseline.

- Repeat this drill three times, with 60 seconds rest between each set.

Lady Magic Tips

- ▶ Stay low on your slides. Don't cross your feet.
- ▶ As you get ready to close out, lower yourself and be on balance. Don't lunge and get beat. Closeout means containment.
- ▶ This is a great conditioner. It will pay off.

SPEED AND QUICKNESS DRILLS

Good defense starts with foot speed, quickness, and knowing angles. These drills will condition you to improve your defense.

DEFENSIVE TURNS

Purpose: To improve your foot speed, anticipation, and quickness. This drill will be easier if you have good conditioning and keep your feet moving, not planted. It takes energy to stop and start.

Procedure: Start out in the proper defensive stance. Run in place, stutter stepping as fast as you can. Do a one-quarter turn to the right and return quickly to your starting point. Do this for 30 seconds. Rest 30 seconds.

- With the same stance, stutter step your feet. Do a one-half turn and return quickly to your starting point. Do this for 30 seconds. Rest 30 seconds. Do the same drill, but with three-quarter turns. Then do full turns, each going to the right side.

- After you have completed all four turns, take a 1-minute rest and repeat all four turns to the left side.

Lady Magic Tips

▶ Keep your feet moving quickly, head and arms up, thumbs pointing to your shoulders. You are using your legs, not your arms, to turn.

▶ Get as many turns as you can in 30 seconds.

▶ On the half, three-quarter, and full turns, you really need to explode and almost jump around in place. Then jump back as quickly.

▶ This is a great drill for quick reaction and explosiveness in different directions.

RAPID-FIRE FOOT DRILL WITH JAB FAKE

Purpose: To play good, solid defense on the ball by keeping your feet constantly moving up and down, like pistons; to learn to attack, jab at the ball handler, and cause her to react; to apply pressure and kill her dribble.

Procedure: Start out in proper defensive position. Quickly move your legs up and down in a stutter or rapid-fire motion. As you are doing this drill for 30 seconds, jab four or five times at the imaginary ball handler alternating with your right and left hand. Then, quickly get back to your rapid-fire stance and footwork. Do three sets, each 30 seconds long. Rest 30 seconds. Repeat.

Lady Magic Tips

▶ Stay low and keep pumping your legs.

▶ Stay on the balls of your feet, arms up by your sides for balance.

▶ Attack quickly with your jab fake. It should be done with your right hand and right foot, or left hand and left foot.

LINE JUMPS

Purpose: To increase foot speed and quickness in front to back and side to side jumping.

Procedure: Facing the baseline, stand next to the sideline or any line. Keep your arms out at your sides for balance. Jump side to side, clearing the line completely. Jump for 30 seconds. Rest 30 seconds.

- Facing the baseline, stand behind the half-court line or any line.
- Jump over the line and back, clearing the line completely. Jump for 30 seconds. Rest 30 seconds.
- See how many jumps you can do in 30 seconds. Record the number and use that figure to improve speed and quickness.
- Complete three sets of 30 seconds each. Rest 30 seconds.

Lady Magic Tips

▶ Slightly flex your knees. Keep your arms out and at your sides for balance and momentum.

▶ Stay on the balls of your feet as you hit the floor. Explode in the opposite direction.

WING DENIAL DRILL

Purpose: To learn to play tight denial defense and to see the ball and the player you are guarding without getting beat. Like anything else, it takes practice.

Procedure: Start on the left low block, in proper denial stance, with your outside (or left) arm in the passing lane. Keep your head looking forward, seeing the ball and your opponent. Keep your knees slightly flexed, your inside arm out in the passing lane behind you. By having that arm out, you look bigger and the space around you looks smaller.

- Slide using a fencing step to the wing area as fast and balanced as you can. When you get to the foul-line extended, quickly use your retreat step, keeping the same form. Try not to cross your feet when sliding.

- Slide to the wing and back five times. As you come back to the lane, quickly open to the ball when your inside foot hits the painted area (low block).

- As you go through the lane and hit the opposite block with your inside foot, pivot and deny out to the foul-line extended. Go up and back five times.

- Complete three sets. Take 60 seconds rest between each. Repeat.

Lady Magic Tips

▶ Keep a good angle while denying to the wing. Your arm should be in the passing lane and be active to discourage the pass.

▶ As you get to the wing, stay low and on balance. Don't lunge at the ball. Contain.

▶ Retreat step. Try not to cross your feet.

▶ In the lane, never lose track of your player. Feel her behind you across the lane.

▶ Pivot quickly and deny the other side. Work hard to react and explode up and back.

DENY DRILL

Purpose: To work on denial defense on the wing, conditioning, and concentrating on keeping your arms up at all times; to learn to see the ball and your opponent.

Procedure: Use lightweight dumbbells, with weight depending on how big or strong you are. (It could be 2, 4, 6, 8, or 10 pounds.) One dumbbell will be on the block and one at the foul-line extended area. Start on the low block in the proper denial position. See the ball and your opponents. Your outside arm is out in the passing lane with a dumbbell in that hand.

- Slide to the wing area, put down your dumbbell, and pick up the one on the floor.

- Slide two or three steps back and open quickly by pivoting on your left leg as if you are protecting against the backdoor cut. Then, slide to the low block.

- Put your dumbbell down and pick up the one on the block. Repeat the denial drill for 30 seconds. Rest 30 seconds.

- Do two sets, one each side for 30 seconds.

Lady Magic Tips

▶ Stay low and balanced. Bend your knees as you put the dumb-bell down. Don't bend at your waist.

▶ See the whole court by using your peripheral vision. Don't cross your feet.

▶ Have your elbow slightly bent to take pressure off the joint.

▶ Remember to keep your palm to the ball, so your thumbs are down when holding the dumbbell.

OTHER DRILLS

These drills round out your defensive training by working on upper and lower body quickness and strength and on your full-court defensive skills.

BOXING DRILL

Purpose: To work on hand speed and endurance. This drill is a lot harder than it looks or sounds.

Procedure: Place boxing gloves on both hands and shadow box for 2 minutes without dropping your hands below shoulder height. Eventually your arms will start getting tired. Here's when you concentrate and focus on conditioning and hand speed. Rest 2 minutes. Do three sets of 2 minutes each. When you take the gloves off, you'll be surprised how light and fast your hands will feel.

Lady Magic Tips

▶ Be quick and have fun.

▶ Intensity and imagination are keys to this drill.

VERTICAL JUMPS (TRACKING)

Purpose: To work on a takeoff with one foot or two.

Procedure: Go to any wall and measure how high you can touch while standing straight up, with your hands high above your head. Mark it or have someone mark it. Do the same as you jump as high as you can off two feet. Use two hands to touch the wall. Mark it.

Track where you started and what type of improvement you have been able to make with your hard work.

- Standing sideways next to the wall, this time measure your jump using two feet. Use your inside hand to touch the wall. Mark it.
- Now you have starting points and you will be able to track your improvement.
- Measure your jumping every few weeks.

Lady Magic Tips

▶ On all jumps, flex your knees at 60- to 90-degree angles depending on your leg strength. Explode up, not out. Use your arms to create more upward power.

▶ Be positive and always give your best effort.

▶ Jump quickly.

▶ Remember, you are working on a gradual steady improvement off two feet.

ONE-ON-ONE (FULL COURT— INDIVIDUALLY)

Purpose: To improve your skills full court.

Procedure: Playing by yourself, start at the baseline, directly under the bucket. It's important to use your imagination. You guard a player; it's one-on-one. Turn the imaginary ball handler a minimum of three times in the backcourt, sliding at an angle to a spot. Then, overplay the ball and slide again at an angle to the opposite side.

- As the ball handler gets to half court, force her to one side of the floor. Now overplay slightly; don't allow the ball to reverse.
- As you funnel the ball to near the key area, the ball handler passes to the wing. You must jump to the ball and make the ball handler cut behind you as you deny any possible pass.
- If the passer stays and doesn't cut, deny the pass back to her from the wing.
- Slide to the baseline, turn around, and repeat the drill.
- Shoot 10 foul shots while resting.
- Repeat three sets (up and back is one set). Take a total of 30 foul shots.

- Use your imagination. You've been on the court before, dogging the ball handler. Work her, turn her.
- Move your feet quickly. Don't cross them. Turn them.
- Stay low and balanced. Keep your hands active as if you're hawking the ball.
- Once you have the ball over to one side of the floor, keep her there.
- On all passes to the wing, jump to the ball and deny any return pass to the guard.
- Be aggressive and work hard.

HORIZONTAL ROPE

Purpose: To develop leg strength and quickness, and improve your vertical jump and balance.

Procedure: Have a 12-inch rope connected to two chairs about 2 feet apart. The rope should be about 6 inches above the ground. As you improve, raise the height of the rope to a maximum of 12 inches. Jump back and forth with both feet for 30 seconds. Take 30 seconds rest. Repeat three sets for 30 seconds each. Take 10 foul shots. Stand on the side of the rope. Jump side to side for 30 seconds. Take 30 seconds rest. Repeat three times, 30 seconds each.

Lady Magic Tips

- ▶ Keep your arms at your sides for balance, but use them to swing upward for momentum as you jump.
- ▶ Bring your knees up high to clear the rope.
- ▶ Hit the soles of your feet and explode in the opposite direction.
- ▶ Keep your head straight and work on your focus and concentration.

NET TOUCH OFF ONE LEG

Purpose: To work on your explosiveness and maximum potential; to steadily increase your vertical leap.

Procedure: Start at the foul line. Sprint to the basket on the left side. As you approach the basket leap off your left leg. Use your left hand on the left side and touch the net, rim, or backboard (whichever you can touch). Sprint back to the foul line to the right side, turn and repeat jump as high as you can, right hand, right leg, right side. Do five backboard touches on each side. Shoot 10 foul shots while you are resting. Repeat three sets—30 jumps total, 30 foul shots.

Lady Magic Tips

▶ As you approach the backboard, jump up, not out.

▶ Dip your knees and drive up as quickly as you can, extending your ankles, knees, and hips.

▶ Remember, it's attitude to want to touch the rim, backboard or net. Go for it.

▶ Use your arms for balance and momentum. Drive them upward as you jump.

TWO-HAND ALTERNATE TOUCH

Purpose: To work your strength, speed, and endurance; to learn to keep your hands up so you will build arm and shoulder strength.

Procedure: Standing under the rim, backboard, or net—whichever is appropriate—jump as high as you can. First, use your left hand. Then, go right back up with your right hand. Alternate touches, five on each side. Take 10 foul shots while resting. Repeat for a total of 30 touches and 30 foul shots.

Lady Magic Tips

▶ Flex your knees at a 60- to 90-degree angle, according to your leg strength.

▶ Extend your lead arm as fast and as high as possible.

▶ Use your opposite leg to help. Drive up high to your target.

▶ Come down on the balls of your feet.

▶ As you land, be ready to use your momentum to explode back up with the other hand.

Summary

There is no greater challenge on the court than being a defensive stopper. It can be you if you apply these points:

- Defensive positioning: body, knees, arms, hands, head, and eyes
- Communication and footwork
- Defensive tips for improvement
- The advantages and weaknesses of player-to-player defense
- Knowing how to overplay the pass, play off the ball, deny the wing (one pass away)
- Getting through screens, knowing when to switch, guarding the post player
- Defensive drills to improve overall defense

CHAPTER
10

Owning the Boards

Rebounding is one of the greatest tests of determination, desire, and fundamentals. It doesn't matter if you are 6-foot-5 or 5-foot-5; proper technique enables you to box out much taller players. If you can outrebound the other team, you have a chance to win the game. If you keep your opponent off the ball, they won't get easy putbacks or fast-break chances.

As athletes get faster, the running game will be in high gear. It's the rebound that starts the break. One of the biggest keys in basketball at every level is who's winning the battle of the boards. The team that does often controls the game. No team ever hit all of its first shots in a game. That's why defensive rebounding is such a major part of the game. If you allow a team to get second, third, and fourth shots at the basket, you will have a tough time winning.

KEYS TO REBOUNDING

There are three keys to rebounding: positioning, boxing out, and using your leverage. Don't be afraid to "hit" your opponent, to make contact with her (your buttocks to her knees). Don't hesitate to, in basketball slang, *lay a body* on someone under the boards while you are jockeying for position. Let your opponent know this is your area and your rebound, and remember to first contest all shots. Put a hand in the shooter's face to distract her. If she is right-handed, put your left hand up. If she's a lefty, your right hand goes up. You never want to cross your body, it will cause you to be off balance and out of position.

Positioning

Work hard to keep your body between the opposing player and the basket. Keep this position as you contest the shot (see Figure 10.1) and after the shot by turning and pivoting. Create some contact so you feel where that player is. Box her out for 2 or 3 seconds (we'll talk about this next). Then, go for the rebound and keep her behind you. Be physical and aggressive on both boards. Jumping ability is important, but not more important than good positioning.

Figure 10.1 Contesting the shot.

Boxing Out

If you are on defense, you should have the advantage because of your rebounding position. Defensive rebounding means boxing out. This is accomplished properly when the defense uses a front or reverse pivot to box out a player. There must be contact. After pivoting, use your rear end to make contact with your opponent (see Figure 10.2) which prevents the offense from going forward to rebound the ball. Move quickly to release from the contact and go to the ball.

In player-to-player defense, each player is responsible for boxing out the person she is guarding. In a zone, players are responsible for boxing out the offensive player in a specific area. Remember to position yourself between the offensive player and the basket. Don't let players push you too far under the basket. That will take you out of good rebounding position.

When covering a shooter after a long-range shot, turn and follow the shot. Pivot and feel where the shooter is. Once you have boxed her

Figure 10.2   Blocking out on the shot.

out, go for the rebound. If you rebound too quickly, the shooter can go around you without any contact. On long, outside shots, if the rebound comes out long and you have rushed to the basket too quickly, the ball can carom over your head.

Leverage

You must get low and have good balance to have leverage. Your feet should be shoulder-width apart. In a "sitting" position box out your opponent at her knees. This allows you to be quicker and to explode to the basket, or to continue boxing your opponent out. You can avoid being pushed out of rebounding position by staying low. The lower you are, the better.

Checkpoints

✓ Pursue the ball. Have determination and desire. Great rebounders think every miss is their rebound.

✓ Box out. Get position quickly and establish your ground if you are small. If you are a post, take the position and box out.

✓ Getting position takes hard work and anticipation. Have your hands ready. Know the angles and percentages from where shots are taken. Positioning is a function of savvy and hard work. Don't let players push you too far under the hoop.

✓ Have balance. Be big. Keep your knees flexed, arms out, and feet shoulder-width apart. Putting your rear end out creates space. Someone might have to go over your back because of that.

✓ Timing is everything. If you jump for the rebound and the ball is still hitting the rim, all your hard work hasn't paid off.

✓ Good hands are a key asset. Grab the rebound and protect it. If you have the ball, be assured players will be slapping at it. Be strong and relaxed. Fingertip control can help get a rebound you didn't think you could get. Great rebounders can give themselves a second chance by tipping the ball to an open area. If you're really good, tip it in the bucket for two.

✓ Protect the ball. That's why we have our elbows, knees, and bodies. Use everything you have to protect the ball. Most importantly, when you do grab the ball, keep it high. Don't bring it down for opponents to steal.

✓ Be big, strong, and aggressive. It's a great combination. Great rebounders have a special desire and determination. They have an attitude and mental toughness. If you're going to rebound, come strong into the paint or don't come at all.

REBOUNDING FUNDAMENTALS

Becoming a good rebounder requires you to react in many ways before and after the shot. We'll briefly look at some ways to do this. We'll also give you some pointers on offensive rebounding, using tip-ins, and rebounding foul shots.

Reading the Shooter's Shot

Reading a shot is a matter of judgment. Is the shot going to fall short or go long? Did the shooter have good rotation on the ball? If the shot was a three-pointer, the rebound should be longer. If it's from the corner, chances are it will rebound to the weak side. Observing a shot can help you get in the correct area for the rebound.

Anticipation

This is part of reading the shot. You can anticipate where the rebound might go and start to establish your position under the basket or maneuver from the perimeter.

Tip-Ins

When you or your teammates shoot the ball, miss, and the ball comes off the rim just slightly in one direction or another, you should try to tip the ball back to the basket—you'll not only get the field goal, but you'll be credited with a rebound as well.

Cradle the ball on your fingertips and tap it back with control. Make sure your fingers are flexed slightly. This will eliminate potential jammed fingers. Having good rebounding position definitely will help when you are trying to tip the ball in. Control is important if you are going to be successful. Jump as high as you can. Your knees, hips, and ankles should be flexed. Your hands must be up and ready to tip the ball. The quicker you get to the ball, the better chance you have to beat your opponent to it and get a clean chance to tip it in.

Rebounding Foul Shots

To prevent the offense from scoring an easy basket, get the rebound off a foul shot. The defense has inside position on both sides of the basket. You must move to box out the offensive players who occupy the second position on each side. You should communicate to your teammates which player or area you are boxing out. The third player (defensive spot) should box out the fourth spot (offensive player) while the other third spot defensive player boxes out the shooter.

Offensive Rebounding

Offensive rebounding is an often overlooked aspect of basketball. With all the work on offensive and defensive schemes, not enough attention is paid to being able to get position for second and third shots off the offensive glass. Regardless of how many offenses you run to get good scoring shots and regardless of how many great shooters your team may have, you're going to miss some shots.

This is a perfect time, especially if you play close to the basket, to pick up easy points on hustle and desire. There are four main areas to recognize where missed shots may fall.

- Perimeter shots usually rebound long because the ball comes off the rim with more power.
- Corner shots tend to rebound long to the weak side.
- Bank shots usually rebound closer to the basket.
- Follow your shot. You are shooting it. You should have a feel for how the shot came off your hand. Were you too strong? Did you have good rotation? Were your arc and follow-through high enough? Be active and get around the person boxing you out.

REBOUNDING DRILLS

Rebounding is the part of the game that allows you to win or lose. Good rebounders are never stationary, always moving and closing in on the basket, and are aggressive on both ends of the court.

SUPERMAN

Purpose: To develop aggressiveness and desire; to improve your jumping and endurance; to combine footwork, passing, catching, rebounding skills, and your ability to protect the rebound.

Procedure: Start by standing on the block outside the foul lane. Face the basket. Toss the ball over the rim to the opposite side of the backboard. The pass needs to be a two-handed chest pass. Aim high over the backboard, then go get it. Be quick and explosive. Rebound the ball with authority using two hands. Take one step in the lane and catch the ball outside the lane on the other side. Start again outside the lane, tossing the ball to the side you started on. Do this drill for 30 seconds. Be intense. Rest 1 minute. Then go for another 30 seconds, followed again by a 1-minute rest period. Complete three sets with a 1-minute rest following each. Shoot 10 foul shots during each rest.

Lady Magic Tips

▸ Be on balance. Land on the balls of your feet, elbows out.

▸ Keep your head up. Look at the ball. Keep your hands up high and be ready to rebound.

REBOUND AND POWER MOVE

Purpose: To increase endurance and strength using pump fakes to draw fouls and complete the play off a rebound. A solid rebounder never changes her mental attitude and desire to be aggressive.

Procedure: Begin this drill by facing the basket. Start in front of the backboard on the right side with the ball in both hands over your head. Jump five times with the ball in this position, touching the backboard if you can. On your last jump, pull the ball down and make a ball fake. Then, go up strong for a power move off both feet.

• Do the same drill on the left side. Remember to jump quickly and explode to the backboard. Be on balance and land on the balls of your feet.

• Ball fake hard. Make it believable. Then execute your explosive power move. Shoot the ball with two hands.

• Complete two sets of 10 on each side. Rest 2 minutes between each set. Shoot 10 foul shots while resting each time.

Lady Magic Tips

▸ There's no substitute for being fierce and aggressive.

▸ When you have good position, balance is important. On rebounds, you are going to be hammered. Stay strong and have a solid base.

▸ Go up strong after the ball fake. Don't anticipate the foul; finish strong.

OFFENSIVE REBOUNDING AGAINST PRESSURE

Purpose: To work on rebounding and scoring, knowing there will be pressure from a defender.

Procedure: Starting at the foul line, toss the ball underhanded to the left side of the backboard using your left hand. Explode to the ball and grab the rebound with both hands. Pump fake, then make the layup.

- Alternate sides. Go back to the foul line and toss the ball off the right side with your right hand. Get the rebound with two hands and make a pump fake. Then make your layup.
- Be intense. Hustle back after each shot. Make five from the left side, five from the right. Repeat this three times. Take a 1-minute rest between sets.

Lady Magic Tips

▶ Be on balance as you grab the rebound.

▶ Pump fake violently as if you are faking the defense.

TIP DRILL

Purpose: Tipping the ball is a great way to gain control of the rebound—maybe not on the first attempt, but on the second or third. There will be times you will tip the ball in cleanly or tip it to yourself or a teammate.

Procedure: Start at the foul line. Toss the ball underhanded off the right side of the backboard with your right hand. Tip the ball with one hand to an open area on the same side. Then, grab the rebounded tip and sprint back to the foul line. Now, toss the ball off the left side with your left hand. Tip the ball with one hand to an open area on the left side. Hustle back to the foul line after each tip is rebounded. Tip five times on each side. Repeat three times. Take a 1-minute rest between sets.

Lady Magic Tips

▶ Tip the ball to an open area. Go get it.

▶ Be aggressive.

▶ Tipping the ball helps you get it out of the lane or congested areas.

Summary

Rebounding can be one of the most challenging skills to learn and execute effectively. It takes a player willing to hustle and get positioning. It takes heart and desire to own the boards. This chapter took you through these areas:

- Positioning, boxing out, leverage
- Defensive rebounding/offensive rebounding
- Checkpoints, tip-ins, reading the shooter's shot, anticipation
- Rebounding drills

CHAPTER
11

Becoming the Complete Player

Many girls want to be good players. Do you dare to be great? Women's basketball is competitive; it's preparation that sets the great players apart from the good. To get to the great level, you must make the game your passion. You must devote endless hours, days, and years to develop your game. Coaches are looking for the all-purpose player who can perform at a moment's notice in a variety of roles. Three areas of the game can spell out a winner.

- A love for the game
- Being in great physical condition
- Accepting all challenges

Most rosters have as many as 15 players—all wanting their chance. All of you are important and each of you plays a role in your team's success. That's why you must blend your skills with those of your teammates to better your team.

If you happen to be the standout on your team, make the commitment to lead by example. Set the tone for each practice and game. If you're not the star, but have worked hard enough to be one of the starting five, you've earned your position. Make sure you keep it by hustling and pushing yourself to be the best team-player you can be. If you are coming off the bench, that's fine. Yours is a special and significant role. Be ready to fill it. That's the beauty of a team sport—the starters start and the role players have a job to perform.

In this chapter, we'll discuss a variety of issues that pertain to your growth as a basketball player. Hopefully, we'll give you the foundation you need to blend your skills with those of your teammates to become the most complete player you can be. Let's begin by looking at 10 steps that can help you achieve and handle the success that will come with your hard work and dedication.

Ten Steps to Stardom

1. **Competitive greatness**—Includes patience, your mental attitude, faith, determination, and fight.
2. **Coachability**—Be hardworking, loyal, enthusiastic. Listen well. Have the ability to adapt to different systems. Be a leader.
3. **Skill development**—Have a will to work at the basics, giving attention to all details. Strive for perfection. Use repetition to achieve success.

4. **Conditioning**—Conditioning includes mental, physical, and emotional training habits; diet; prevention of injuries; and the ability to take on all challenges.

5. **Confidence**—Lead by example. Respect all, fear no one.

6. **Practice habits**—Be the first one there, the last to leave. Be cooperative, have discipline, be alert, and have enthusiasm and team spirit.

7. **Loyalty**—Be loyal not only to yourself, but to your school, coaches, and teammates. There's nothing more important.

8. **Goal setting**—Plan your improvement. Reach each level of your goals, little by little, until you achieve where you want to be.

9. **Ambition**—Have the confidence and desire to be the best. Work hard. Be better than others. Make your dreams a reality.

10. **Being a good sport**—Show respect, integrity, and good judgment in how you treat teammates and opponents, coaches and officials. Have self-control.

PRACTICE, PRACTICE, PRACTICE

If you can't tell by now, to truly be a solid basketball player, you must practice. Taking a positive approach to practice, your teammates, and your coaches is necessary right from the start. Never say the dreaded words: "I can't." Always say "I'll strive."

Other players can't give you confidence. They can encourage you, but you know if you have put in the hard work and dedication. When you have done your homework, being self-confident feels good!

Self-confidence exudes enthusiasm and you play with an attitude. It's attitude that builds winners. Have you ever noticed the great ones always come through? They make things happen instead of waiting for them to happen. It's called producing results. Results start in practice.

I have six rules to practice. If these are words that you use to describe yourself and your team, you're on your way.

1. Self-confidence comes from experiencing success. Winning builds an attitude and belief that you will and can always win.

2. Desire means self-improvement, welcoming all challenges, and a will to do what it takes to win.

3. Leadership is a quality you earn from your teammates. If you show you can lead, others will follow.

4. Aggressiveness means being tough, physical, and assertive. Your actions will force others to play hard.

5. Determination is a special characteristic. You want to succeed. Don't accept defeat. Always strive to be better.

6. Responsibility is being accountable. You don't point fingers.

Preparing for Practice

Look forward to practice. This is where questions will be answered and your knowledge and skills developed. You need a proper mental attitude before you even walk into the gym. Be competitive and focused. If you don't understand something, ask questions. You will be more open to try things your coach's way if you understand what's expected. Respect the older players. Learn from someone you respect as a good role model.

I always used practice to challenge myself and to work on my weaknesses: my left hand and outside shot. I always was the first player in the gym because I wanted to work on those weaknesses. Being good wasn't enough; I had an insatiable appetite to be the best.

Your practices have been well-planned by your coaches. There's so much to teach in a short amount of time. The most important part is being organized and getting from drill to drill, while making sure you give your best effort each time.

Start thinking about how you want to improve during these sessions. Is there a teammate who is hard to guard? Or an offense you don't quite understand? Like anything, preparation and mental readiness can help you physically. Get there early enough to get taped, warm up, stretch, shoot, and work on a few weaknesses.

Have Fun, but Stay Tough

Even though you are working hard and concentrating you can have a good time. Talk, laugh, have fun and enjoy each other, your coaches, and practice. Help keep practices loose and spirited. Never lose sight that basketball is only a game. And if you are working hard, concentrating, and staying relaxed, you will be able to give your best effort. If you're unhappy or tight, it will take away from your ability to give your best effort.

Keep in mind, however, that even though you're having fun, you still must compete with your teammates. Be tough physically and strong mentally. Occasionally, teammates will take it easy against one another because they don't want to get hurt or make a teammate look bad. That's very nice of you, but it won't make either of you better. Challenge each other to the best of your ability. Make each other work hard and play hard. It's the only way to improve.

Push your teammates to be better. Don't expect anything less. It could at times get so physical that tempers or emotions flare. So be it. It's part of the game. The most important thing is not to carry a grudge off the court. If you got knocked down or picked too hard, deal with it in practice. Don't take if off the court and divide your team. That will cause more problems than you can imagine.

Listen Up

We all have questions during a practice or a game. When your coach is talking or a teammate has asked a question, listen! It might be the same question you have but didn't ask. Understanding your coach's system is very important. If you are not sure about something, ask the coach. It could be the difference between you and your team succeeding and falling short. And most of all, it's disrespectful to talk when someone else is. If you listen, you might be able to follow up with another thought that could help someone else on the team understand.

Ready, Let's Go

When the whistle blows, sprint to your coach to show that you're eager and ready to get started. Most often, the beginning of practice is running—not at full speed, but to loosen up. That's why, prior to the start, stretching and getting loose is important. The last thing you want is to pull a muscle going through a three-person weave. You really can prevent annoying, nagging injuries.

Practices can seem like an eternity, so it's important to break them down by establishing your own minigoals. For example: *Just 11 practices until the first preseason scrimmage. Then, just 6 practices until we tip it off for the season opener.* Establish minigoals within practice: *I'll work to my maximum effort in the first drill. Then, I'll rest.* Your next goal: *I'll give the same effort and intensity.* Practices will move quickly and you'll get the most out of each aspect if you break things down and concentrate on every part. It's hard when you look at 2 hours and think, "Man, I've got to concentrate for that long." If your concentration is in short, snappy bursts, practice can be fun and you will be able to give it your all.

PLACES TO PLAY

Don't limit yourself to playing only when your team officially opens practice. Play year-round. When the weather is nice during the summer, you'll find numerous opportunities for practicing. In this section, we'll talk about some places to play.

Summer Leagues

Somewhere in your town or area, there's a summer league. Usually games take place once or twice a week. You are mixed with players you don't know. It's competitive, but a more relaxed environment. These leagues keep you in shape mentally and physically throughout the summertime. Friendships are formed with players you didn't know. Ask your friends and coaches if they know of any such leagues. If not, call your local YMCA or park and recreation department.

Basketball Camps

Basketball camps are a great investment in your future. They give you the opportunity to compete, be pushed, and challenge yourself against different types of players. There is nothing better than drilling on the fundamentals of the game. Improvement comes with repetition. That's exactly what camps offer. It allows you the chance to compete with kids outside your area to see how good you really are.

I use my camp in Dallas to promote skill development and provide an arena to develop self-esteem and confidence. My campers receive instruction in the following areas:

- "Fun"damental skills
- Promotion of physical abilities
- Discipline, leadership, and responsibility
- Game situations
- Being good sports
- Drug awareness: "Drug-free, the way to be"
- Positive reinforcement, confidence, and self-esteem

Basketball camps should be fun and challenging, not to mention great places to make longtime friends. Plus, many camps across the nation are scouted by college coaches. It's a great opportunity to get noticed. Information about specific camps appears in the appendix.

When selecting a basketball camp that best suits you, there are some objectives you should think about. Some of you are already good basketball players and want to improve on the skills you already have. Some might want to learn the basic skills of the game. Now here's where all your options come into play.

- Sleep or day camp? Do you want to go to a week-long sleep-over camp or a week-long day camp? Maybe you are more interested in a three-day mini-day camp. There are a variety from which to choose.
- Cost. This may or may not be a factor in selecting the camp of your choice.
- Staff. What coaches or players will be there to teach and demonstrate?
- Enrollment. Find out how large camp is and how many instructors there are for each camper. The ratio should be around 8:1, players to coaches.
- Individual all-skill camp. This is where you can work on both ends of your game, offense and defense.
- Individual position camps. These are terrific to work specifically on your position—guard, forward, post.
- Recruiting camps. You can get a lot of exposure at many of these camps. During the proper time period, coaches can evaluate talent at these camps.

- Team camps. This is a chance to work together in the off-season. They can be both fun and beneficial to you and your team.
- Girls only or coed camps? Both have benefits. Competition versus guys is a good workout and improves your game. You can see your overall improvement better versus girls.

Playing Against Guys

Prior to puberty females and males can play on the same team in any sport, provided they have had the same skill training. The physical changes in size and strength manifest themselves at about 11 years in females and 13 years in males. After these ages males, in general, are taller, heavier, and show greater speed, strength, power, and size due to the influence of testosterone. In many sports this is a major problem since skill, agility, and coordination are primary determinators of success.

After puberty there are valid questions about contact or collision sports. In early adolescence, some girls have the ability to physically dominate boys. Therefore, matching by size, weight, and skill rather than by gender may be necessary. The evidence seems to indicate that grouping athletes into competitive categories based not on gender, but on skill level or size, provides the greatest opportunity for growth and development for both gender groups.

However, at this age boys and girls are very sensitive to their perceived inadequacies, such as lack of size or skills. It is always important to help males and females feel they could compete—win, lose, or draw—without having their masculinity or femininity questioned.

If you are comfortable playing against males, it is a great way to improve your game. Their size, strength, and quickness will truly challenge you. However, you can challenge them with your court sense, finesse, and fundamental skills. Take advantage of your strengths. Playing against guys can only help you improve. Here are some tips for competing against guys:

- Play hard.
- Use the opportunity to improve.
- Don't ever quit. Concentrate and stay focused.
- Don't back down physically.

- Don't worry about them; worry about your game.
- Be confident.
- Once you have earned their respect, they have helped you improve.

Getting Into Pickup Games

It's easy to find pickup games. Go to the local park, YMCA, recreation center, or health club. Go to your school or play in your driveway. Take a bunch of friends to the park and play. You will usually meet other people there. Mix it up. Try to play against people who push you. Play hard, be physical, and work on areas of your game you usually neglect in your team's practices. Expand your creativity on the court. Remember it's street ball. Don't call every little foul. Take it and move on. Here are some tips for getting into a game:

- Take your own ball.
- Yell "Next!" or quickly sign your name up on the board.
- Pick a good team.
- Be confident and play hard.
- If you're shooting to see who plays, make it. That way you won't have to rely on being picked.

Basketball Festivals

Hoop-It-Up is the official three-on-three street basketball tour of the National Basketball Association. These traveling 48-hour basketball festivals are the essence of the playground game: a hoop and a net. There are no gyms and no refs—just the opportunity to create spectacular moves. The Gus Macker series also provides a chance for competition, practice, and fun.

Every summer, thousands of male and female players of all ages and abilities compete against others of similar age, height, and experience in these events. Depending on the event, you might find three-point shooting competitions, free throw contests, and chances to raise money for local charities.

GAME TIME

Now it's time for all the hard work and practices you've been through to be put into action. Game time is about results and giving your best effort. What a great feeling to run out onto the court for pregame warmups, having family, friends, and fans cheer you and your teammates on. You're pumped. Your adrenaline is flowing. You're breaking a sweat in layup lines, getting loose and relaxed. You also should be staying focused.

So many things can affect you during the game. Maybe the outcome has critical implications for postseason play, maybe you're matched up against your archrival, or maybe there are factors surrounding a teammate or coach that cause a lot of external eyes to focus on your game. Whatever the situation, you must concentrate on playing your best and ignore the hype. Here are some tips that might help you keep your focus before, during, and after the game, and when facing special circumstances.

Pregame

Everyone has her own way of preparing for the game. I always wanted to be at my locker early to relax, take my time, put on a T-shirt and shorts to go out and shoot around, loosen up, and think about the game and my responsibilities without a lot of people around. I usually returned to the locker room as my teammates were first arriving for the game.

Usually, coaches want you in the locker room ready to change and get taped 90 minutes before game time. You should be eager to be in the locker room after you get dressed, taped if necessary, and have stretched a little. Remember, it's now time to give your attention to the coach. Usually your coach has matchups and plays on the chalkboard. This is the time to think about what your matchup or responsibility will be. Your coach is setting the offense and defense. Concentrate on what's being said. If you have any questions, be sure to ask. Now is the time. This is a very positive moment for you and your teammates and coaches. It's just you getting ready to do battle with your opponent. If the game plan is carried out and executed you have a good chance for victory.

After the information is given, it's time to get ready. Some players are loud and some are quiet as you head out of the locker room toward the court. It's a great emotional time to get pumped up: high-fiving, talking, playing music in the locker room and on the court. Once you hit the court, you should have this incredible desire to meet all challenges. Think about everything your coach said in the locker room. Your coach may have told you that No. 10 is your player. She likes to drive and her weakness is that she can't shoot with her left hand. Think about what that means to you. If you understand your responsibility, you can produce results by running plays correctly, shutting down offenses, rebounding. That all comes from the constant practices and communication between your coach, yourself, and your teammates. Play for today and take it one game at a time.

Halftime

This is a time to reflect on what has happened in the first half. If you're up, try not to be too satisfied. Games can turn around quickly. If you're down, let your coaches map out what they feel has taken place. The stat sheet usually doesn't lie. It will reflect key areas: shooting, rebounding (offensive and defensive), and turnovers. Your coach will give suggestions or make adjustments for the second half. Once you have the information, talk it over with your teammates. Always be positive. Then relax. Stretch. Try not to get stiff. Keep your warm-ups on if you're cool. Then, get out to the court for warm-ups. Staying focused and having concentration throughout is very important to your giving your best effort.

Postgame

Hopefully, you left everything you had on the court. In talking about all your hustle and effort, you should be drained after a game.

No matter if you win or lose, after the buzzer sounds shake hands with your opponents and the referees and head to the locker room. Of course, the mood will reflect whether you won or lost. If you won, enjoy it. Your coach probably will gather you in the locker room for his or her final thoughts about the game. Many times you learn more about your team and yourself from losses. They expose weaknesses. Winning sometimes disguises them. Shower, change, and relax. It's over. There will be another game.

Revenge Isn't Always Sweet

During my freshman year, our team had a tumultuous relationship with our coach, Pam Parsons. She left after the season and went on to become the head coach at South Carolina. Heading into my junior year, we eyed the South Carolina matchup, to be played in Columbia.

Old Dominion was 23-0 heading into the game. Our confidence and play was at an all-time high, although our all-American center, Inge Nissen, twisted her ankle and didn't make the trip. Nothing meant more to us than revenge. We'll show her. Ever heard of trying too hard? Our focus was Coach Parsons, not her team. We got spanked by 25 points. I had a glorious game—6 for 25 from the floor. To make matters worse, a fight broke out at center court. I think our poor play and the tension of the game got to us. I tried to break up the fight and got tossed from the game. The showers didn't seem like a bad idea at that point. Revenge doesn't mean a lot; just play the game that you prepared for in practice.

Don't Believe the Hype

Hype is for the media, fans, and people selling tickets and merchandise. When two teams play, there's no way around it. Someone is going to win and someone is going to lose. Keep your focus on what you have to do to win. Never get caught up in trashing your opponent to the media. What you or your teammates think in private is your business. The games are emotional enough. Don't give your opponents extra incentive. It's legendary for coaches to put up articles in the locker room to get their teams fired up. Don't give anyone more incentive with your words.

The Marquee Matchup

It's part of the hype—star versus star, all-state versus all-state. TV, radio, and newspapers are becoming more involved with covering sports. If you are a great player, an all-American, a Gatorade Player of the Year, that's great. There will be other great players to compete against. The biggest problem is thinking you have something to prove. Don't fall into that trap. You will prove your point by following the game plan. The most important thing is to give your best effort as a team.

The Big One

This can mean crosstown rivalries, conference or district rivals playing in a big game that gets them to the next level, or the championship game. It is important to be relaxed so you can perform to your best level of play. Again, the media and big crowds seem to change how important a game is. It's important to keep your routine. Don't overdo it. Your coaches will help you prepare mentally and physically. Don't put added pressure on yourself. Think of big games as opportunities—ones that other players and schools would love to have. During my senior year in college, the Soviet Union, the world champs, were touring the states, routinely beating our best collegiate teams by 30 to 40 points. Our arena downtown, Norfolk's "Scope," was sold out: 10,000 plus for the game. National champs versus world champions. Our coach, Marianne Stanley, told us to relax, play hard, and enjoy the game. We did and loved every minute of it. We were so pumped when the game started. The excitement carried us to a tie game at the half. Unfortunately, foul trouble for me, Inge Nissen, and Anne Donovan and a great Soviet attack led to the world-champion Soviets winning by ten.

 Some Simple Advice

At the 1993 women's basketball Final Four in Atlanta, Texas Tech all-American Sheryl Swoopes and I were talking during practice. (I was covering the tournament for CBS radio.) We talked about the pressure of playing in the finals against the other heralded player in the tournament, Ohio State's Katie Smith. I shared a few words of advice with Sheryl: "Remember, Sheryl, it's just another game. Get caught up in the hype and you'll be fighting more opponents than just Ohio State. Katie and Ohio State are great. Don't worry about them. Concentrate on what your job is." I think Sheryl was relaxed. She set an NCAA tournament record—47 points—as Texas Tech beat Ohio State, 84-82, for the NCAA title.

COACHABILITY, ATTITUDE, BEHAVIOR

More than anything, it's important to respect your coach. Your coach wouldn't be in that position if he or she wasn't qualified for the job. Be coachable. Don't get stuck with being labeled "uncoachable." Many players who aren't as good will get a break or chance because of the tag "She's very coachable, a team player, willing to learn."
Being coachable is what I call "A.R.T."

A = **Attitude**. Have a willingness to listen and learn. Always give your best effort to show you're a good sport. It's how you handle yourself in all situations.

Acceptance. Be willing to learn your coach's style and system and believe in it.

R = **Respect.** Show it in a variety of ways: by practicing hard, by listening to your coach's philosophies for the team, and by treating your coach with consideration. It also means never talking about your coach or team. Stick up for the team.

T = **Trust.** Know that what your coach is telling you will lead to improvement as a team and individually.

Team. Winning as a team is more important than achieving individual goals.

Taking criticism. Handle it and make it a positive message. Use criticism of your game, practice habits, and attitude to improve your overall performance on and off the court.

Accepting a Role

If you think you're not important because you're a reserve, you're dead wrong. Reserves are vital to a team's success. You provide daily competition for the starters. You push them to be better. You will continue to improve if you see your role as a positive one. You have to be sharp and ready to enter a game at any time. You must know every phase of the game and there's nothing better than to cheer your teammates on. It doesn't matter if you play 1 minute or 25. You have a role to play; do it to the best of your ability. You are essential to your team's success, attitude, and character. Role players make teams winners. They, above all, ensure the success of a team.

The Bench

Back in 1975, when I was on the Pan-American and Olympic teams, I was a sub, a reserve, a benchwarmer. My pride would frequently get hurt when I didn't play in games. You see, I practiced every day and put in just as many hours of sweat and pain as the others. But my teammates were more experienced and better skilled in many areas. Each night I couldn't wait to get to the next practice. I was going to play hard and get better. My attitude and desire pushed my teammates as well as myself. My competitiveness almost made them want to kill me. No, I wasn't a star, but I tell you what: Anytime you want to look at my gold medal or Olympic silver medal, I'll share it with you. Being a reserve built character and incentive. Hard work, desire, and luck did the rest.

Showing Dedication

Coaches are looking for players who have talent, especially physical talent. But they are also looking at players who are hard workers, who love the game of basketball, and who are dedicating themselves to constant improvement. They also are looking for players who want to win, players who want more to win than have the highest scoring average. Coaches want players who can make other players on their team better. They want players who display good attitudes and are willing to be positive to help teammates. What you say and do to a teammate goes a long way in the overall success of your team.

Coaches also are looking for student-athletes who are willing to work hard on the court and excel in the classroom. They care and want you to be well balanced in terms of your studies and how you perform on the court.

On-Court Demeanor

Being a good sport counts. Talking trash, taunting, showboating, and abusing officials seem to be out of control. The game you play should be spirited and teams should give all-out effort. But whatever happened to being a good sport? It's OK to talk and have confidence, and to use your confidence as a psychological tactic. "When you guard me, I own the three-point line. Come out at me and I'll take the jumper." Or, "Are you going to guard me or what?" It doesn't have to be cursing or degrading talk. Remember that there may be payback. Chances are someone will be talking trash to you one day. Keep it in the spirit it was intended.

Many of your teammates and opponents believe that being a good sport relates only to how they treat their teammates. It has to go beyond that. Many athletes have said they didn't realize their behavior until later. Just think for a minute how you want to be treated. If you're guarding a player who blows by and makes a shot, you don't want her to come back in your face, talking trash and taunting you. How would you feel? However, if you make a great play or someone on your team does you can celebrate; just don't degrade your opponent.

Think About It

If you trash talk, taunt, or abuse the officials, you are likely to get into a fight, which proves nothing, and will probably get tossed from the game. You and your team may receive technical fouls. It could take you out of the game mentally so you can't perform at your best level. If you get thrown out, you are of no help to your team. You've let your teammates down. If you're looking to go to college, coaches will notice your attitude and wonder why you're not playing. Your own coach could discipline you. Abuse the officials and you're a marked player. If you have a question, ask it. How you ask it will determine how you're dealt with. Respect the referees. It's all judgment and it's a tough job. Believe me, the calls will even out. How many times have you hacked someone and the ref didn't see it? Just because you see fights, trash talking, and showboating on television doesn't mean you have to do it. Be your own person.

Being a Role Model

There's no greater feeling than being respected for how you conduct yourself. Being a role model causes others to look up to you for what you have achieved. Just think of all you can project as a solid role model: being a good sport, hardworking, reliable, encouraging; keeping your teammates up; having a good attitude; being responsible, competitive, and trustworthy. Now that's something to strive for.

What makes a good leader? If you apply the following points, you will be a leader or well on your way to being one. A leader is a person who has authority or influence over people. A leader is

- someone who takes charge,
- someone willing to make decisions,
- someone who stands for her word,
- someone who is flexible and willing to accept suggestions from others,
- someone who is consistent and understanding, and
- someone who is hardworking.

Promoting Yourself and Your School

It is important that your coaches allow you to make yourself available to the media and to the community in which you play. Be positive and personable. When you make an appearance, speak with enthusiasm about your team, coach, and the prospect for success. Don't underestimate how much this rallying of the community can mean to a team.

Look at the magic Texas Tech's Sheryl Swoopes created not only with her skills, but also with her personality during her team's championship run in '93. Sheryl was like a magnet attracting hordes of fans and media. She was accessible, engaging, and warm and humble at the same time. That blend of personality has been a terrific way for Sheryl to promote herself and women's basketball.

This brings me to the media. The media can bring your team or program a great deal of exposure. The media have a responsibility to provide news and information to the public. Be accessible. Remember, it is important to fulfill your responsibilities to the media whether you win or lose. If you don't talk to the media when you lose, why should they want to hear from you when you win? Help make their job easier and good things can happen.

Many college programs have radio and television packages. Even high schools are being carried on cable television. Your sports information office can be invaluable in sharing interesting facts about you. They can arrange interviews with the media and serve as the liaison. It's proper promotion that allows you and your team to get noticed.

Working Through Problems With Coaches

This is a very important area because there will, undoubtedly, be times when you won't see eye to eye with your coach. Remember, you are playing for your coach in his or her system. Try to be flexible and understanding as to what is required of you. Small problems tend to become larger problems when there is a communication breakdown between player and coach. It can affect not only you and your performance, but the team's performance as well.

Let's say something is bothering you about your coach. The first thing you should do is go talk to him or her. Express your concerns, whether it's a personality problem or a problem with your playing. Share your thoughts in an adult manner. This might help your coach understand a problem he or she didn't know existed. If you keep it to yourself, it can't be solved. The bottom line is that you must try to work out any and all problems in a player-coach relationship. It will definitely help you in all other relationships you have in the future. You should always try to find common ground. Don't assume coaches know there's a problem. Tell them. If you are not ready to talk to the head coach, one of the assistant coaches would be a good start. They might be able to be a buffer between you and the coach. They can also share insight into how you should handle a situation. Basically, assistant coaches can help solve a minor problem before it becomes a major one. Rely on their friendship and advice.

Finally, remember you can make a player-coach relationship work. You might not always agree with them, but no matter what, show coaches the courtesy and respect they deserve. They are there to help make you a better student, athlete, and person.

Working Through Problems With Teammates

Dealing with teammates is similar to dealing with coaches. It can be more difficult because you're working with many personalities.

If you have a problem with someone on your team and it is a legitimate one, take her to the side and discuss it. Again, use the same behavior you would want someone to use with you. Try not to embarrass her in front of your other teammates or coaches. Don't fight with her; that would not solve anything and could result in injury to you or her. Express your points, then listen to what she has to say in response. Many times there are simple misunderstandings between each other. A rift between two teammates can split a team.

There is a natural tendency for friends to take sides. If you are not involved in the problem, stay out of it. Working on what you have to do for the team is more important than getting in the middle of another person's situation. If there is a problem, discuss it. Share your side. Hear her side and make some compromises if necessary. The main thing is to work it out before it disrupts the focus of the team. You're never going to agree with everyone; it's a matter of how you choose to handle your relationships with others.

BEING RECRUITED

Every athlete has her own story of how she was recruited—what she looked for and what her objectives were in selecting a school. Let me tell you, when you are 16 or 17 years old, it is tough to make a decision that will impact you for the rest of your life.

With so many choices available, this has become a tough and tedious process. You have to research all areas of each university you might be interested in. It's challenging to be 17 or 18 years old and have to determine where you are going to spend the next 4 or 5 years of your life. You may be attending a local college or one that is far away from friends and family. Being recruited can be very exciting and a confidence builder, but it also can be frightening—frightening in having to make such an important decision with guidance usually coming only from coaches and family.

Getting Ready for Recruiting

Your high school coach has an important responsibility in the recruiting process. The high school coach is the direct link to the college coach. If you are an athlete who wants to play basketball, it's the coach's responsibility to become familiar with the Xs and Os of recruiting. It will take extra time, paperwork, and selling you, the athlete, but the benefits for your coach, the community, the school, and you are worth the effort.

During the summer, your coach should get you involved in a local summer league or an AAU team. The college coaches are out during the summer months, and they are not as limited in how many times they may call or see you. July is an important month. Many scholarships are decided during the summer. If your local community or town runs a summer league, send a schedule to the colleges.

Summer is also the time for your coach to talk to you about the NCAA Clearinghouse and make sure you have started the process. The NCAA now requires all seniors to complete an NCAA initial-eligibility Clearinghouse form. If you have any questions about the certification process, contact the NCAA Clearinghouse at Box 4044, Iowa City, Iowa, 52243-4044, or call (319) 339-5003. Most high school counselors have these packets in their offices. Remember, you will not be able to set up visits without completing this process. These rules apply to Division I and Division II schools only.

The preseason is the time to send out fall schedules with a cover letter containing vital statistics, conference period, athletic period, etc. Juniors should sign up for the PSAT. Hopefully, seniors will already have taken their tests in the summer. If not, do so as soon as possible.

This is the time colleges will be setting up their school, campus, and home visits. These will be set up before September 17. This is a good time to sit down with your coach and set up a calendar for all of the visits. Most quality programs will work through your high school coach, as well as you the athlete.

The contact period typically runs from September 17 through October 8. Follow all rules established by the NCAA regarding visits. It is important for the high school coach to be at the home visit. Coaches should encourage the athlete to have a list of questions for the college coach. It is also a good idea to limit the home visit to 2 hours. Your coach should encourage you to narrow your choices to a top five. The campus visits can become confusing and time-consuming. By narrowing your choices, you have a better chance of picking the university that is best for you.

The NCAA allows you to sign a letter of intent before your senior season. This has both advantages and disadvantages. There are several advantages: It allows the athlete to focus on her senior season and not be bothered by recruiters all season; it guarantees her a scholarship even before the season starts; and she knows she is the university's top choice. Disadvantages are these: An athlete may settle for a university she might not have truly wanted; and an athlete might have a terrific senior year and increase her value to a top Division I program.

The best way for you to handle recruiting is ensure that you get exposure. Do anything you can to help get a scholarship. Send letters.

Get to know the college coaches in your state. Work summer camps and attend college clinics.

Making Your Decision

There is nothing more precious in the world than one's honor and loyalty. When you finally narrow your choices and select a school, be proud. The school is making a financial and educational commitment to you, and that commitment is a two-way street. I see too many athletes transfer for reasons like these: "I'm not getting enough playing time"; "I hate my teammates"; "It's too far away from home." These are situations to which proper thought should be given prior to signing.

Remember, nobody owes you anything. Show humility, not arrogance. Give, do not take. Just because you are a high school star does not mean you are a college starter. Yes, there are some who will adjust more quickly than others. Be receptive to learning. Do not announce to a coach that you deserve to start. Earn that right. Show the coach in practice how much you want to start. That is more satisfying. It annoys me that recruits ask: "Will I start?" or "How many minutes will you play me?"

Do not ask or expect a coach to break the rules regarding recruiting. Although it happens repeatedly, it is wrong. Have a sense of honor. Know what you can have and ask for it—nothing more, nothing less. It amazes me when athletes who have been taken care of by schools, coaches, or boosters later reveal wrongdoings that create major problems for that institution. They are now gone so it does not affect them; it affects only the current and future athletes of the school. Why do that to your alma mater?

As corny as it sounds, you are in charge of your own destiny. Allow friends and family members to offer you advice on what school to attend, but make the ultimate decision yourself. You are the one who has to live, play ball, go to school, and make the necessary adjustments for the next 4 years. Your parents are not going to school with you. They may not like the same things you do. Here is your chance to make a good, solid independent decision. Weigh all the factors, make your choice, and stick with it.

In reaching this important decision, here are some questions student athletes should ask themselves:

- Does the school meet my academic needs?
- Have I selected the right school for all my needs?
- Is the coach a good person and a good coach as well?
- Does my game fit the system?
- What are my teammates like?

Academics.   Academics should be at the top of your list of questions to coaches, academic advisers, and school officials. You are being awarded a scholarship because of your athletic ability, but you must take seriously your opportunity for education. Your letter of intent is a contract. For 4 or 5 years, you will receive a paid education in exchange for your time, commitment, loyalty, and hard work in representing your institution. Think about what field interests you. No matter what it is, give it plenty of thought. It will soon matter if you don't like it. Like anything you do, have an organized plan for the classroom of where you want to be and how to achieve it.

Knowing the graduation rate of the athletes at your institution is important. It gives you insight into the commitment the school has to its student-athletes. It also will give you an indication of how many years it has taken for other athletes to receive their diplomas. Many coaches will tell you that accurate graduation rates cannot be calculated because transfers and dropouts, for example, count as nongraduations. Tell them you understand that and ask for a breakdown. Numerous transfers and dropouts could tell you something about the program.

Things to Ask

1. What is the coach's graduation rate as coach at this school?
2. What is your team grade point average?
3. Is a study table required? How many hours or days does it meet?
4. Is tutoring available? If so, from whom and at what cost?
5. Considering my high school grades, reading ability, and college admission test scores, can I compete academically at this institution?
6. Does the school offer a complete program in my field of study? Or will I be offered softer courses designed to keep me eligible?

7. Do you have an academic athletic advisor?

8. If there is a conflict with a class and practice, how do you handle it?

9. How much class time is missed during the year due to basketball?

10. What happens if I can't maintain the GPA required?

Personal Needs.   Examine your personal preferences. In what area of the country would you like to attend college? It can be scary to go far away from home. Do you want friends and relatives to be able to watch you play? Or, do you want to break those apron strings and see how you develop away from the security of home? Are you warm- or cold-blooded? Do you want to attend a big or a small school? Some athletes love the big-time schools, complete with nationally recognized football programs and a host of other sports. Others are more suited for a smaller city, nestled in the country. The number of students and other factors should help you decide what environment will ultimately make you happy.

Things to Ask

1. Do I want to spend the next 4 to 5 years of my life in this college environment?

2. Given my ethnic background and recreational interests, can this college and its surrounding community provide for my social needs?

3. Do the athletes live separately from other students, or do they mix with the school socially and academically?

4. Can my parents, relatives, and friends come to see me play? How important is it for the college to be close to home?

5. Exactly what does the scholarship cover and what does it not cover?

6. Will the school find me a well-paying summer job that conforms to my career plans?

7. If I become injured and am unable to play, will the school continue my scholarship and continue to help me to obtain a degree?

8. Does the institution have an active organization of alumni and boosters who help athletes with career planning?

9. Are other athletes at the school who come from my environment and background happy with the social structure?

10. Will my scholarship cover a fifth year if I need it to get my degree?

11. How many days do I get off for Thanksgiving and Christmas?

12. What happens to my scholarship if I sign a national letter of intent, then get injured during my senior year of high school?

13. What major cities and airports are near your school?

14. How safe is the campus?

The Coach. Decide what type of coach you want to play for. Examine whether your skills fit the coach's philosophy. If not, are you willing to make adjustments? If the coach stresses defense and you're good at that, you could have a good match. If you're a half-court player in a run-and-gun philosophy, you're probably not going to be happy. Also look at the coach as a person. Many terrific coaches have never won national titles. Look for qualities in a coach that you value: loyalty, honesty, integrity, dedication, etc.

Things to Ask

1. Is the head coach the kind of person whom I want to be the most important person in my life for the next 4 years?

2. Is the coaching staff really willing to place academic demands in higher priority than athletic demands?

3. Is the coach respected by his or her peers, players (current and former), fans, media, and the community?

4. What is the coach's game philosophy? Practice philosophy?

5. How long has he or she been coaching and what are his or her successes?

6. What is the coach's philosophy on conditioning and strength training? Is there a strength coach?

7. What is the coach's experience? Who are the assistants and what are their strengths?

The Team

Do you want to go to an established winning team and be one of many great athletes who came through that program? Or, do you want to go to a lesser known school and be part of building a tradition?

What about exposure? Are you interested in national recognition? Can you handle the limelight? Are your skills good enough to play at a major college program? Do not let anyone kid you. Combining basketball and academics is a full-time job. A scholarship means commitment, not convenience. Some young athletes who are extremely talented in high school find it difficult to handle the demands very well.

Things to Ask

1. How many other players are being recruited at my position?
2. Do I have the quickness, strength, and skills to play regularly at this level of competition?
3. Do my skills and playing experience fit with the style and tempo of this program?
4. Does the school have a "revolving door" reputation with players coming and going? How many players have left and why?
5. What is the breakdown of the team by class?
6. Where does the team practice? Are the games played there?
7. How long are your practices?
8. Who is in your conference?
9. Do you have a postseason tournament?
10. Does your conference receive an automatic bid to the NCAA tournament?
11. What was your team's record over the last few seasons? Where have you consistently finished in the conference, region, national championships?
12. How does your team travel?
13. Is your program supported by the president of the university, its athletic director, professors and faculty, and the community?
14. What is the game schedule for the coming years? Are you playing top-ranked opponents?

What College Coaches Look for in a Recruit

Coaches look at many things when recruiting. Mainly, they want to put together a team of individuals that can achieve success both on the court and off. In general, college coaches are looking for athletes who have a commitment to excellence—people who are self-motivated, have positive attitudes, and exhibit above-average skills and abilities. They want to know if you're coachable and if you are receptive to instruction.

You'll be a strong candidate if you've taken and met academic requirements, which include test scores, core courses, GPA, and so on. Obviously, coaches want to know if you have an interest in their institutions, and if so, if you will sign early or late, and why. Some other questions coaches have include the following:

1. What kind of individual are you? Will you fit in with my program and philosophy? What's your background?
2. Are you participating in AAUs, BCI, and so on?
3. Who is helping you with the recruiting process (family, coach, etc.)?
4. Are we in your top five?
5. Do you have the total package?

Summary

Learning the fundamentals of basketball is just the beginning for you. The complete game is physical, mental, and emotional.

- Game time is what you have been waiting for. It's a time to learn what is going right and wrong and how to improve.
- Try not to get caught up in the hype of a game. Keep your focus.
- Accept your role on your team—whatever it might be.
- A true athlete lets her play do her talking. Never taunt your opponent.
- Find out where to play. Get involved in pickup games.
- Promote yourself and your school.
- Be prepared for recruiting. You have homework to do.

SUMMER CAMPS

The following summer camps are a sampling of what's available throughout the United States. Check with your local colleges and universities for information on camps that might not appear on this list.

Nancy Lieberman-Cline Basketball Camps

For more than 12 years, we have developed young girls' skills, confidence, and self-esteem through individual improvement on and off the court. For more information about Nancy Lieberman-Cline's basketball camps in Dallas, see the ad in the back of the book or write: Nancy Lieberman-Cline Basketball Camp, Box 795054, Dallas, TX 75379-5054; 214-612-6090.

Five-Star Camps

For information, write: 315 Fairfax Drive, Winston-Salem, NC 27104; 910-768-4550.

WBCA Summer Camps

WBCA offers four regional camps for the nation's best up-and-coming female high school players. During the 4 action-packed days, these players have a chance to showcase their skills against players with similar talent. The camps focus on developing the total person through education sessions and seminars. For more information, call 404-279-8027, ext. 110.

West

Blue Star West, Santa Clara University, Santa Clara, CA 95053; 215-727-9450.

Bruce Haroldson's Pacific Lutheran University Summer Basketball Camps, Pacific Lutheran University, Tacoma, WA 98447; 206-841-8849; after June 21, 206-535-8706.

Cougar Cage Camp, Bohler Gym M-9, Washington State University, Pullman, WA 99164-1602.

Cowgirl Basketball Camps, University of Wyoming, Box 3414, Laramie, WY 82071-3414.

Falcons Sports Camp, United States Air Force Academy, Colorado Springs, CO 80840-5651.

North Coast Girls Basketball Camps, Inc., University of Denver, Denver, CO 80210; 216-775-8730.

Summer Basketball Camp, The Head-Royce School, Oakland, CA 94602; 510-531-1300

University of Utah Basketball Camp, University of Utah, Salt Lake City, UT 84112; 801-581-7037.

WBCA West Summer Camp, California State Polytechnic University at Pomona, Pomona, CÁ 91768; 404-279-8027.

West Coast Camps Girls Camp Shootout, California State University, Dominiguez Hills, CA 90747; 818-349-0935.

Southwest

Blue Star Southwest, Baylor University, Waco, TX 76798; 215-727-9450.

Midwest

Blue Star Midwest, Indiana State University, Terre Haute, IN 47809; 215-727-9450.

Blue Star Position Camp, Indiana State University, Terre Haute, IN 47809; 215-727-9450.

Girls Basketball Camp, Mankato State University, Mankato, MN 56001; 507-389-6111.

High Intensity—The Camp of the '90s, University of Indianapolis, Indianapolis, IN 46227; 317-888-4645.

Indiana University Girls' Basketball Camps, Indiana University, Bloomington, IN 47405; 812-855-3954.

Lady Redbird Basketball Camps, Illinois State University, Redbird Arena, Normal, IL 61761.

Marian Washington Lady Jayhawk Basketball Camp, University of Kansas, P.O. Box 3302, Lawrence, KS 66044; 913-864-4938.

Michigan All State Girls' Basketball Camp, Inc., Northwestern Michigan College and Traverse City Senior High School, both in Traverse City, MI 48098; 616-947-4598.

Summer Basketball Girls' Camps, The University of Oklahoma, Norman, OK 73019; 405-325-8322.

University of Nebraska-Omaha Lady Mav Basketball Camps, Omaha, NE 68132; 402-554-2300.

USA Superstar Basketball Camp, Anderson College, Anderson, IN 46012; 704-298-4565.

WBCA Midwest Summer Camp, Washington University, St. Louis, MO 63130; 404-279-8027.

Wisconsin Coaches Scouting Service, Lakeland College, Sheboygan, WI 53082-0359; 414-334-4402.

East

Atlantic Cape Camps, Marcucci Farms, Williamstown, NJ 08094; 609-629-8243.

Blue Star East, Lehigh University, Bethlehem, PA 18015; 215-727-9450.

Blue Star Northeast, State University of New York at Buffalo, Buffalo, NY 14260; 215-727-9450.

Blue Star Southeast, University of North Carolina, Chapel Hill, NC 27514; 215-727-9450.

Championship Basketball Camp, Salem State College, Salem, MA 01970; 508-741-6570.

Eastern Invitational Basketball Clinics, Trenton State College, Trenton, NJ 08650-4700; 717-992-5523.

Future Stars International, State University of New York at Oneonta, Oneonta, NY 13820; 610-783-6336.

Future Stars International, Swarthmore College, Swarthmore, PA 19081; 610-783-6336.

Keystone State Camp, Albright College, Reading, PA 19604; 717-323-2072.

Keystone State Camp, Juniata College, Huntingdon, PA 16652; 717-323-2072.

Metro Index Girls Basketball Camp, California University of Pennsylvania, California, PA 15419; 412-343-7099.

University of New Hampshire Girls' Basketball Camps, UNH Field House, Durham, NH 03824.

WBCA East Summer Camp, University of Rochester, Rochester, NY 14627; 404-279-8027.

South

Blue Star South, University of Tennessee at Memphis, Memphis, TN 38163; 215-727-9450.

Lady Techster Basketball Camp, Louisiana Tech University, Ruston, LA 71270; 318-257-4111.

Norm Benn's Florida Southern Basketball Camps, Florida Southern College, Lakeland, FL 33801-5698; 813-680-4250.

WBCA Mideast Summer Camp, Baylor School, Chattanooga, TN 37405; 404-279-8027.

AIDS FOR BETTER BASKETBALL

- Shooting—Ace Hoffstein's Shot Correction Guide for Men and Women. Call 800-866-7468.
- The Big Ball—A great training tool for basketball players of all levels and ages. The Big Ball can be used for shooting, ballhandling, rebounding, and passing. Call 800-776-PLAY.
- Jump Rope or Heavy Rope—Used for conditioning, improving arm strength, and increasing foot speed.
- Blinders—For ballhandling so you cannot look at the ball.
- Gloves—Handle the ball with worker's gloves in your drills. Then take them off. You will have a better feel for the ball.
- Toss Back Machine—This can be quite effective for passing drills, shooting, and rebounding.
- Strength Shoe—Used to increase speed, quickness, jumping ability, and lower leg strength. Call 800-451-JUMP.

PUBLICATIONS, VIDEOS, AND ORGANIZATIONS

Publications

AAHPERD/NAGWS Publications
Call 800-321-0789 for ordering information.

A Century of Women's Basketball
Joan S. Hult and Marianna Trekell, eds. Stock #0-88314-490-5. $24.95 ($22.50 for AAHPERD members).

Title IX Toolbox
Stock #303-10021. ($12.95 for AAHPERD members).

Girl Scouts of the U.S.A. Publications
420 Fifth Ave., New York, NY 10036 or fax request to 800-643-0639

Developing Health and Fitness: Be Your Best!
CAT#2610. $2.75.

Playing Fair: A Guide to Title IX in High School and College Sports

Elementary School "Support Girls Participation" Classroom Writing Activity and Certificate Program

Racism in College Athletics: The African American's Experience
Dana D. Brooks, EdD and Ronald Althouse, PhD. 319 pp. $38, ISBN: 0-9627926-2-4.

Women's Sports Foundation Publications
Call 800-227-3988 for ordering information.

Parents' Guide to Girls' Sports

Videos

Girl Scouts of the U.S.A. Publications
420 Fifth Ave., New York, NY 10036 or fax request to 800-643-0639

Be Your Best Video
Hosted by Janet Evans, 1988 and 1992 Olympic gold medalist. CSP#40-500-11. $9.95.

Black Women in Sports Foundation
Box 2610, Philadelphia, PA 19130

It's Amazing Grace

Women's Sports Foundation Publications
  Call 800-227-3988 for ordering information.
  Aspire Higher

Organizations

National Association for Girls & Women in Sport
  1900 Association Drive, Reston, VA 22091-1599; 703-476-3452.

  The National Association for Girls & Women in Sport (NAGWS) is a nonprofit, educational organization designed to serve the needs of administrators, teachers, coaches, leaders, and participants in sports programs for girls and women.

  NAGWS's focus is advocacy, leadership, and coaching. The association strives to accomplish its goals via programs including the Wade Trophy (awarded to the most outstanding female senior collegiate basketball player), annual conventions, leadership conferences, publications including the *NAGWS's Volleyball Rulebook* and the *NAGWS Title IX Toolbox*, mentoring programs, National Girls and Women in Sports Day, and officiating enhancement.

Women's Sports Foundation
  Eisenhower Park, East Meadow, NY 11544; 800-227-3988.

  The Women's Sports Foundation is a nonprofit educational organization that promotes and enhances the sports experience for all girls and women.

  The foundation gives girls and women the information they need to make the most of their sports opportunities and to gain opportunities where they do not currently exist. Educational services include a resource center, a toll-free line for women's sports information, conferences, videos, and educational guides. Grant programs help athletes prepare for national and international competition and help establish new or improved sports programs for girls, among other purposes. Awards programs include both national and local awards to bring attention to the achievements of girls and women in sports. The foundation actively advocates equal opportunity for women in sports.

USA Basketball
  1750 E. Boulder, Colorado Springs, CO 80909; 719-632-7687.

  As the sport's national governing body, USA Basketball is dedicated to help young basketball prospects train and develop into future Olympians. USA

Basketball includes hundreds of male and female athletes from the high school, college, and professional levels. USA Basketball assembles teams for the Olympic games, World Championships, World University Games, Junior National Teams, and U.S. Olympic Festival teams.

Women's Basketball Coaches Association
4646 B. Lawrenceville Highway, Lilburn, GA 30247; 404-279-8027.

Founded in 1981, the purpose of the WBCA is to promote women's basketball by unifying coaches at all levels to develop a reputable identity for the sport and to foster and promote the development of the game in all of its aspects as an amateur sport for women. A membership with the Women's Basketball Coaches Association assures you of direct affiliation with the only professional association that deals specifically with coaches of women's basketball. The WBCA is involved in many areas of recognition and promotion of women's basketball.

Amateur Athletic Union (AAU)
3400 W. 86th St., Indianapolis, IN 46268; 317-872-2900.

The Amateur Athletic Union offered its first national basketball champion-ship event for women in 1926. Since its inception in 1888, the AAU has been a leader in providing competitive opportunities from the local to the national level. Today, the AAU offers a full range of competitive basketball opportunities beginning at age 10 and under, progressing to the post-college athlete. In addition to participation opportunities, the AAU offers the individual interested in coaching or giving back to the sport an avenue to participate.

The AAU Girls' Basketball Committee oversees the national program for ages 19 and under. AAU Girls' Basketball has offered National Champion-ships since 1973. For the purposes of national championship competition, the AAU conducts programs in seven age divisions: 11 and under, 12 and under, 13 and under, 14 and under, 15 and under, 16 and under, and 18 and under.

The Women's Basketball Hall of Fame
118 N. Liberty, Jackson, TN 38301; 901-423-8349.

The Women's Basketball Hall of Fame will be the mirror and memory of women's basketball, and thus is designed to be an informational and educational resource center, to showcase the current state, and to project a vision of the future of women's basketball.

It will portray and preserve the rich history of the first 100 years and provide a place to present the continuing history of women's basketball. The Hall of Fame will become the information center for women's basketball with book, film, and video libraries and displays that capture the evolution of rules, uniforms, and every phase of the game's development. Furthermore, it will recognize the achievements of individuals who have significantly contributed to its rich history.

INDEX

ABOUT THE AUTHORS

Nancy Lieberman-Cline

Robin Roberts

Nancy Lieberman-Cline has been a dominant force in amateur and professional basketball since the early 1970s. In 1975 she won a Gold Medal at the Pan-American Games. As a member of the 1976 U.S. Silver-Medal-winning team, at the age of 18 Nancy became the youngest basketball player in Olympic history, male or female, to win a medal. She was also a member of the 1980 Olympic team, (which did not compete due to the boycott).

After a standout career, leading her team at Old Dominion University to two consecutive National Championships and being named a three-time Kodak All-American, Nancy was the number one draft choice for the Dallas Diamonds, the professional women's basketball team. She led her team to the 1984 Championship in the Women's American Basketball Association. She made history again in 1986 as the first woman to play in a men's professional league, signing with the Springfield Fame of the United States Basketball League. Another triumph followed when she joined the 1987-1988 Harlem Globetrotters/ Washington Generals World Tour. In 1993 she was the first woman inducted into the New York City Basketball Hall of Fame.

Nancy's talents extend beyond the basketball court. From 1981 through 1984 she served as Martina Navratilova's conditioning coach, revolutionizing the way women train. She has worked as a network and cable broadcaster and color analyst for men's and women's basketball games, including NBC, CBS, ESPN, Prime Network, HSE, and the SportsChannel. Nancy owns Events Marketing, Inc., which promotes sporting events across the country.

Each year Nancy conducts several weeks of basketball camps for young girls across the country and donates her time and effort to numerous charities and special organizations. She lives in Dallas, Texas with her husband, Tim, and their son, T.J.

Robin Roberts's affiliation with ABC and ESPN has made her one of the most versatile commentators in the business. Since joining ABC in 1995, Robin has covered a variety of sporting events for the network and hosted the *Wide World of Sports*. For ESPN she hosts *Sunday SportsDay*, anchors *SportsCenter*, and contributes to *NFL PrimeTime*. She hosted the network's coverage of the men's NCAA Final Four, and the NCAA Women's Basketball Tournament, and she called play-by-play for the East Regional Final in the Women's NCAA Basketball Tournament.

Prior to her career as a sportscaster, Robin made her mark at Southeastern Louisiana University. She was a standout performer on the women's basketball team, ending her career as the school's third all-time leading scorer (1,446 points) and rebounder (1,034 rebounds). She earned her bachelor's degree in communications, graduating with honors.

Roberts received the 1993 Excellence in Sport Journalism Award for Broadcast Media and the 1992 Women at Work Broadcast Journalism Award for her contributions to the image of women in broadcast journalism. She is active as a speaker for charity and civic functions across the country. Robin lives in Farmington, Connecticut.

Kevin Warneke, who assisted the authors in preparing the manuscript, is a former newspaper reporter and editor. He serves as a magazine editor and part-time journalism instructor at the University of Nebraska at Omaha. Warneke writes for several sports magazines and covers high school sports for a daily newspaper in Nebraska.

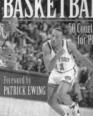